Frommer's™

Greek Islands

i with your family

From golden beaches to ancient legends

by Jos Simon

JOHN WILEY & SONS, LTD

UK Publisher: Sally Smith
Executive Project Editor: Daniel Mersey (Frommer's UK)
Commissioning Editor: Mark Henshall (Frommer's UK)
Development Editor: Donald Strachan (Frommer's UK)
Content Editor: Hannah Clement (Frommer's UK)
Cartographer: Tim Lohnes
Photo Research: Jill Emeny (Frommer's UK)

Wiley also publishes its books in a variety of electronic formats. Some content that appears in print may not be available in electronic books.

British Library Cataloguing in Publication Data
A catalogue record for this book is available from the British Library

ISBN: 978-0-470-51861-8

Typeset by Wiley Indianapolis Composition Services
Printed and bound in China by SNP Leefung Printers Ltd.

5   4   3   2   1

Contents

About the Author

Born and raised in Pwllheli on the Ley Peninsula, Jos Simon ventured into the world beyond Snowdonia as an LSE student in mid-60s swinging London. Having married a Greek, he embarked on a teaching career in various parts of the UK, his life enriched by Greek in-laws, Greek food and Greek holidays. Early retirement brought new challenges as a freelance travel writer, specialising (of course) in stories about Greece. As a result of continued frequent Hellenic touring, with children, then alone, then with grandchildren, writing about Greece for UK magazines, and researching this book, he has come to feel like an honorary Greek.

Acknowledgements

For help and support in writing this book my thanks are due:
at John Wiley & Sons, to commissioning editor Mark Henshall for firm but friendly guidance and Donald Strachan for perceptive, sympathetic development editing; to Hannah Clement for introducing me (a poor pupil, alas) to the arcane mysteries of templating and to Jill Emeny for good-natured help with photographs and maps.

In arranging research visits to the Greek Islands, to a host of professionals who clearly love Greece as much as I do – Sarah Belcher at Travelpr (for Sunvil), Bernadette Askouni at Ionian Island Holidays, Natalie Humphreys of Aegean Homes/Sapphire Villas, Carole Pugh of Four Corners PR, Anna-Maria Pachis of Sunvil Holidays in southern Corfu, and Caroline Thaw of Ionian Island Holidays in northern Corfu. Thanks also to Nick McKenna, managing director of Sunisle Holidays for being willing to help (sorry I didn't get back to you). Especial thanks to Linda Diamandis (again of Sunvil) and Frankie Miles (author of *Crete on the Road*) for a hundred suggestions of where to go in Western Crete, and to Nigel Khan, who shone the light of his computer expertise into the darkest corners of my digital ignorance, and to Jonathan Sutch for smooth, totally professional fact-checking.

Finally, as ever, heartfelt thanks to my family – sister-in-law Litsa and her husband Mike for insights into Greek life (and accommodation between islands), son Daniel for help with Greek wines, daughter

Catherine for fact acquisition/checking in Chapter 2 and lifts to the airport, and wife Doulla for note-making/translating in the field, hours spent on the phone to the Greek Islands, and general support. Oh, and my grandchildren Lazaros and Eliza for cheering me up when I started to feel that I'd lost my way.

Dedication

For my brother Jeff – how he'd have loved all this travel writing stuff! We all miss him.

An Additional Note

Please be advised that travel information is subject to change at any time and this is especially true of prices. We therefore suggest that you write or call ahead for confirmation when making your travel plans. The authors, editors and publisher cannot be held responsible for experiences of readers while travelling. Your safety is important to us however, so we encourage you to stay alert and be aware of your surroundings.

Star Ratings, Icons and Abbreviations

Hotels, restaurants and attraction listings in this guide have been ranked for quality, value, service, amenities and special features using a star-rating system. Hotels, restaurants, attractions, shopping and nightlife are rated on a scale of zero stars (recommended) to three (exceptional). In addition to the star rating system, we also use five feature icons that point you to the great deals, in-the-know advice and unique experiences. Throughout the book, look for:

FIND	Special finds – those places only insiders know about
MOMENT	Special moments – those experiences that memories are made of
VALUE	Great values – where to get the best deals
OVERRATED	Places or experiences not worth your time or money
GREEN	Attractions employing responsible tourism policies

The following **abbreviations** are used for credit cards:

AE	American Express
MC	Mastercard
V	Visa

A Note on Prices

Frommer's provides exact prices in each destination's local currency. As this book went to press, the rate of exchange was €1 = £0.72. Rates of exchange are constantly in flux; for up-to-the-minute information, consult a currency-conversion website such as www.oanda.com/convert/classic. In the Family-friendly Accommodation section of this book we have used a price category system.

An Invitation to the Reader

In researching this book, we discovered my wonderful places – hotels, restaurants, shops and more. We're sure you'll find others. Please tell us about them, so we can share the information with your fellow travellers in upcoming editions. If you were disappointed with a recommendation, we'd love to know that too. Please write to;

Frommer's Greek Islands with your family, 1st Edition
John Wiley & Sons, Ltd
The Atrium
Southern Gate
Chichester
West Sussex, PO19 8SQ

Photo Credits

Cover Credits

Main Image: © Jack Barker
Small Images (L-R):
© James Davis / TTL
© Leigh Beisch – Foodpix / Photolibrary Group Ltd
© Sam Howard / TTL
© Terry Harris / PCL
Back Cover: © Jos Simon

Front Matter Credits

Pi: © Jack Barker; piii: © James Davis / TTL; © Leigh
Beisch – Foodpix / Photolibrary Group Ltd; © Sam Howard / TTL;
© Terry Harris / PCL

Inside Credits

Courtesy of Alamy: p179 (© Clairy Moustafellou – IML Images
Group Ltd)
Courtesy of PCL: p1, p71 (© Clive Sawyer); p39 (© Colin Paterson);
p116, p221 (© John Miller).
Courtesy of TTL: p11, p214 (© Steve Outram); p65 (© Stuart
Black); p83, p96, p107 (© Jan Wlodarczyk); p143 (© Philip
Enticknap); p211 (© Lee Frost); p215 (© James Davis); p219
(© Steve Day).
© Jos Simon: p4, p5, p6, p7, p8, p9, p10, p47, p49, p57, p59, p61,
p63, p69, p74, p78, p79, p82, p87, p91, p97, p100, p102, p104,
p109, p111, p113, p119, p123, p124, p125, p127, p131, p137,
p139, p147, p148, p149, p152, p153, p156, p157, p161, p164,
p171, p172, p178, p182, p193, p195, p196, p200, p204, p205,
p210, p229.

1 Family Highlights of the Greek Islands

Since I first visited the country in the summer of 1965, with a group of fellow students in a battered old van, I've been in love with Greece. A month after returning to England, I met a Greek girl. We married. We honeymooned in Greece. Through my mother-in-law's cooking I learned to love Greek food. My wife and I often drove around Greece – with toddlers, then teenagers, then on our own, then with our grandchildren. Eventually, I started to write for *Greece Magazine*. My passion for Greece is no fad.

I can't begin to say how beautiful Greece is. Physically, of course – all those rugged mountains, cobalt seas and picturesque fishing boats. But it's not just that. The Greeks successfully combine 21st-century savvy with a deep feeling for what's important in life. Thought and argument. Politics. Honour. Philosophy. Above all, family and children. In what other country would restaurant staff hold a baby so that the parents could finish their meal, or a group of adolescent youths stop to play with, dandle and admire a three-year-old boy? Both these things happened to my daughter and her kids when holidaying in Greece.

It's undoubtedly the case, too, that the Greeks seem to be well disposed towards Brits. This is partly because of British support for Greece during its War of Independence from the Turks in the 19th century (you'll come across many streets, and Greeks, named after Lord Byron), partly because the British and Greeks were comrades-in-arms during World War II. Whatever the reason, there is often a genuine warmth in the way in which Greeks greet Brits which hasn't been tarnished by the over-familiarities of mass tourism.

Okay, so much for Greece, but why the islands? First some statistics: there are 3000 Greek Islands, about 170 of them inhabited. They are scattered across a staggering 750 000 square kilometres of the Eastern Mediterranean.

The cold facts, however, don't come anywhere near reflecting the grip that this scattering of islands has on the European imagination – especially on those who live in colder northern climes. Consider: sea so clear that boats seem to float in mid-air. Craggy men in tavernas, playing *tavli*. Old women leading donkeys laden with firewood. Blue-and-white cottages climbing steeply from azure seas, crescents of golden sand beneath lofty bare grey mountains. You know the kind of stuff.

There's another side to the Greek Islands, it's true. Mass tourism, giant hotels, coast-to-coast villas, battery-farm holidays and dance-til-you-drop, alcohol- (and worse) fuelled youth excess.

Fit all this around the range of things you do on holiday – sightseeing, barbecues on the beach, arcade games, going to the pictures, buying presents, having family arguments – and the task of organising a successful trip starts to seem like the labours of Hercules. Don't fret – that's where we can help.

So, which islands are the best for families? Out of 170 inhabited islands, only very few are big enough to cater for the variety of tastes and ages found in the average family. If you're looking for beach-and-taverna simplicity almost any one will fit the bill. If you just want a sea-and-sun resort holiday, almost any country on the Mediterranean can give you what you want. Or the Caribbean.

But if you want that balance of a comfortable place to stay with lots to do, some interesting trips out, some Greek history and culture, nice views and good places to eat (or fix your own packed lunch), together with information about everything from car hire to Internet cafés, or where the best playgrounds and theme parks are – in other words, a family holiday which can appeal to everybody in the clan – look no further.

The islands that come up with a string of hits are Corfu, Crete and Rhodes. They have all got a terrific tourist infrastructure, yet they're big enough to have retained their own Greek culture. They have an extended and complicated history with all sorts of interesting back-waters to explore. That they all have strong – and positive – connections with the UK is an added plus. That's why you can watch cricket on the green in Corfu, visit the site of the British-led kidnap of a German General in Crete, or climb Mount Smith in Rhodes.

The fourth island covered here, Evia, has everything that I love about a holiday destination. It's interesting in itself. It has lots of history. It's typically Greek – though most inhabitants in the south of the island are Albanian in origin. It's totally untouristy – many guide-books don't even include it – yet, owing to its popularity as a destination for Greeks, it has a reasonable tourist infrastructure, and offers access to other wonderful places like the Sporades, the Pelion peninsula, the area around Marathon, and Athens itself.

Enough said. Let's take a look at the pick of the bunch.

BEST FAMILY EXPERIENCES

People-watching on the Esplanade in Corfu Town at one of the Liston's cafés (see p. 47).

Looking down from Kanoni at the jets thundering in across the convent of Vlacherna to land at Corfu Airport (see p. 55).

Spending a family day at one of Corfu, Rhodes or Crete's splendid water parks (see p. 4).

Spotting Jersey tiger moths from the paths, steps and bridges of the Valley of the Butterflies in Rhodes (see p. 112).

Walking through the damp, dark tunnel (or not!) at Epta Piges in Rhodes (see p. 111).

Riding a donkey up the hill to the Acropolis at Lindos in central Rhodes (see p. 103).

Sweating in the Mustafa Hamam Turkish Baths in Rhodes Town (see p. 93).

Wandering around Chania's wonderful Naval Museum, looking at the fascinating exhibits (see p. 139).

Having family competitions at ten-pin bowling, pool, go-karting or mini-golf in Golden Fun Park, just outside Chania, whilst the younger children are being entertained by staff (see p. 142).

Feeding the animals or riding a pony at 'The Ark', just outside Vamos in Crete (see p. 147).

BEST CHILDREN'S ATTRACTIONS

Aqualand (Corfu) A huge water park right in the centre of Corfu, accessible from everywhere on the island, with a wide range of slides, tubes, pools, food and drink outlets – the works. A great family day out (see p. 57).

Lunar Park (Rhodes) A noisy funfair in the centre of Faliraki,

with all the rides and stalls you're ever likely to want (and some that have disappeared from the UK). You'll either love it or hate it (see p. 102).

The Water Park (Rhodes) This has all the slides and rides that now seem standard in holiday water parks – perhaps they're all built by the same firm. Wherever you're staying in Rhodes, it's worth a day trip (see p. 102).

Hydropolis Water Park (Corfu) Almost on a par with Aqualand, with many of the same slides and rides, Hydropolis, on the north coast of Corfu, is less accessible and less widely advertised, and usually less crowded. It also has the advantage that it's next to the Gelina Village Resort, with a small zoo and a nice beach (see p. 63).

Golden Fun Park (Crete) A brand new facility, with enough to do for all the family, outdoor (bouncy castles, go-karts) and indoor (pool, ten-pin bowling)

Aqualand, Corfu

Asterakia, Evia

to make it an all-weather attraction (see p. 142).

Asterakia (Evia) A lovely little funfair on the banks of the Euripos – a bit like a travelling fair that stays put. Particularly suitable for younger children, with enough to keep teens and adults happy as well (see p. 187).

BEST CASTLES

The Greeks don't make much of their castles – many are just shells, slowly crumbling under the assault of time and the weather. Yet it needs only a little imagination to bring them back to life, and, for obvious defensive reasons, they usually have wonderful views.

The Old and the New Fortresses (Corfu) Corfu
Town's two huge fortresses are worth visiting, not only in their own right, but also for the terrific views they offer across the town, the surrounding countryside and the sea (see p. 41).

Gardiki Fortress (Corfu)
Totally abandoned in the middle of the countryside near Corfu's Lake Korission, the Gardiki Fortress, with its overgrown stonework and goats, is wonderfully atmospheric (see p. 70).

The Palace of the Grand Masters (Rhodes) Looking
like a fictional fairytale version of what a medieval castle should be (thanks in part to restoration work done by the Italians), the Palace of the Grand Masters gives an idea of the presence and sheer bulk of ancient fortifications (see p. 95).

Monolithos Castle (Rhodes)
Though there's not much to see when you actually get into it, from a distance the castle has a fairytale aspect, perched on its impressive crag above the Mediterranean (see p. 107).

Palace of the Grand Masters, Rhodes

Fortezza (Crete) Within walking distance of the centre of Rethymnon, the Fortezza represents an enticing combination of warfare and piracy (see p. 157).

Frangokastello (Crete) On the south coast, Frangokastello is an impressive shell dominating a lovely sandy beach. It comes with a scary ghost-story, too (see p. 154).

Kara Baba (Evia) Massive and empty, Kara Baba Fortress stands high above Evia's capital, giving wonderful views across the narrow straits (see p. 187).

BEST WILDLIFE EXPERIENCES

The Shell Museum (Corfu) On the outskirts of Benitses, the Corfu Shell Museum has a fine collection of seashells, stuffed sharks, crabs, lobsters and other denizens of the deep (see p. 68).

The Hydrological Institute (Rhodes) Otherwise known as the Rhodes Aquarium, it sits on the northernmost tip of the island, and offers close-up views of fish you might otherwise only glimpse whilst snorkelling (see p. 98).

The Ostrich Farm (Rhodes) Ostriches, of course, but also lots of other animals, including camels you can ride (see p. 113).

The Bee Museum (Rhodes) All you need to know about our honey-producing friends – including hives made of Perspex so you can see what's going on inside (see p. 114).

Valley of the Butterflies (Rhodes) Not butterflies but Jersey tiger moths, fluttering in their thousands in this stunning little valley (see p. 112).

A resident of The Ark, Crete

The Ark (Crete) Though principally an ostrich farm, the Ark has lots of other animals to look at and ride, all set in beautiful grounds with views of the White Mountains (see p. 147).

Nautilus (Evia) A well-organised little shell and sealife museum just outside Agiokampos on Evia's north coast (see p. 193).

Diving (all islands) Whichever island you're on, there's always the opportunity of seeing wonderful Mediterranean fish swimming in crystal clear waters, either with your own snorkelling equipment, or with one from the many diving schools.

BEST PICNIC AREAS

You can have a pleasant picnic virtually anywhere in the Greek Islands, especially on beaches or in woodland – all you need is a place to sit and some shade.

Mon Repos (Corfu) Acres of woodland with free access just south of the capital; pick your spot and tuck in (see p. 56).

Epta Piges (Rhodes) Streams, rocks and waterfalls, ducks quacking and peacocks keening, all under the shade of the trees (see p. 111).

Spili (Crete) Spili's platia (square) is a lovely place to unpack the sandwiches – lots of shade and plenty of cold running water from 25 lion-head spouts (see p. 162).

Prokopi (Evia) The road between Prokopi and Madouni is ideal picnic territory, with little pebble beaches along the river and lots of shade (see p. 190).

BEST BEACHES

The Greek Islands have hundreds of great beaches – part of the fun is finding your own favourite. A few, though, have something extra special.

Sidari (Corfu) Unique because of the sinuous shapes of the sandstone cliffs. Older teenagers might want to swim the *canal d'amour* to find eternal love; parents, of course, have already found it (see p. 62).

Paleokastritsa (Corfu) One of Corfu's loveliest villages, Paleokastritsa also boasts a choice of wonderful beaches and coves – not particularly sandy, but in the most perfect setting you could ask for (see p. 64).

Agios Gordios (Corfu) On Corfu's west coast, the beach at Agios Gordios is sandy, the view of the cliffs delightful, and if teenagers get bored, they can wander up into the village (see p. 69).

Prassonissi (Rhodes) A great vista of sand, sea and windsurfing right on the southern tip of Rhodes, the double bay of Prassonissi is a delight (see p. 117).

Elli Beach (Rhodes) If your ideal beach is packed with holidaymakers and locals sunning themselves, Elli Beach, which stretches from Mandraki Harbour to the Aquarium in Rhodes Town, is for you. Ablaze with sun-umbrellas, electric with the *zeitgeist*, it's perfect for people watching. Don't expect peace and quiet, though (see p. 98).

Trianda Bay (Rhodes) The pebbly beach itself at Trianda Bay, on Rhodes' northwest coast, isn't up to much, but when you consider the wealth of things for kids to do – a playground at one end, Planet Z indoor play area at the other, and lots of restaurants and cafés in between – you can begin to appreciated its family potential (see p. 105).

Loutro (Crete) Loutro, on Crete's south coast and accessible only on foot or by boat, has a lovely little beach right in front of the stacked white and blue houses of the village. It's a sheltered spot, you can get drinks and food at the cafés and tavernas, and there are boats for hire. You couldn't be anywhere else but a Greek island (see p. 153).

Maleme (Crete) Facing north along the coast, west of Chania, the beach at Maleme is long and uncrowded, with loads of child-friendly cafés and bars – there's

Paleokastritsa, Corfu

Loutro

nowhere better to watch the sun go down (see p. 141).

Loutra Edipsou (Evia) Do what the Greeks do in this town in northern Evia – bring your kids to the beach, let them swim or play on the sand or in the children's playground, whilst you have a drink in the adjacent cafés and bars (see p. 193).

Karystos (Evia) The beach west of Karystos, on Evia's southern tip, goes on for miles, and is therefore never crowded. It's one of the best beaches anywhere in the Greek Islands: clean, sandy, with parking along its whole length (see p. 200).

BEST VIEWS

The Kaiser's Throne (Corfu)
If it's good enough for Kaiser Wilhelm II, it's good enough for us. Above Pelekas in western Corfu, the views of country, coast and the Ionian Sea are spectacular (see p. 71).

The Monastery of Theotokou (Corfu) From the terrace of this beautiful monastery, enjoy vistas of surf-ringed rocks and cliffs like something out of an 18th-century Romantic painting (see p. 65).

Filerimos (Rhodes) Climb up the spiral staircase inside the giant cross and, vertigo permitting, look out across Rhodes' west coast – terrific (see p. 115)!

Monte Smith (Rhodes) After a gentle climb (or road-train ride) to the summit of Monte Smith, Rhodes Town lies before you like a pictorial map (see p. 99).

Askifou (Crete) As you top the rise and start to drive down towards Askifou, your first glimpse of the plateau's patchwork of fields–so unexpected in the arid mountains of western

The Kaiser's Throne, Corfu

Crete–takes the breath away (see p. 150).

The Venizelos Graves (Crete)
Eleftherios Venizelos chose this site for his grave partly because of its historical significance, but also, surely, for the view across Chania. Try to be there at sunset (see p. 140).

Derveni Gorge (Evia)
Approaching the Derveni Gorge from the south, mountains hang against the sky, and everywhere is the smell of pine and the clang of goat bells (see p. 190).

Myli (Evia) The drive up to Myli, above Karystos, opens up a view of the town and the sea beyond. If you're feeling fit, climb up to Castel Rosso, or even to the summit of Mount Ochi – the view gets even better as you get higher (see p. 200).

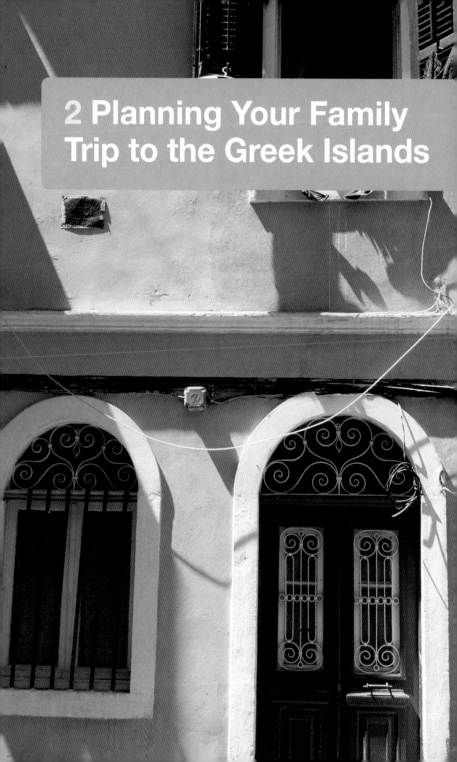

2 Planning Your Family Trip to the Greek Islands

GREECE

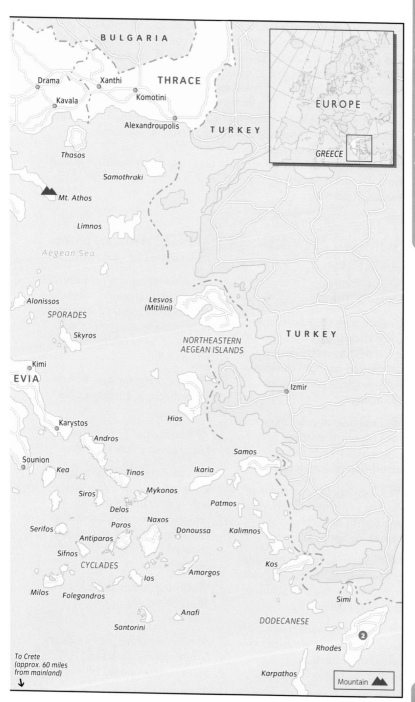

Anybody organising any kind of family holiday has a hard furrow to plough. You have to keep in mind the overall budget, the time constraints, the logistics, and above all, the needs and tastes of a group of disparate human beings aged from birth to... whatever. Do it well and you'll get scant credit. Do it badly and you'll never hear the end of it. No matter if you're dad or mum, granddad or grandma or a teenager who's defiantly taken on responsibility for the whole holiday: whoever you are, my heart goes out to you!

Only you can plan a successful holiday for your particular family. Its blend of ages, interests and skills, the dynamic relationship between its members, are unique.

I, however, can offer pointers for planning family holidays gleaned from decades of arranging my own, and from the experiences of friends. Read on!

SOME PLANNING BASICS

Before going

Consult with the whole family when deciding on a destination – it has to suit everybody. Once a destination has been chosen, let the youngsters play their part in the planning:

● Deciding whether to go for a package or organise the holiday yourselves, whether to tour, island-hop or stay in one place.

● Choosing between airlines/ car hire companies/ hotel/villa/ apartment, or between tour operators. See p. 32.

● Contacting tourist boards to get pamphlets, maps and general information sent (children love receiving mail!). See p. 17.

● Collecting guidebooks, novels, DVDs and so on about, or set, in the area you're going to, so that the family can get a rough idea of what the place is going to be like. (see box p. 34)

● Researching their own interests (animals, history, science), then putting together scrapbooks of 'things I want to see or do'. For more on Greek history, see Chapter 8.

● Discussing the type of food you're likely to encounter. See p. 32.

● Having family quizzes at home about the destination.

● Learning a few useful Greek words or phrases, and (particularly important this) trying to get at least one member of the family up to speed on pronunciation and reading Cyrillic script. See Appendix, p. 230.

● Listing names and addresses of people to whom you want to send postcards.

● Downloading the Frommer's family activity pack from *www.frommers.co.uk*

Once there

Once you're on holiday, there are all sorts of ways to keep everybody amused:

● Limerick competitions (sample first lines: 'There was a young man from Corfu', 'A silly young woman from Crete')

● Most tacky piece of tourist tat, with an upper price limit and a prize. I still remember my son's triumph in Cyprus with a plastic donkey cigarette dispenser – you pumped the tail, and the cigarette emerged from ... well, I'm sure you can guess!

● Best photo competition: much easier and virtually cost-free with digital cameras, though you need to make decisions about age ranges, categories, and who will act as judge.

● Buy a load of postcards and stamps, so that it's easy to get cards written and sent with the minimum of fuss.

● Keep a log to which everybody contributes.

However, it's still down to the adults to make sure:

● That there's plenty built into each day's plans to interest everybody.

● That younger children have time to run around, climb things and have a laugh.

● That allowance is made for teenagers who would probably rather be with their friends, by letting them bring a friend along on holiday or making sure they

have the means to stay in touch – a mobile phone for texting, access to e-mail.

● That teenagers can have time on their own, and the opportunity to meet people their own age.

When you get home

It's a nice idea to put together a record of the holiday. It's easy enough to incorporate everybody's log entries, photographs and bits and pieces of souvenirs into a scrapbook. You can even produce a booklet, using software such as Microsoft Publisher. The youngsters will moan, the teenagers will consider it terminally uncool, but they'll come back to it time and again in the future.

THE REGIONS IN BRIEF

Each of the islands has a character all of its own. The first three (**Corfu**, **Rhodes** and **Crete**) are major destinations for UK holidaymakers – the route maps of the main airlines that serve them look like plates of spaghetti. A local or regional airport is, therefore, almost certain to offer **direct flights**. The three have much in common, but much also that is unique. The fourth island, Evia, is one that very few people have heard of – that's the point. It offers a different experience, for families seeking the unchanging side of Greek life and of Greece as it used to be.

Corfu

The queen of the **Ionian Islands** off Greece's northwest coast, Corfu is the closest to the UK, with the shortest flight times. Famed for its beauty and the exuberance of its plant and animal life, it is divided into the mountainous north, with pretty bays and fishing villages, and the more sedate and agricultural south. Between them stands **Corfu Town**, the cosmopolitan capital, dominated by two giant fortresses and a busy working port. Corfu has always had a close relationship with the UK – it was ruled by the British for the first part of the 19th century, and you'll see a lot of architecture and sculptures in the British imperial mould. You might even see a game of **cricket** on the Esplanade. You'll also see a lot of Venetian influences, which accounts for the capital's beauty. One of the earliest Greek islands to welcome tourism, it offers a variety of hotels, villas, apartments, cafés, restaurants and shops, together with a wealth of nice places to visit. It's big enough to offer plenty of variety, small enough for you to be able to see most of it in a week or two.

Rhodes

From the western edge of the Greek archipelago to the eastern... Rhodes is in some ways similar to Corfu: much the same size, dominated by an historical capital city, much **greener** than you'd expect for an island so far south. Like Corfu, it's also in the holiday mainstream. The principal island of the **Dodecanese** group, Rhodes is defined by the 200 years it was ruled by the Knights of St John, and the short period of the 20th century when it was under the control of Mussolini's Italy – you can see the results of both everywhere.

The capital (**Rhodes Town**) lies at the island's extreme northern tip. Southwards, the regions are clearly delineated – a hot and arid north-east coast, a cooler, wetter and greener north-west coast, an attractively mountainous interior, dotted with picturesque villages, and a pleasantly rural south. Like Corfu, there's a healthy stock of places to stay, eat and go and things to do, with most of the developed holiday areas being in the northern half of the island, though with the south slowly catching up. Again like Corfu, the island is big enough to offer lots of contrasts, yet be do-able in a week or two.

Crete

The largest of all the Greek islands, Crete is the only one that is not part of a group. Indeed, it's big enough to be a country in its own right. Stretching along Greece's southernmost line of latitude, the resulting heat is mitigated by the effect of strong **seasonal winds**. The most history-rich of Greece's islands, everywhere you are aware of the past – of the great **Minoan** civilisation, of rule by the Venetians and the Ottoman Empire, of the bitter

War of Independence and successive rebellions until Crete finally joined the new Greek state in 1913, and of the vicious fighting against the Nazi occupation during World War II.

Long and narrow, Crete is divided into four administrative areas, divided by mountain ranges and ruled from its four main towns – (from east to west) Agios Nikolaos, Iraklion, Rethymnon and Chania. The most developed part is the north coast, accessed by the National Road. Each area stretches down to the south coast, which is dotted with fishing villages and is joined to the north coast by good-quality main roads. Inland, Crete consists of lofty mountain ranges scored by gorges, fertile valleys and plateaus. Though it's difficult to generalise, **Western Crete** seems to be more child-friendly and family-oriented than the east, so this is the area covered throughout this book.

Evia

Almost as big as Crete, Evia hugs the east coast of central Greece just **north of Athens**. Attached to the mainland by two bridges near the capital, **Chalkida**, there are also numerous ferry crossings, which take anything from 30 minutes to an hour.

Evia is different from the other three islands in almost every way. It stands at the heart of Greece, rather than at its western, eastern or southern limits. Although it does have a tourist industry, it is aimed largely at the Greeks themselves, who visit the island for the hot springs and mountains, the small resorts and beaches, and the relaxed pace of life. Hotels and apartment blocks tend to be relatively small, menus are usually Greek and don't try to be 'international', road signs, especially away from the capital, are in **Greek script**. Although many people in Evia speak English, especially those who work in tourism, many in towns and villages outside the capital don't. What Evia offers UK families is both beautiful scenery and total immersion in **Greek life**.

VISITOR INFORMATION

The **Greek National Tourism Organisation** can provide information needed about travelling to, from and within Greece: see *www.gnto.gr* or contact their offices:

Greek National Tourism Organisation, 4 Conduit Street, London W1S 2DJ
☏ *020 7495 9300*,
www.visitgreece.gr

and in the US:
Olympic Tower,
645 Fifth Avenue, Suite 903,
New York, NY 10022
☏ *212 421 5777*,
www.greektourism.com

However, tourist information is not one of Greece's strengths. The provision of information offices in Greek towns and villages is hit-and-miss, and where they do exist what they can offer in terms of information about attractions is often a little thin.

Entry Requirements and Customs

Entry requirements

European Union and US citizens need only a valid passport to travel to Greece – no visa is required. You may stay for up to 90 days. For longer visits you need a residence permit from the appropriate office. For further information, contact the **Embassy of Greece in London** (📞 *020 7221 6467*) or the Greek Consular office in Washington (📞 *202 939 1306, www.greek embassy.org*).

Customs

The import of **plants in soil** is strictly prohibited as well as narcotics, firearms and parrots! While most sports and camping equipment have no restrictions it should be noted that only one windsurf board per person may be imported duty free and a note of it will be made in your passport to ensure that the board is exported.

When travelling into Greece from the UK or Ireland visitors over the age of 18 may bring in:

800 cigarettes or 200 cigars or 400 cigarillos or 1 kg of loose tobacco.

10 litres of alcoholic beverage or 90 litres of wine and 110 litres of beer.

When travelling from Greece to the UK or Ireland there is no need to pay tax or duty on items that were bought in Greece, as long as local tax was paid on purchase. This applies to purchases for personal use only and customs are likely to question you about goods that exceed the following limits:

3200 cigarettes or 400 cigarillos or 200 cigars or 3 kg of loose tobacco.

110 litres of beer or 90 litres of wine or 10 litres of spirits or 20 litres of fortified wine.

When travelling within the **European Union** you are permitted to pay tax-free prices on fragrances, cosmetics, skincare, photographic goods, electrical goods, fashion and accessories, gifts and souvenirs.

When entering Greece from the US, over-18s may bring in the following:

10 kilos of food and drink; 200 cigarettes or 50 cigars or 250 grams of tobacco; 1 litre of spirits or 2 litres of wine; 50 grams of perfume; 500 grams of coffee; 100 grams of tea.

When travelling into the US, the first $800 worth of gifts are duty free (every 30 days). For the next $1000 worth a flat rate of duty is charged. Any items above this $1800 limit are charged at the normal rates for that commodity.

For any valuable personal items (electronic equipment, jewellery) that you intend to take

TIP 〉〉 **Exporting Antiquities** 《

The export of **antiquities** out of Greece is strictly prohibited. Any genuine antiquity, particularly religious objects including icons, needs special permission to leave the country and you must provide receipts and a full explanation of how it was acquired. In addition, an **export certificate** must be provided for any object that dates from before 1830. This should be provided by the dealer or shopkeeper responsible for the sale.

with you to Greece, take proof (receipts, insurance documentation or similar) that they were purchased in the US, otherwise you might be charged at the above rates on your return. Alternatively, register the items (free) with your nearest Customs office, or at the airport of departure.

Further information is available on *www.cbp.gov* ☎ *877/ 287-8667.*

Money

Currency

The **euro** has been the official currency in Greece since 2002. There are seven denominations of notes: €500, €200, €100, €50, €20, €10 and €5. Coins come in denominations of €2, €1 and 50, 20, 10, 5, 2 and 1 cents. You may hear the cents being referred to as *lepta*, which was to the Drachma what the cent is to the euro. Although euros differ slightly in appearance from country to country, they are legal tender throughout the Eurozone. In smaller shops and restaurants there can sometimes be a problem using large denomination notes, so ensure you carry smaller notes with you. Most banks and travel agents and

the Post Office offer foreign currency and traveller's cheques.

> **INSIDER TIP** 〉〉
>
> When you arrive on your Greek island, you'll need a €1 coin at the airport to secure a trolley, and there are often long queues at airport cashpoints.

Credit cards and cash machines (ATMs)

Credit cards are widely accepted in Greece – look out for the labels posted on the shop door. However, in many places this seems more theoretically than practically true. Many Greek retailers, waiters and so on seem reluctant to accept plastic. Fuel station attendants (still widespread in Greece – self-service pumps are uncommon) have pockets full of cash to make change on the spot, and get fed up if you insist on paying by card.

The most convenient and safe way to obtain cash while on holiday is to get it from a cash machine (ATM), just as you do at home – with your normal bank card or credit card. Look out for the useful ATM locators on providers' websites before you go (*www.visa.co.uk* and *www. mastercard.co.uk*). Enter as much information about your intended location as you can provide, and it gives you addresses telephone numbers and a map of the closest ATMs.

Credit and debit card companies charge a fee for currency exchange. Depending on how the charges work, it may prove-cost effective to withdraw cash in larger sums (on debit cards only) and use it for transactions, rather than using the card direct. Check with your card provider before you go.

Another option worth investigating is a **pre-paid credit card** that you charge up just like a pay-as-you-go mobile phone. The Visa card offered by the Post Office costs a one-off £10. Top the card up by phone, with a limit you set, and if it is lost or stolen, the card and any remaining balance will be replaced. See *www.postoffice.com*

Traveller's cheques

Though now something of an anachronism, traveller's cheques can still be a useful back-up. You'll have no problems changing them at banks and larger hotels, and many (but by no means all) other establishments accept them.

Thomas Cook also offers an **American Express traveller's cheque card** that works in a similar way to the pre-paid Visa card (see above). It's available to any child aged 13 or over and can be used anywhere that accepts American Express. See *www.thomascook.com*

Banking hours

Banking hours are generally 8am until 2pm, but check with the closest bank when you arrive.

If you need money in an **emergency** you can have it transferred to you through **Western Union,** (*www.western union.com*). This can be done through an agent, over the phone or online.

The Greek Islands on a budget

● Booking flights (or even hotels) **online** couldn't be easier; if you can be flexible with times and whether or not you fly

---

TIP ▶▶ **Keep Copies of Everything** ◀◀

Before you go, **photocopy** your passport, traveller's cheques, credit cards (both sides), travel insurance details, itinerary and airline tickets. Carry one copy with you and leave a duplicate and your mobile number with someone back home.

For each of your credit and debit cards, copy down the emergency phone number. You'll probably find it on the back of your card in minuscule print.

It's worth taking the contact details of your card provider's global assistance service in case your credit card gets **lost or stolen**.

direct you might be surprised how much you save – try: *www.cheapflights.co.uk*, *www.skyscanner.net* or *www.flightline.co.uk*. If you see a hotel or aspect of a package deal that appeals, contact the hotel **direct** to see if they can offer it for less.

● Tour operators often offer a flight/hotel/car rental package more cheaply than you could do it yourself (see box p. 238).

(see box p. 238)

INSIDER TIP 》

Phone or e-mail a hotel that you've seen in a guidebook, brochure or online and check availability. Check again closer to the time and if there is still available room you'll be in a good position to haggle.

● Study hotel tariffs carefully – some charge for cots, while children of certain ages are free in some but get only a discount in others, and so on. Hotels often put up their prices during **local festivals**, so avoid staying unless you're actually going to the festival.

● Fish restaurants often show prices by the kilo, making it difficult to know how much your meal is going to cost. Ask... or order something else!

● Check prices before entering a restaurant. There is no need to **tip** lavishly – it's not expected. Whatever small change is left is usually enough.

● Some **museums** are free on certain days, often Sundays. Over-60s and students usually pay the child rate – ask.

● If you can, visit out of season as it's a lot cheaper. However, some attractions may be closed.

● If using taxis, establish a price before getting in – it's sometimes negotiable.

What things cost in the Greek Islands

Though not as cheap as it once was, Greece still has the edge over northern Europe and the US in value for money. In most tavernas a couple can have a three-course meal with wine for €35-50, bus fares between towns are between €3 and €6, taxis €5-15 for local trips, museums are rarely more than €3, daily car hire starts at about €25 and petrol is around €1 per litre. The Greek government also introduced a law that ensures you shouldn't pay more than €0.50 for a regular sized bottle of water. Hotel prices are also reasonable when compared with UK equivalents.

When to Go

Weather

The Greek Islands enjoy a **Mediterranean climate**, with hot summers and cool, wet winters. Corfu is wetter than Crete, and has a shorter holiday period. The west coast of Rhodes is wetter and cooler than the east. All areas of Greece enjoy hot summer months, with temperatures averaging 30-35°C (85-95°F) but frequently reaching highs of 40°C (104°F) and more. Other

Comparative Temperatures and Sunshine on the Greek Islands		Jan	Feb	Mar	Apr	May	Jun	Jul	Aug	Sept	Oct	Nov	Dec
Corfu	Temp	14	15	16	19	23	28	31	31	28	23	19	16
	Sun	4	4	6	7	9	11	12	11	9	7	5	4
Rhodes	Temp	15	15	16	19	23	27	29	30	27	24	19	16
	Sun	3	4	5	6	9	11	13	12	10	7	4	3
Crete	Temp	16	16	17	20	23	27	29	29	27	24	21	18
	Sun	3	5	6	8	10	11	13	12	10	7	6	4
Evia	Temp	11	12	13	18	22	26	28	27	25	20	16	13
	Sun	3	4	5	8	10	12	13	11	9	6	4	3
Temp = average daily temperature in Centigrade.													
Sun = average daily hours of sun.													

variables need to be taken into account: some islands (e.g. Crete) have strong seasonal winds, which can make them seem cooler, and correspondingly increase the danger of getting serious sunburn or sunstroke. The combination of strong winds and heat in the summer can also cause forest fires.

For weather forecasts, check out *www.bbc.co.uk/weather*, *www.met office.co.uk* or *www.weather.com*.

Public holidays in Greece

New Year's Day

Epiphany 6th January

Clean Monday Varies (see p. 23)

Easter Varies

Independence Day 25th March

May Day 1st May

Pentecost Monday Varies

Assumption of the Virgin 15th August

Ochi Day 28th October

Christmas Eve

Christmas Day

St Stephen's Day 26th December

During any of these, government offices, banks, post offices and many museums, restaurants and tavernas are closed. The dates of some public holidays vary because they are linked to the date of Easter (see below).

You may be forced by school holidays to take Greek Island holidays in July and August. The pluses are that the weather's at its hottest and all attractions are open. The disadvantages are, of course, overcrowding in many places, and top price for everything. Spring and autumn are cheaper and less crowded.

An **Easter** holiday in the Greek Islands is especially enjoyable – with lots of eating, drinking and dancing going on, mild weather, spring flowers and birdsong.

Children's favourite Greek Island events

The Greeks love children, and it isn't unusual to have everyone from teenage boys to old ladies engaging them in conversation and clucking over babies. If your child is crying, you won't be treated to stares of disgust – but to offers of help. Consequently there are plenty of public **festivals** not specifically aimed at children that yours will love nonetheless.

January

New Year's Day 1st January is a celebration of **St Basil**, who, like Father Christmas, gives out gifts. Tradition dictates that eating Vassilopita, a special basil cake, is a must. Watch the children's faces as they wait to see if their slice contains the hidden coin that will bring them luck for the year ahead.

Epiphany ★★ 6th January is a holiday that celebrates the **Baptism of Christ** with the blessing of water and the vessels that hold it. All over the Greek Islands you will find priests throwing a cross into water – either the sea, rivers or lakes – and people swimming out to recover it. Children will love hearing the legend of the **Kallikantzari**, goblins that spend their year attempting to cut down the tree that holds the Earth. As with all hard-working goblins, they take Christmas off and during the 12 days of Christmas like nothing

better than to cause mischief and play tricks. The blessing of the waters sends them back to the underground where the renewal of the tree sees them start again until next Christmas.

February

Karnavali Widely celebrated in many parts of Greece, it involves drinking, dancing and general merrymaking, with dressing up and marching bands. In Corfu it has an **Italian** flavour; in Crete its own particular spin.

Apokreas and Clean Monday (or Pure Monday, Ash Monday) ★★ Apokreas is the period of eating, dancing and celebration that leads up to the beginning of **Lent**. It ends on Clean Monday, a public holiday. Since you're supposed to be off the meat, eggs, oil and dairy products for Lent, Apokreas is kind of a three-week pancake day whose dates vary with Easter. It's also carnival time. Traditionally everyone dresses up and people have to guess their identities. The final weekend of Apokreas is the most popular for masked balls and children's parties, culminating in parades across Greece on the Sunday. On Clean Monday, families pack Lent-friendly picnics, eat in tavernas and go kite-flying.

TIP **Easter Holidays**

In 2008 and 2009 Greek Orthodox Easter is on a different date from the 'Western' Easter so you can take a holiday whilst dodging Greek Easter prices.

Rethymno Carnival ★ Art, culture, dancing, theatre and traditional Greek customs are all part of this **Cretan** carnival. Enjoy a grand parade, treasure hunts, a graffiti festival and fancy dress balls – and on Shrove Thursday a huge open-air party.

March

Greek Independence Day and the Feast of the Annunciation

This dual celebration of Greek independence and the day that Archangel Gabriel told Mary that she was pregnant is a busy day that sees **military parades** and religious celebrations throughout Greece. As with any Greek celebration or public holiday, children are not only welcome but practically revered.

April

Easter ★★★ Orthodox Easter is a major celebration everywhere in Greece. Good Friday sees a procession with big crowds; it's a day of mourning when church bells ring slowly throughout. Saturday is for preparation: just before midnight everyone, including children, goes to church for the miracle of the **Resurrection**. Afterwards they slowly make their way home with a candle and hundreds of people heading along the streets from every church is a truly moving sight. Easter Sunday is a day of celebration marking the end of Lent. Lamb is spit-roasted over hot

coals; dyed red eggs are a traditional snack. **Corfu** has its own version of Easter, with marching bands and the hurling of pots into the street.

Feast of St George This feast day of the patron saint of **shepherds** is an important rural celebration with dancing and a traditional feast.

May

May Day Another day for family picnicking. It's traditional to head to the country to pick flowers and make wreaths.

June

Rhodes Flower Festival. This two-day contest for the most beautiful garden, balcony and shop window in Rhodes includes an open-air concert, activities for children, dancing and a flower-themed art and photography exhibition.

Rhodes Cultural Summer Festival (to September) This festival varies year to year, but always involves a range of events including dance, theatre and music. Look out for events at the **Medieval Moat Theatre** for added atmosphere. Go to the 'Events Calendar' at *www.rhodes.gr* for details of what's on when.

July

Rethymnon Wine Festival (Crete) Wine and Cretan folklore music as the sun goes down.

Renaissance Festival of Rethymnon (July–August)

A rich festival that includes theatre, dance, music and the visual arts. Past highlights have included theatre by **Cretan playwrights**, as well as Shakespeare and Molière. Musicians from around the world perform. For further information see *www.rfr.gr*

August

Feast of the Assumption of the Virgin 15th August marks the day the Virgin Mary ascended into Heaven, a huge holiday in Greece – the third-biggest religious day after Easter and Christmas. People return to their home towns and villages; the entire country is closed for celebrations, church services and festivals. Family gatherings and feasts make this a wonderful time to be in Greece. Travel can be difficult so book well in advance.

Paleochora Music Festival (Crete) Song contests and music are performed on an **open-air stage** in the village – with a lively party atmosphere.

September

Feast of the Exaltation of the Cross (Ypsosis tou Timiou Stavrou) This autumnal feast, on 14th September, marks the last of the outdoor summer festivals and feasts.

October

Ochi Day ★ 28th October is a public holiday that commemorates the reply given by General Ioannis Metaxa in response to Mussolini's demand for surrender during World War II. Ochi ('no' in Greek) Day is a celebration involving military parades, folk music and dancing.

Elos Chestnut Festival (Crete) This tiny Cretan village celebrates the edible **chestnut** with local entertainment, *usually* around 15th October, but check ahead.

November

Tsikoudia Festival, Voukolies Tsikoudia, or raki, a distilled spirit, is honoured in this late autumn festival. Try it in many variations, including raki made with honey, along with other local produce.

St Minos Parade Iraklion honours its patron with a parade along Kalokerinou. **St Minos** saved Christians from being slaughtered by Turks in the 19th century.

December

Christmas Christmas Day and 26th December are public holidays in Greece. Traditionally Christmas is not as big as Easter, but Western customs are infiltrating: turkeys and Christmas trees are quite common. Christmas is a time for families, singing and feasting.

New Year's Eve Children sing and adults drink and eat.

What to Pack

Even in the summer heat, it's worth packing a **light jacket** or jumper for cool evenings. If you have a child who will be in a buggy, then don't forget a light blanket for the same reason.

For trips to a Greek monastery, or if you will be attending an Orthodox religious festival, you will need to **cover up** shoulders and legs. Sunglasses, hats and suncream are essential in the summer; ditto a warm coat and jumpers in winter.

Pack a collection of each person's clothing in each suitcase, so if one goes missing no one has to suffer the indignity of having no clean clothes, teenagers having to wear their parents clothes or, even worse, vice versa.

In-flight hand luggage, take small cartons of ready-made formula for babies, which saves you the bother of having to mix it and ensures your baby has sealed sterile food. If you're **breastfeeding**, pack a light sheet or muslin to allow you some privacy. This will also be useful later in Greek restaurants, where discretion is recommended, and can be useful for blocking the vision of a curious baby. A must for hand luggage is enough **nappies and wipes,** not only for the flight but extras in case it is delayed. Flights can be boring for young children once the excitement wears off, so pack colouring books, pens and pencils, sticker books and notebooks as well as story books. Reveal your stock of distractions slowly in order to get maximum value time from them. Noisy toys are best avoided, and don't forget your child's favourite **comfort toy**. Older children and parents might enjoy small travel games, mp3 players, books and magazines.

Check restrictions on hand luggage before you fly – there may be security checks that affect what you can take on board. For all you need to know see the **Department for Transport** (*www.dft.gov.uk*) and **British Airports Authority** (*www.baa.co.uk*) websites, or in the US the Federal Aviation Administration (*www.faa.gov*).

Health, Insurance and Safety

Health

No **vaccinations** are needed for Greece, but it's worth checking that your children's inoculations are up to date. It also may be worth considering a vaccination for **tick-borne encephalitis** (TBE) if you are camping, rambling or travelling to forested areas.

A big health risk in the summer is the **sun**. Drink plenty of water, wear a high SPF sun cream, cover up where possible and wear a hat and sunglasses. It is highly recommended that you stay out of the sun during the hottest part of the day – you can be burned even through a parasol.

Travellers from the UK need to apply for a **European Health Insurance Card** (EHIC), which entitles EU citizens to free or reduced cost healthcare. The card is valid for five years and allows you the same treatment as a resident of Greece if you become ill or have an accident during your trip. Each person travelling needs their own card and it's free. You can apply at *www.dh.gov.uk/travellers*, on ☎ *0845 606 2030* or pick up a form at the Post Office. A postal application should take up to 21 days and telephone and online applications take up to seven days.

The EHIC card isn't a substitute for travel and health **insurance**. Be sure to check carefully for exclusions on your policy and that you are covered for any activities that you are planning. It may be worth checking home insurance policies or credit card perks to find out if you are already covered for things such as contents away from home; you may find it is more cost effective to extend one or more of these policies than buying a new one. If you are not covered, comprehensive cover can be found at a reasonable price online. Shop around: **Moneysupermarket** (*www.moneysupermarket.com*) compares prices and coverage across a bewildering range.

The **hospitals** and medical centres in Greece are of varying standards and services may be limited on the islands – the ambulance service in particular can be rudimentary. Find out about medical facilities close to where you will be staying before you travel. Many of the big resort hotels have **doctors on call**.

Safety

Crime rates in Greece are relatively low, but tourism does attract pickpockets and thieves, especially in crowds. Stay as vigilant as you would at home, and keep valuables in the **hotel safe**. Ditto passports. You should always keep a photocopy of the main page somewhere separate from the passport itself. **Sexual assaults** are rare, but they do occur: older teenage daughters should be warned against drinking too much, going off alone with strangers and leaving drinks unattended. For up-to-date travel safety information visit *www.britishembassy. gov.uk* or *www.fco.gov.uk,* and in the US *travel.state.gov*.

Road safety

There are high numbers of **road traffic accidents** in Greece – the death rate on Greek roads is three times higher than in Britain. Extra care should therefore be taken whether driving or walking. Hiring motorcycles, mopeds, scooters or quad bikes really isn't a good idea, especially if you're not experienced – the rate of serious and fatal accidents involving tourists on these forms of transport is frightening. If you do hire a moped, scooter or motorcycle you should be aware that Greek law requires you to wear a helmet (or a full face helmet/helmet and goggles if you are on a quad bike). Failure to wear a helmet is also likely to invalidate any travel insurance. A full driving licence is needed to drive a moped

TIP ›› **Greek Laws** ‹‹

Indecent behaviour, possession of even small quantities of drugs, drink-driving and carrying an offensive weapon (such as knuckle-dusters or a knife with a blade bigger than 10 cm) are crimes punishable by a large fine or **imprisonment**. It is also imperative you are **identifiable**, so carry photo ID at all times.

and it needs to cover category A1, light motorcycle, not category P which is valid in the UK for driving a moped up to 50cc.

Travelling Safely with Children

Ensure that everyone has the name, address and phone number of the hotel or apartments you are staying in. This can be put in the pocket of younger children along with your mobile phone numbers. Remember to include dialling codes.

Make younger children aware of what to do if they get lost. Make these as similar as possible to any safeguards you have in place at home so they are then more likely to remember them. Common recommendations are that they should find someone in uniform or to go to a shop and ask for help.

Hold hands with small children, especially in busy areas where you can lose them in seconds.

Dress young children in bright colours, and take a buggy for any who have recently stopped using one at home. This is not just a safety issue – small legs can find it difficult to keep up, especially when sightseeing.

Safety measures also need to be put into place for older children,

with clear procedures in the event that you get separated. Arrange a time and place that your child can find easily. Perhaps give older ones a phone – with strict limits on chatting to friends back home!

Specialised Resources

Single parents

UK companies such as **Small Families** (📞 *01763 226567*, *www.smallfamilies.co.uk*) specialise in single-parent family holidays. **Websites** that are worth a look for travel advice (before you leave), friendships and member discounts are *www.singleparents. org.uk* and *www.oneparent families.org.uk* has now merged with the original single-parent family resource *www.gingerbread. org.uk*. They provide excellent travel advice as well as a **lone parent helpline** 📞 *0800 018 5026*.

Be aware that under UK law if you have joint parental responsibility without a residence order you need the consent of the other parent to take your child abroad. If you have joint parental responsibility with a residence order you can take your child abroad for up to a month without consent. If in any doubt call the lone parent helpline above.

Families with special needs

The following UK-based organisations offer help and advice for families travelling with a member who has special needs.

Tourism For All *www.holidaycare.org.uk* (📞 *0845 124 9971*) and the Royal Association for Disability and Rehabilitation *www.radar.org.uk* (📞 *020 7250 3222*).

The 21st-century Traveller

Greece has a well-developed **Internet** culture. Many hotels offer Internet access, either in a dedicated 'internet corner' somewhere, or 'in-room' access via the TV or your own laptop. Even the ferries across the Adriatic from Italy have Web access.

To connect your laptop to the Internet there are two main ways:

● Sign up for a net-roaming account that gives you an ISP that you can use worldwide without changing settings on your computer or struggling with local access numbers.

● Get a pay-as-you-go connection from a Greek Internet Service Provider.

There are **Internet cafés** all over the islands. The charge is generally reasonable – €1 for 15–20 minutes. Local people usually know where the nearest one is; also try the places named in the 'Fast Facts' for each of the islands.

Before you travel let your **mobile phone provider** know you are going abroad and check that there is no **international call bar** on your phone if you want to use it. Find out from your phone network which Greek network they recommend – when you first switch you phone on in Greece you may be given a choice; one may be cheaper. Remember you will pay to receive calls while abroad. You may also pay to receive voicemail, even if you never pick it up. Check with your provider and disable the system temporarily if necessary. Greek mobile phone networks include Cosmote, TIM, Vodafone and Q-Telecom.

TIP ▶ **i-Kids** ◀

If you're worried about your children wandering off in a town, or just want to give them the freedom of the campsite, consider a **GPS-based i-Kids handset** (*www.i-kids.net*). If your phone has WAP and GPRS capabilities, you can track their movements and send them text messages. Each child handset has an alarm button that will dial your phone if pressed, and can store up to three other numbers for them to dial. You can even pre-set a radius beyond which they're not to roam: if they go too far, you'll get a text message. In the UK the handset costs £99.99 from **mobiles2go** (📞 *0844 800 9133*, *www.mobiles2go.com*). An 18-month contract costs £15.75 per month.

Alternatively buy a local sim card to slot into your phone. You can buy these from any mobile phone or electronics shop, even from some kiosks, for about €15. If you intend to make lots of local calls, this will almost certainly save you money, but remember to get your handset **unlocked** before you leave – any small mobile phone shop in the UK will do it for about a fiver.

Payphones in Greece tend to be card phones. Cards can be bought at shops and kiosks and come in varying denominations from €3 upwards.

Accommodation Options

The variety of accommodation – in type, location, price/quality and provider – is vast, especially in Corfu, Rhodes and Crete (on Evia you're more restricted). Before committing yourself to a specific holiday, you need to keep certain considerations in mind.

Type

What will suit your family best – a hotel, a villa or an apartment? Each has its own advantages, and its own drawbacks.

Villas offer privacy, the exclusive use of bathrooms and showers, often a pool, terrace and barbecue area, the ability to prepare your own meals, and, within reason, the freedom to make as much noise as you like. On the downside, villas can isolate you, with little opportunity for your children to make new friends.

You'll also have to find your own food. The Greek Islands are not blessed (or cursed) with UK-style hypermarkets; to some extent, you'll live like a local. This chance to experience the 'authentic' side of island life may be something you'll treasure. Finally you will almost certainly need to **hire a car**.

Resort hotels, on the other hand, provide such a wealth of activities and facilities on site that you might well enjoy a terrific holiday without setting foot outside the premises. The best offer a heady cocktail for all ages – kid's clubs, games and sports, beach activities, courses, discos, evening entertainment. Add the provision of babysitters in many and the wide variety of excursions on offer, and you can quite understand their popularity. There are also lots of opportunities for **making friends**. On the downside, noise and congestions, especially during high season, can be a nuisance, with rowdy neighbours, queues in the cafeteria and heaving swimming pools. Unless you can afford a suite, rooms can sometimes begin to feel very restrictive. You will also need to make an effort to go out and find the 'real' side of island life.

Apartments ideally combine the independence of villas with the opportunities for meeting other families of the resort hotel – many are grouped around a common swimming pool with a pool bar. However, they also combine some of the disadvantages listed above.

In many areas the distinction between resort hotels, villas and apartments is breaking down – in addition to rooms and suites, hotels offer apartments and bungalows within the grounds, combining access to a wide range of facilities with greater privacy. Increasingly villas and apartments are sited so that they offer easy access to local restaurants and swimming pools.

Other options include accommodation arising from the Agritourism movement (see, for example, the cottages in Vamos included in 'Family-friendly Accommodation' in Crete, or have a look at *www.europe-greece. com*. Camping is also viable – in Corfu and Evia it would be possible to take your own car/tent/caravan. In the other islands, realistically, you're confined to bungalows in campsites.

Location

In addition to considering the type of accommodation to best suit your family, you need to think about its location. What are the transfer times from the airport? Is it reasonably close to the main attractions? On Rhodes, for example, if your main goal is the capital, you don't want to be facing a 50-km drive from the southern tip of the island every time you visit. Is it within walking distance of the beach, the local village or a bus stop? For families with teenagers, it's useful to be able to offer them some independence. Look out too in this book for recommendations in this guide as

to which parts of which islands are particularly family friendly.

Price/quality

By and large, you get what you pay for. There's plenty of excellent accommodation out there, and loads of good deals, especially if you dodge high season. But take care. Tariffs are sometimes so complicated that it's difficult to do a valid comparison. Is a rental car included? Is it half-board, B&B or room only? Are there charges for extra beds or cots? Are there any other hidden costs? Watch out also for the 'wide-angle lens' trap (a photo makes a room look bigger than it is) and even the 'digitally enhanced' trap (all sorts of nasty things are edited digitally). As with so many things, the Internet has revolutionised this aspect of holiday planning – check websites like TripAdvisor (*www.tripadvisor. com*) which offer the uncensored views of guests who have already stayed there. There are also online holiday forums where you could post queries about accommodation you're thinking of booking (for example, *www. holidaytruths.co.uk*).

Provider

It is a simple matter nowadays to arrange every detail of your holiday on the Internet. But certain advantages arise from using tour operators – they do all the work, arrange hassle-free transfers from the airport, provide local reps who can be a valuable source of information and can use local contacts to help resolve problems that may arise. They also offer support and restitution if things go wrong. (for details of tour operators, see Appendix, p. 238.

Getting There

By plane The vast majority of people visiting the Greek Islands do so by plane – it has never been so easy, or so inexpensive, to fly. The principal providers of scheduled flights to Greece from the UK are **British Airways** (℡ *0870 850 9850, www.british airways.com*) and **Olympic Airlines** (℡ *0870 606 0460, www.olympicairlines.com*). BA flies from Heathrow, Gatwick and Manchester.

The main no-frills airlines with routes to the Greek Islands are:

Thomsonfly: *www.thomsonfly.com*

Flythomascook: *www.flythomas cook.com*

Airtours: *www.airtours.co.uk*

XL: *www.xl.com*

From the US, only two airlines offer direct flights: Olympic Airlines (℡ *800 223 1226*) and Delta Airlines (℡ *800 241 4141, www.delta.com*) fly nonstop from JFK to Athens.

Getting around

For more details on individual islands, see 'Getting around' in each of the relevant chapters: **Corfu**, p. 44; **Rhodes**, p. 87; **Evia**, p. 183; western **Crete**, p. 132.

Eating and Drinking in Greece

Eating in Greece is a social activity – it's said that, if a couple are dining alone, they're either in love or have no friends! *What* is eaten could be described as a theme with variations. Many of the dishes that make up Greek cuisine are common across the mainland and islands and, indeed, in Greek households and restaurants throughout the world. The great staples of Greek cooking are fish, meat, cheese, pasta, olive oil and bread. This is reflected in the statistics – Greece eats more meat, per head of population, than any other country in the EU, it eats the most cheese, and is second only to Italy for pasta consumption.

But beyond this common theme there are regional variations, from slightly different ingredients or ways of cooking to dishes which are exclusive to that region or island. In restaurants, ask the waiter if there are regional dishes on the menu – people are proud of their culinary traditions. Look out for:

Corfu: *pastitsada* (spicy braised beef or veal and pasta); *sofrito* (beef and onion with garlic and herbs); *bianco fish* (fish and potatoes); *bourdetto* (fish stew); *sikomaedoa* (fig pie).

Rhodes: *pitaroudia* (chickpea patties); *pirgouri balls* (veal and couscous balls); *lakani* (veal with course wheat); *chicken with loukoumi* (stuffed chicken with pasta); *dolmades with pirgouri* (cabbage leaves stuffed with pork and couscous).

Before you go:

- Look online for policies or advice regarding flying with children which apply to your airline.
- If you have a baby, ask if you can book a bassinet.
- Introduce first-time flyers to likely **scenarios** (check-in, security, the safety talk, a bumpy ride) by playing 'let's go to the airport'.
- Read your toddler the 'Going on a Plane' chapter from *The Little Book of First Experiences* (Usborne, £5.99) before you go.
- Put together a 'survival' kit of disposable nappies, bottles, wipes, snacks, drinks, toys, books, stickers, paper and pencils (but check the frequently changing regulations concerning what you are allowed to take in your hand luggage).
- Let the children have their own backpacks – they love it, and it reduces the load on you.
- Get to the airport in plenty of time and use automatic check-in – it saves queuing. However, if you have young children it might be an idea to check in at the desk. When you do so, ask if the flight's fully booked. If not, the booking clerk may agree to block out the seats next to you, giving you more room.
- Use reins or a harness for toddlers, and dress them in bright, clashing colours – it'll make them easier to see if they wander.

During the flight:

- Tell cabin staff when you're about to change a nappy – they may be able to help by showing you to a changing table.
- Scented nappy sacks are useful for all sorts of things – dirty nappies, of course, but also soiled clothes, used wipes and general rubbish.
- If given the choice, opt out of airline food and bring your own, especially with fussy children. Persuade them that you're having a picnic.
- Feed babies as you take off and land – it can help to avoid ear discomfort.
- For children who haven't learned how to 'pop' their ears, use ear plugs or cotton wool.

These websites are packed with more good ideas:
www.travellingwithchildren.co.uk, *www.family-travel.co.uk*, *www.babyflying. co.uk/travel_tips.htm*.

Crete: *saligaria stifado* (snail and onion stew); *kouneli stifado* (rabbit and onion stew); *horta* (wild greens); *lamb kriotopita* (lamb and cheese pasty); *myzithra* (soft cheese); *staka* (cheese, often cooked).

Evia: *bougatsa* (cream cheese pie with cinnamon).

Wherever you are in Greece, breakfast isn't made much of – most Greeks will make do with a cup of coffee, a slice of bread with honey or preserves, perhaps rice pudding.

Getting the Children Interested in the Greek Islands

Greece has long been a source of fascination to the British (and Americans) and as a result there's a wealth of published memoirs, travel books and novels in English relating to Greece, some of which are included below. All the books suggested can be obtained from good bookshops or online from Amazon (*www.amazon.co.uk*). Some are aimed specifically at children; others, more suitable for adults and older teens, would be a good source of information and anecdotes, which can then be passed on to the rest of the family.

Specifically for children

- Terry Deary, *The Groovy Greeks* and *Greek Legends* (Scholastic). Irreverent and very funny.
- Francesca Simon, *Helping Hercules* (Orion). Hilarious retelling of Greek myth. Great fun.
- Anthony Horowitz, *Myths and Legends* (Kingfisher). A cracking introduction.
- Caroline Lawrence, *The Colossus of Rhodes* (Orion Children's Books). Atmospheric novel aimed at Y5 and Y6 children, with lots of accurate detail.

General

- The 1963 film *Jason and the Argonauts* and the 1981 *Clash of the Titans* have worn remarkably well, and are a fun introduction to Greek mythology. The more recent *300*, *Last Stand of the 300* and *Troy*, though not well reviewed, are still a good way of introducing Greek history. All are available on DVD from Amazon.
- A.R. Burns, *The Pelican History of Greece* (Penguin). Useful short introduction to Ancient Greece, though it's now quite old.
- Lawrence Durrell, *The Greek Islands* (Faber and Faber) – a personal introduction to all the Greek islands, written in 1978.
- John L. Tomkinson, *Traveller's Greece* (Anagnosis Press) – a wonderful collection of extracts from historical first person narratives covering the whole of Greece and the islands.
- Suzanne Slesin et al., *Greek Style* (Thames and Hudson) – a wide-ranging illustrated guide to Greek design and domestic culture.

Corfu

- Edward Lear, *The Corfu Years* (Denise Harvey, Greece). An account of the famous nonsense-verse author's travels in mid-19th century Corfu.
- Gerald Durrell, *The Corfu Trilogy* (three books, including *My Family and Other Animals* (Penguin). Light-hearted description of people, plants and animals in 1930s Corfu by the famous zoologist.
- Lawrence Durrell, *Prospero's Cell* (Faber and Faber). Sensitive account of the author's life in 1930s Kalami, in northern Corfu.

- Henry Miller, *The Colossus of Maroussi* (most recently Summersdale) – Corfu (and Crete) on the eve of World War II.

Rhodes
- Lawrence Durrell, *Reflections of a Marine Venus* (Faber and Faber). His experiences in post-World War II Rhodes.
- Willard Manus, *This Way to Paradise: Dancing on the Tables* (Lycabettus Press). Life in Lindos in the mid-20th century.

Crete
- Edward Lear, *The Cretan Journal* (Denise Harvey, Greece). His journals for mid-19th century Crete.
- Nikos Kazantzakis, *Zorba the Greek* (Faber and Faber). The book from which the film was adapted. Neither is suitable for children.
- Evelyn Waugh, *Officers and Gentlemen* (Penguin). Novel set during the Battle of Crete.
- George Psychoundakis and Patrick Leigh Fermor, *The Cretan Runner: His Story of the German Occupation* (Penguin). About the German occupation of Crete.
- W. Stanley Moss, *Ill Met by Moonlight* (Cassell Military Paperbacks). An exciting factual account of the abduction of General Kreipe by one of the kidnappers. There's also a 1957 film of the same name starring Dirk Bogarde.
- Lawrence Durrell, *Dark Labyrinth* (Faber and Faber). Novel set in Crete just after World War II.
- Rory MacLean, *Falling for Icarus: A Journey Among the Cretans* (Viking).

Evia
- Sara Wheeler, *Evia: Travels on an Undiscovered Greek Island* (Tauris Parke Paperback). Account of life on Evia.

Greek publishers
In addition, a number of Greek publishers offer a range of Greek books for adults and children translated into English, which can be bought directly from them:
- Kedros 3, G. Gennadiou Street - 106 78 Athens (📞 *21 03 80 97 12*, *www.kedros.gr*).
- Lycabettus Press (📞 *21 06 74 17 88*, *www.lycabettus.com*).
- Anagnosis Books (📞 *01 06 25 46 54*, *www.anagnosis.gr*)

Useful websites
- Movie buffs wanting to know if any films were set in places they intend to visit should have a look at *www.imdb.com/LocationTree*.
- A good selection of books in English aimed at children, on Greek history and mythology, can be found at *www.hellenicbookservice.com/classics/Children.htm*

Lunch is likely to consist of stews like *kleftiko* or *stifado* or staples like *moussaka* and a salad, or might simply consist of dips and bread, or snacks like *tiropittes* and *spanakopittes* (respectively cheese and spinach pies). The main meal of the day is eaten in the evening, often, especially at the weekend, in estiatoria or tavernas. Although Greeks eat late – usually after 9pm – they will invariably have their children with them. Evening fare consists of *mezedes* (mixed starters) shared by all, followed by the individual meals ordered – grilled meats or fish, things like *keftedes* (meatballs) or *dolmades* (stuffed vine leaves) accompanied by potatoes and vegetables, and a *choriatiki* (village salad) and bread. Or, rather than the single 'meat and veg' we're used to in the UK, it's common for a succession of dishes to appear at the table throughout the evening, with everybody helping themselves – all-night mezedes. The Greeks don't go in much for sweets or puddings – sticky honey and almond-based cakes, ice-cream, that's about it.

Drinking in Greece takes second place to eating, and is an adjunct of it. **Ouzo**, probably Greece's most famous aperitif, tastes of aniseed, turns milky when mixed with water, and is always served with a small dish of something to nibble. **Beers** are served ice-cold, are popular with Greeks, especially in summer, and are drunk in quantities which are, by British standards, very modest. The most popular spirit is made from fermented grape skins, and

goes under many names – **raki** is the most common. As for wine, Greece was for a long time looked down upon by aficionados, and was most associated with **retsina**, a white wine with a strong taste of resin, often served in functional aluminium containers. Recently, however, and especially since 1985 (when a group of Greek wine producers returned from training in France, prompting a boost in EU and private investment in Greek vinyards) – Greece's wine reputation has been growing rapidly, with its modernised technology and its own **appellation** system (20 for table wines, eight for sweet white wines). Wine buffs get particularly excited by the fact that a lot of Greek wine producers use traditional indigenous grape varieties that may well go back to ancient times, rather than imported international ones.

Of the Greek islands, **Crete** is by far the biggest wine producer – names to look out for are Peza, Archanes, and Dafnes. **Rhodes**, too, is winning a growing reputation for wine – the big two producers are CAIR, just outside Rhodes Town, and Emery in Embonas. The most famous Rhodean wine – Villare – is made from the athiri grape which only grows well on the slopes of Mount Ataviros. Other islands where the local wine is well worth looking out for are **Kefalonia** and **Zakynthos** in the Ionian islands, **Limnos** and **Samos** in the north-eastern Aegean islands, and **Paros** and **Santorini** in the Cyclades.

FAST FACTS: THE GREEK ISLANDS

Business hours Opening hours in Greece can be complicated. Many shops and businesses are closed for afternoon siesta between 2pm and 5.30pm. **Supermarkets** tend to open 8am–8pm, sometimes 9pm during high season. They close at 6pm on Saturdays and are closed Sundays and holidays. **Shops** open 9am–2pm Monday to Saturday, then on Tuesdays, Thursdays and Fridays open again 6pm–9pm. This may vary depending on the season. As with supermarkets they are closed on Sundays and holidays. **Tourist shops** often open later at night than normal shops, especially in season.

Offices keep to the same hours as shops, but are not open Saturdays.

Petrol stations open all-day Monday to Saturday, though very rarely past 10pm. Sundays and holidays are a matter of luck.

Main **Post Offices** are open 8am–8pm Monday to Friday and 8am–2pm Saturday. Other Post Offices tend to open 8am–2pm Monday to Friday.

Pharmacies keep the same hours as shops Monday to Friday; they're closed weekends. If you need one outside of normal hours, there will be a list (probably in Greek) in the window.

Most **mechanics** work 9am–4pm Monday to Friday, and some on Saturday mornings.

Currency See 'Money', p. 19.

Drinking laws The minimum **drinking age** in Greece is 18; the minimum purchasing age is 17. This only applies to drinking in bars: there is no age limit for purchasing alcohol in shops or drinking off the premises. Alcohol is available in restaurants, some cafes and supermarkets as well as bars. High spirits are expected in Greece but extreme **drunkenness** is rarely tolerated.

Electricity Electric sockets are 220 volts/50 Hz and take a two-pin round plug, so **adapters** are required. Buy before you leave home.

Embassies and consulates

The **British Embassy** is at 1 Ploutarchou Street, 106 75 Athens (☏ *21 07 27 26 00*). For local **vice-consulates** see the relevant island chapter.
US Embassy – 91 Vasilisis Sophias Avenue, 10160 Athens (☏ *21 07 21 29 51; www.athens. usembassy.gov*).

Emergencies General emergency, ☏ *112*. Police ☏ *100*. Ambulance ☏ *166*. Fire department ☏ *199*. Tourist Police ☏ *171*.

Internet access See 'The 21st-century Traveller', p. 23.

Language See Appendix, p. 230.

Mail All shops that sell postcards also sell stamps (they're €0.65), so buy them at the same time.

Maps Good maps of the islands are available from good bookshops in the UK. **Tourist offices** in all four islands covered in this book also provide maps.

Mobile phones See 'The 21st-century Traveller', p. 23.

Newspapers and magazines Most British national daily and Sunday papers can be bought in shops and kiosks in cities, large towns and tourist areas. They are often a day or two old. A cheaper alternative is *The Athens News*, a Greek English-language newspaper available all over Greece.

Pets Cats and dogs must be micro-chipped, registered and have had a rabies vaccination no more than 12 months, but longer than 30 days, previously. You will need an **EU pet passport** from your vet. If you also want to bring them back to the UK get a blood test done 30 days after the rabies vaccination. See *http://ec.europa.eu/food/animal/liveanimals/pets/index_en.htm* for the latest EU rules on the movement of animals; *www.defra.gov.uk/animalh/quarantine/index.htm* explains UK regulations for bringing your pet home. Airlines also require a **fitness to fly certificate** from your vet.

Pharmacies Always marked by a large green cross sign, with the timetable for out-of-hours opening displayed on the door. See also 'Business Hours', p. 37.

Police In general, use the **Tourist Police** – they are marginally more likely to speak English. See 'Emergencies', above.

Smoking Smoking in Greece is widespread and although you may see no smoking signs, they are often ignored. An increasing number of hotels prohibit smoking in rooms – you have to use the balcony.

Taxes All purchases include VAT of between 4% and 18%.

Telephones To telephone Greece from the UK, dial *0030*, from the US dial *01130*. Then dial the number (which should start with a 2). However, some Greek numbers (perhaps older ones) don't follow this rule. For all numbers in this book, preface the given digits with *0030*. To call abroad from Greece dial 📞 *00* then *44* for the UK and *1* for the US and Canada. In the UK then dial the area code (omitting the first 0), followed by the phone number. To make a call within Greece use the area code followed by the phone number.

Time zone Greece is on **Eastern European time**: GMT + two hours in winter; BST + two hours in summer. Clocks usually go forward and back at the same time as the UK.

Tipping It is customary to leave tips of 10% in formal **restaurants**, though in tavernas and cafés a few coins will suffice. It is also good practice to round up to the nearest euro on small drinks bills. Although it is not usual for Greeks to tip **taxi drivers**, tourists are expected to tip 5-10%. Hotel **chambermaids** should be left about €2 per night at the end of your stay.

Water Greek water is **safe** to drink.

3 Corfu

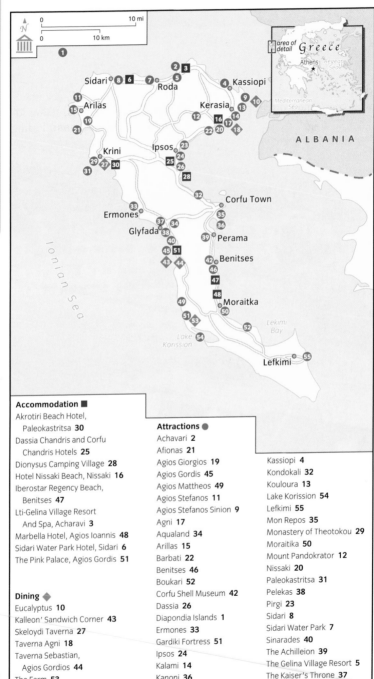

Accommodation ■

Akrotiri Beach Hotel,
  Paleokastritsa **30**
Dassia Chandris and Corfu
  Chandris Hotels **25**
Dionysus Camping Village **28**
Hotel Nissaki Beach, Nissaki **16**
Iberostar Regency Beach,
  Benitses **47**
Lti-Gelina Village Resort
  And Spa, Acharavi **3**
Marbella Hotel, Agios Ioannis **48**
Sidari Water Park Hotel, Sidari **6**
The Pink Palace, Agios Gordis **51**

Dining ◆

Eucalyptus **10**
Kalleon' Sandwich Corner **43**
Skeloydi Taverna **27**
Taverna Agni **18**
Taverna Sebastian,
  Agios Gordios **44**
The Farm **53**

Attractions ●

Achavari **2**
Afionas **21**
Agios Giorgios **19**
Agios Gordis **45**
Agios Mattheos **49**
Agios Stefanos **11**
Agios Stefanos Sinion **9**
Agni **17**
Aqualand **34**
Arillas **15**
Barbati **22**
Benitses **46**
Boukari **52**
Corfu Shell Museum **42**
Dassia **26**
Diapondia Islands **1**
Ermones **33**
Gardiki Fortress **51**
Ipsos **24**
Kalami **14**
Kanoni **36**

Kassiopi **4**
Kondokali **32**
Kouloura **13**
Lake Korission **54**
Lefkimi **55**
Mon Repos **35**
Monastery of Theotokou **29**
Moraitika **50**
Mount Pandokrator **12**
Nissaki **20**
Paleokastritsa **31**
Pelekas **38**
Pirgi **23**
Sidari **8**
Sidari Water Park **7**
Sinarades **40**
The Achilleion **39**
The Gelina Village Resort **5**
The Kaiser's Throne **37**

The first thing that hits you about Corfu is its extraordinary, stunning beauty. This should come as no surprise – why else was it the first Greek island to attract holidaymakers in large numbers? But any idea that it has been ruined by overdevelopment, engulfed in a sea of concrete and clubbers, is miles from the truth. Corfu is big and varied enough to offer holidays suited to all tastes, and all ages.

Shaped like a leg of pork (not very romantic, I know, but I can't think of a better simile), it lies in the Adriatic Sea off the Greek northwest coast, the trotter opposite Epirus, the ham off Albania. Being so far north, it's the coolest of Greece's islands, and the **greenest**. It differs from the template in other ways, too. Like its sisters in the Ionian Sea, it was never part of the Ottoman Empire, so you won't encounter Turkish influences. It was ruled by Britain from 1815 to 1864, so some things have a familiar feel, from sash windows, to dignified civic statues, to cricket on the green. Periods under Venetian, Italian and French domination have also left their mark. The result? A capital, **Corfu Town**, whose diversity of architecture is a delight, and an entire island which displays hints of each invader, whilst remaining essentially Greek.

The two halves of the island are different in character and atmosphere. The north is mountainous, dramatic and urbane, the south hilly and gently rural. There's a suspicion that the people of the north look down upon southerners as peasants, who in turn regard northerners as effete posers. Floating between north and south, in Corfu Town the island is a sure-fire winner, with narrow lanes, fine museums and two stupendous fortresses, all wrapped up in elegant arcades and fine sea views. The **Old Town**, for all its tourist shops and cafés-cum-bars-cum-restaurants, is still quite lovely.

There's no doubt that the whole of Corfu has turned to the holiday industry as its staple, and it has a well-developed infrastructure, with a wide range of accommodation, restaurants and attractions. Yet it's still remarkably easy to come across ordinary Greek life – the strident street-market vendor, the priest taking coffee with his wife, the moustachioed farmer riding his donkey, the woman in traditional headgear, the fisherman mending his nets, the schoolyard loud with the shouts and laughter of children.

On any holiday here, a visit to the capital is a must. Beyond that, the best course is to choose the north or the south for detailed exploration. Some places, like **Kavos**, are better left to the clubbers. Others have been largely taken over by tourism, but retain much to commend them – **Sidari**, on the northwest coast, springs to mind. But apart from this, there are exquisite bays, little fishing ports, sandy beaches, meandering rural lanes, the lake of **Korission** and the highlands of **Mount Pantokrator**, all just waiting to be explored.

Olive Trees

Olive trees are widely cultivated in Corfu – there are thought to be three to four million on the island. Different strains are used to grow olives for eating and olives for oil. Although Corfu has some of the tallest (Corfiots don't prune them in the same way as people in the rest of Greece), they can't lay claim to the oldest—one tree in Crete has been reliably ring-dated at 3000 years old (see p. 142).

ESSENTIALS

Getting There

By plane The vast majority of Brits will fly into Corfu Airport, a mile or so south of the town. A favourite destination for planes flying from the UK's expanding number of regional airports, it's quite a spectacular introduction to the island – you land on a single runway that has been built out into the sea, so there's water on both sides. The long, thin runway with a bulge at the end for turning planes around makes it look, from the air, like a huge thermometer. If you're sitting near a right-hand window, do look out – seconds before you land, you'll see Corfu's most famous landmark, the tiny convent of Vlacherna, sitting on its islet, attached to the mainland by a boat-lined causeway.

It's not a big airport, so continuing on your way once you've arrived is easy. The coach and hire car enclosures are right outside the terminal, as is the taxi rank. Cab fares pan out at around €8–10 into the centre – negotiate before you get in.

Flights to Corfu can be arranged through British Airways and Olympic Airlines, and also through a growing number of holiday companies that offer both package holidays and flights only. To Corfu there are Thomsonfly flights from 16 regional airports, XL from 12, Flythomascook from nine and Airtours from eight. The best airports as regards choice, with all four companies using them, are Gatwick, Bristol, Birmingham, East Midlands, Newcastle and Glasgow, but some also use Stansted, Luton, Cardiff, Norwich, Manchester, Liverpool, Doncaster, Leeds, Durham, Belfast and Exeter.

By car Corfu is probably the only Greek island where taking your own car is feasible. If it's a holiday exclusively in Corfu, then it would probably still be best to fly to the island and hire one. But if Corfu were part of a wider touring holiday – say Italy and Corfu, or Corfu and mainland Greece, with a caravan or motor caravan, then driving to Corfu becomes a real possibility.

The drive across Europe brings you to ferries from the eastern Italian ports (Venice, Brindisi and Bari), which, on their way to Igoumenitsa and Patras, often call in at Corfu's

New Port (check out *www.via mare.com*). Many of these boats allow you to pay rock-bottom deck prices and sleep in your own caravan or motor caravan. They even provide electric hook-ups and toilet/shower facilities. Do check when you book, though, that the ferry you've chosen stops at Corfu, and that it has provision for 'camping on board'!

On arrival in Corfu, drive down the ramp and out of the port, then turn right. In a couple of kilometres, a well-signposted intersection will take you either north along the east coast towards Kassiopi, south towards Lefkimi, or across the island towards the west coast.

Being one of the earliest destinations for UK mass tourism, there are lots of guidebooks to the island though they don't, of course, concentrate as this one does on the needs of families with children. I don't feel that Corfu is particularly well served by the Internet – the information on a lot of the sites is rather thin – but you could try *www. allcorfu.com, www.corfu-island.biz, www.gnto.gr* and *www.gnto.co.uk*

Tourist information is not, as I've noted elsewhere, a Greek strength. Despite a lot of time

Writers on Corfu

The Corfiot air seems to inspire writers. Dionysios Solomos, though born on Zakinthos, favoured Corfu from 1828 up to his death in 1857. His house in Corfu Town is now a museum (see p. 54). Although he wrote many sonnets, his most famous work is his 'Hymn to Freedom', the first two verses of which are now the **Greek National Anthem.** English humorist, writer and illustrator **Edward Lear** introduced 19th-century English readers to the pleasures of Greece in general, and the Ionian Islands in particular, through works like *Journal of a Landscape Painter in Greece and Albania* (1851) and *Views in the Seven Ionian Islands* (1863). **Lawrence Durrell,** most famous for his novels, wrote a highly influential book about Corfu – *Prospero's Cell* – describing his stay in 'The White House' (see p. 60) with his young wife in 1937–38. It gives a wonderful sense not only of place (the northeast coast of the island) but also of time (the brief calm before the storm of World War II). In the 1970s Durrell published *The Greek Islands* – a quirky personal survey of all the islands. Gerald Durrell, Lawrence's younger brother, first came to the island in 1935, with his mother and the rest of the family. Already a budding naturalist, he revelled in his freedom to wander far and wide across the island in search of birds, animals and insects. His book about this period – *My Family and Other Animals* – and later films, are perhaps the best and most accessible introduction to Corfu. He went on to become a famous naturalist, conservationist and zoo owner.

surfing the Net, and even more time walking around Corfu Town, I'm still none the wiser as to Corfu's tourist information provision. I visited several places where existing guidebooks led me to expect offices – to no avail. I did find a small kiosk in Sanrocco Square, but it was shut, and there was no indication of the dates or times of opening. When I asked local people where the tourist information office was, they usually looked bemused and shook their heads. The only suggestion was that it was out of town, and I'd have to catch a bus. At which time I lost all patience and gave up.

My point here is that, even if there is a tourist office, it isn't much good if it's this hard to find.

When you get to the island, there are two local English language magazines which are a very useful source of up-to-date information about what's going on in Corfu:

The Corfiot (€2), a well-established monthly magazine, which, although with rather low production values and aimed specifically at expat residents, does contain a lot of useful stuff.

Island (€3.50), a new, far glossier lifestyle magazine for Corfu – the first issue was May/June 2007. A mixture of travel (both within Corfu and elsewhere), health and beauty, fashion, cookery, car and restaurant reviews.

Getting Around

On foot and by taxi Within Corfu Town most things worth seeing are within easy walking distance. If you do need to travel further afield within the capital, grab a taxi. There's also a tourist road-train which runs around Corfu Town and especially out to the attractions just to the south – Mon Repos and Kanoni.

By bus For transport outside the capital, there are two types of bus, and they're easy to use because they're colour-coded. The blue buses serve suburbs and villages close to the capital. The main terminus is in Sanrocco Square, but you'll find bus stops in various parts of Corfu Town, including on the Esplanade. For the rest of Corfu, there's a network of green buses which connect all parts of the island to the capital.

Most hotels and resorts also offer excursions by coach, which is a good option if you plan to stay in one place but have the odd trip out.

By car For a more thorough exploration of the island, your best bet is to hire a car. Pre-booking will avoid disappointment, especially in high season, but outside July and August you should find it reasonably easy to rent a car on the spur of the moment.

Corfu's main roads are of good quality, though there are very few stretches of dual carriageway – think good UK A-road standard. Side roads can vary from good to very poor, and can change from one to the other and back within a few hundred yards. So you can be bowling along a fine stretch of tarmac, only to be shaken to the core as you hit a giant pothole. In visiting some of the more isolated attractions you might even find yourself inching along a dirt track with cliffs to one side and a drop to the sea on the other. Don't forget: your car rental insurance probably won't cover tyres and exhausts! When planning days out by car, bear in mind that you're unlikely to be able to average much more than 30 mph.

Parking can be chaotic, especially during high season. Corfu Town has three main areas where you might find somewhere – the large car park off the dual carriageway between the Old and the New Port (€1.0), on the Esplanade itself (€3) and at the kerb along the coast road south of the Old Town (free). Outside the capital, parking is easier, so if you're staying at one of the resorts and visiting the capital, it might be easier to leave the car behind and catch a bus.

By moped, motorbike or quad-bike There are rental places for these all over the island. But, though I *have* seen families out on motorbikes (dad and child on one, mum and child on another), I don't really think that they can be recommended for families – a pothole that damages a car's exhaust could kill a motorcyclist.

By boat Most of the places you're likely to stay are on the coast, so look out for trips to the mainland or other islands and along the coast. In particular, many places along the east coast offer boat trips to Corfu Town – a pleasant way to visit the capital without having to negotiate traffic and parking.

Planning Your Outings

On visits to Corfu Town, base yourselves on the Esplanade. It has got everything you need – wide open spaces, a fair-sized children's playground and a central position which gives access to virtually everything you're likely to want to visit. There's a wide choice of cafes and restaurants – good for refreshment but also for toilets. Wherever you are in Corfu, the best source of toilets is cafés and tavernas, though you really need to at least have a drink: they're likely to take a dim view of people who use their facilities without buying anything.

As always in Greece, take plenty of water with you. If you forget, bottled water is cheap – 50 cents is the norm. This is because the government, horrified by the scandalous prices sometimes charged, fixed a maximum price for water. Though large supermarkets are still relatively rare, there are plenty of mini-markets where you can put together a basic picnic. Also look out for bakeries selling fresh bread, and *zacharoplastios,* which offer a wide choice of cakes. Food in your hand is also generally available – *tiropites* (cheese pasties) and *spanakopites* (spinach pasties) are particularly nice.

Children are welcomed everywhere. In fact, they're usually made much of. And there are playgrounds all over the place – often with only one or two pieces of equipment, sometimes rather down-at-heel, yet Greek children make full and enthusiastic use of them. Discrete breast-feeding is acceptable in most places.

FAST FACTS: CORFU (SEE ALSO CHAPTER 2)

Airport see 'arriving by plane'.

American Express Accessed through Greek Skies Travel Agency at: 20A Kapodistriou, Corfu Town ☎ 26 61 03 34 10.

Banks and ATMs there are cash machines throughout Corfu Town. In the rest of Corfu, most locals will know where the nearest one is.

British Vice Consulate 18 Mantzarou Street, 491 00 Corfu Town. Open Mon-Fri 8am– 1.30pm. ☎ 26 61 03 00 55/02 34 57.

Buses Blue buses ☎ 26 61 03 15 95. Green buses ☎ 26 61 03 06 27.

Business hours see Chapter 2. Tourist shops stay open for long hours, tavernas and restaurants often close when the last customers have left.

Credit cards all larger establishments (hotels, restaurants, shops) accept the main credit cards, but a lot of smaller ones don't. And even when they have the technology to accept them, you may find a reluctance to do so. In service stations, for example, there are usually pump attendants, and they'd far prefer taking cash – they always seem to have enough money on them to give change – to returning to the office to process a credit card.

Internet access big hotels usually offer Internet access, either in-room or in a dedicated 'Internet corner' on the premises. Internet cafés and bars are common in most towns visited by tourists, often with just two or three machines. In Corfu Town, the bigger Online Café at 28 Kapodistriou and Netoikos at 14 Kalachairetou are the most accessible.

Police 19 Leoforos Alexandros, Corfu Town ☎ 26 61 03 95 75 or just dial ☎ 100.

Post Office 26 Leoforos Alexandros, Corfu Town ☎ 26 61 02 55 44.

EXPLORING CORFU

Any exploration of Corfu divides itself naturally into three areas – Corfu Town, the north of the island, and the south. In a week it's reasonable to have a look at Corfu Town plus either the north or the south. In a fortnight you could sample the best of the whole island.

Top 10 Family Experiences

1. Sipping drinks in a **Liston** café and watching the world go by (see p. 79).
2. Watching the jets come in over the convent of **Vlacherna** (see p. 55).
3. Spending the day at **Aqualand**, **Hydropolis** or **Sidari Water Park** (see p. 57 and p. 63).
4. Enjoying a long, lazy lunch in **Agni** whilst the children play on the beach (see p. 60).
5. Walking around **Theotokou monastery** in Paleokastritsa – the contemplative life with majestic views of sea and cliffs (see p. 64).
6. Touring the **Achilleion** for an insight into European history at the end of the 19th century (see p. 67).
7. Choosing a shell at the **Corfu Shell Museum** as a souvenir of the holiday (see p. 68).
8. Clambering over the deserted remains of the **Gardiki Fortress** (see p. 70).
9. Enjoying the awesome views across Corfu from the **Kaiser's Throne** at Pelekas (see p. 71).
10. Building sandcastles and doing water sports on one of Corfu's **family beaches**.

Corfu Town

The Esplanade

By far the best way to explore Corfu Town with a family is to base yourselves in the great lozenge-shaped area called the **Esplanade** that forms the heart of the Old Town. It is said to be one of the largest public squares

The Esplanade

CORFU TOWN

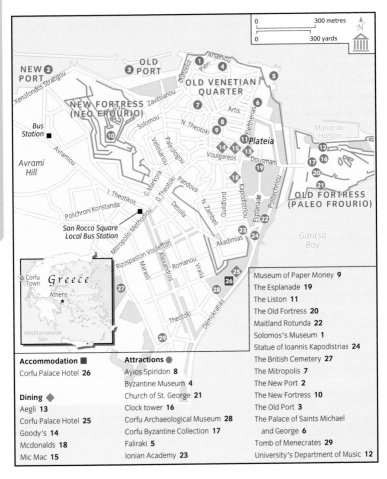

0	300 metres
0	300 yards

NEW **②** PORT

OLD **③** PORT

Arseniou
Pieri **①**
Donzelot
④

⑤

OLD VENETIAN QUARTER

Xenofondos Stratigou

Zavitsianou

NEW FORTRESS (NEO FROURIO)

⑦

Artis

⑥

Eleftherias

Bus Station

Solomou

N. Theotoki

⑧

⑨

⑩

Mandraki Harbor

Avrami Hill

Avramiou

Velissariou

Paleologou

Plateia **⑪**

⑭ ⑮

Voulgareos

⑬

Dousmani

⑲

⑫

⑰ ⑯

⑳

I. Theotikos

G. Markora

G. Theotoki

Pandova

N. Zambeli

Guildford

Kapodistriou

⑱

㉑

OLD FORTRESS (PALEO FROURIO)

Polichroni Konstanda

Dessila

Esplanade

Politechniou

㉒

Garitsa Bay

San Rocco Square Local Bus Station

Mitropoliti Methodiou

Akadimias

㉓

㉔

Rizospaston Voulefton

Marasli

Alexandros

Romanou

Vraila

㉕

㉖

Corfu Town

Greece

Athens
Aegean Sea

Mediterranean Sea

㉗

Theotoki

㉘

Demokratias

㉙

Museum of Paper Money	**9**
The Esplanade	**19**
The Liston	**11**
The Old Fortress	**20**
Maitland Rotunda	**22**
Solomos's Museum	**1**
Statue of Ioannis Kapodistrias	**24**
The British Cemetery	**27**
The Mitropolis	**7**
The New Port	**2**
The New Fortress	**10**
The Old Port	**3**
The Palace of Saints Michael and George	**6**
Tomb of Menecrates	**29**
University's Department of Music	**12**

Accommodation ■	**Attractions** ●
Corfu Palace Hotel **26**	Ayios Spiridon **8**
	Byzantine Museum **4**
Dining ◆	Church of St. George **21**
Aegli **13**	Clock tower **16**
Corfu Palace Hotel **25**	Corfu Archaeological Museum **28**
Goody's **14**	Corfu Byzantine Collection **17**
Mcdonalds **18**	Faliraki **5**
Mic Mac **15**	Ionian Academy **23**

in Europe. Here there are acres of grass under the shade of the trees for children to run around on, and great ranks of cafés and restaurants with inside seating, toilets and outside tables under the arcades for older family members to rest and people-watch.

The Esplanade is an ever-changing kaleidoscope of colour and movement. Horse-drawn carriages clip-clop along the surrounding roads, balloon-sellers ply their wares, children's electric cars buzz around the park, a road-train departs for the south of the town with clanging bell, and there are youngsters everywhere, playing football, skipping, running races, swinging from the bandstand and climbing trees. On some summer Sundays you'll catch Corfiots playing **cricket** at the northern end of the Esplanade (see 'Cricket in Corfu', p. 50).

And if you walk across the grass to the shady park that edges the eastern Esplanade, you'll come to a fair-sized **children's playground**, spread out under the trees. Though at first it looks absolutely secure, watch out for its rear fence – it's not very high, and there's a drop down towards the moat of the Old Fortress beyond.

Whilst the younger children let off steam out on the grass, teenage and adult family members can join the throng along the **Liston** ★★, the impressive flagged arcade that overlooks the northern half of the Esplanade. Built during French rule, and apparently a copy of Paris's **Rue de Rivoli**, it is occupied by a series of chic cafés and restaurants with outdoor tables where young people sit, seeing and being seen, while their elders congregate under the shade of the arcades. Waiters shuttle back and forth carrying trays of drinks, and hawkers thread their way through the tables, selling CDs of dubious provenance. The roadway of the Liston is traffic-free except for delivery vehicles, which exercise great care, so children can play safely on the flagstones.

> **INSIDER TIP** ▶
>
> Some guidebooks criticise supposedly **high prices** charged by the establishments of the Liston – it's nonsense! They're only slightly higher than elsewhere in the town, and worth every cent in atmosphere.

Once established on the Esplanade and the Liston, explore the rest of Corfu Town at leisure – everything worth looking at is within walking distance, even with a buggy.

Vlacherna and 'Mouse Island'

Cricket in Corfu

You might well not expect to hear the sound of leather on willow or cries
of 'howzat!' in Greece, but one of the legacies of British rule in the Ionian Islands
is the popularity of **cricket** on Corfu. The game doesn't exactly loom large in the
Greek consciousness – most Greeks would be surprised to discover that there is
a Hellenic Cricket Federation, or that Greece has belonged to the European
Cricket Council since 1995. HQ for the HCF is Corfu, and 13 of the 15 Greek
cricket clubs are from the island (the other two are in Athens and Thessaloniki).
Ironically, the stalwarts of the Greek game are largely of **Pakistani** origin.

East and south of the Esplanade

One of the easiest places to visit
from the Esplanade is the **Old
Fortress**, which looms over its
eastern edge (see below). At the
southern end of the Esplanade
stands the **Maitland Rotunda**,
a memorial to the first British
High Commissioner of the
Ionian Islands. Beyond it is the
Statue of Ioannis Kapodistrias,
a Corfiot who became the first
President of independent Greece
in 1827 (see below). The road
that marks the entire western
length of the Esplanade is
named after him.

There's also a memorial to
Frederick North (1769–1828), a
famous British politician and
lover of Greece whose title – Earl
of Guilford – gave the name to
the street which parallels the
southern stretch of Kapodistriou.
Just beyond the Kapodistrias
statue stands the pink building of
the **Ionian Academy**, a centre of
learning established by the Earl
in 1823. It operated until 1865.
A further five minute's walk
south brings you to the **Corfu
Archaeological Museum**, definitely worth a visit, especially for
its Gorgon Frieze (see p. 52).
Southwest of the Old Town

Easter in Corfu Town

If you get the opportunity to experience Easter anywhere in Greece,
jump at the chance. In addition to colourful **religious processions**
through the streets, often accompanied by icons and the remains of
saints, there is plenty of eating and drinking, and children will love the
tradition where eggs are hard boiled and dyed bright colours, then
cracked against each other — a bit like playing conkers.

In Corfu there's the addition of music by the city's three **marching
bands**, and a ceremony where people wait on their red-bedecked balconies with earthenware pots full of water, then hurl them onto the
streets and pavements below. A spectacular **firework display** ushers
in Easter Sunday on the stroke of midnight.

Ioannis Kapodistrias (1776–1831)

A native Corfiot doctor, Kapodistrias made himself a name as a diplomat, first in the service of Alexander I of Russia, then as a leading supporter of Greek independence from the Ottoman Empire during the War of Independence. He became the **first President** of the new independent Greek Republic, did sterling work in setting up the new country's central administration, and made a start on combating the squabbling clans that had fleetingly allied to win independence. He was **assassinated** in Nafplion by the brother and son of one of the clan chiefs (from the notoriously violent Mani peninsula) whom he had imprisoned. A statue in his honour stands at the southern end of the Esplanade in Corfu Town.

centre, and a brilliant place for a sit down and some quiet contemplation, is the **British Cemetery**, off Zafiropoulo, with lots of grass and flowers, a great sense of peace, imposing military monuments, and graves dating back almost 200 years. Their inscriptions are a fascinating slice of colonial history.

The Old Fortress ★ ★
AGE 5 AND ABOVE

Immediately east of the Esplanade.

Towering over the eastern edge of the Esplanade is the Old Fortress, surrounded by water and attached to the rest of Corfu Town by a bridge. Built on the promontory's twin peaks, originally by the Byzantines, it was extensively modified by the Venetians (including the digging of the moat to separate it from the mainland), with some additions by the British. Look out, in summer, for impressive sound and light shows.

Boats line the moat between the fortress and the Esplanade,

and a small exhibition – the **Corfu Byzantine Collection** – occupies a room on the left of the main gate. Beyond that, to the right is a wide open space dotted with rusting cannon barrels, and enclosed by the fortress wall. The large building that looks like a Greek temple, tucked below the lighthouse-topped cliff, is in fact the **Church of St George**, built by the British in 1840. This was where Prince Philip, the Duke of Edinburgh, was christened (see p. 56).

To the left after you pass through the main gate is an administration building and an elegant **clock tower**, beyond which is a large white building – usually with bikes chained to its railings – which houses the **Ionian University's Department of Music**. As you walk along outside you might hear a percussion lesson at one end, a young women's choir practising in the middle and violins at the other.

Below the castle walls yachts lie in the little harbour of

Mandraki. The views from all parts of the fortress, out to sea, along both coasts and across Corfu Town, are divine.

Open *8.30am–7pm (summer), 8.30am–3pm (winter) Tues–Fri.* **Adm** *€4 adults, €2 concessions.*

Corfu Archaeological Museum ★ AGE 5 AND ABOVE

1 Armeni Vraila, ☎ 26 61 03 06 80. A five-minute walk beyond the southern tip of the Esplanade.

Whilst the detail of the Corfu Archaeological Museum's collection of sculptures, metal and clay objects would be of interest only to students of Ancient Greek history, some of the exhibits are spectacular enough to appeal to younger children. In particular, see the famous **Gorgon Frieze**, the huge 17m pediment of a Temple of Artemis unearthed south of the capital, and the stone lion of Menecrates, thought to have crowned the circular **Tomb of Menecrates** – another five-minute walk beyond the museum. The tomb contained an Ancient Greek about whom little is known, except that he drowned. Both date from the 6th century BC.

Open *8.30am–3pm Tues–Sun.* **Adm** *€4 (free on Sundays).*

West of the Esplanade

West of the Esplanade is a maze of narrow alleys that make up the bulk of the **Old Town.** Buzzing with tourist shops selling kumquat preserves, olive-wood carvings, icons, worry beads, T-shirts, baseball caps, jewellery, leather goods, toys and a thousand other things, there are also pleasant squares, cool arcades, cafés, bars and restaurants.

At the heart of the Old Town stands Corfu's most famous church, **Ayios Spiridon.** Surrounded by the swarm of commerce, its lofty bell tower, with blue clock and characteristic red dome, soars upwards above neighbouring buildings, making it an excellent navigation aid if you get lost. And you will get lost – the Old Town is like a rabbit warren.

Inside, the church is gloomy – indeed, after the glare outside it's difficult to see anything. But at the front you'll undoubtedly see a line of locals, queuing up to kiss the **silver reliquary** which contains the mummified remains of

---

FUN FACT ⟩ **Britain & Corfu** ⟨

The Ionian Islands were a British military protectorate from the end of the Napoleonic Wars in 1814–15 until 1864, when they were ceded to the Kingdom of Greece. Though austere and autocratic (despite the nominal retention of Corfiot assemblies), the succession of British High Commissioners did greatly improve the administration and prosperity of the islands, and much of their influence can be seen around Corfu, from government buildings, to statues of British statesmen, to cricket on the green.

St Spiridon (c. 270–348 AD)

The patron saint of Corfu never actually visited the island whilst he was alive. A poor Cypriot shepherd, he entered a monastery after his wife's death to devote his life to God, and rose to be a bishop. His remains, having been moved to Constantinople, were smuggled out of the city when it was occupied by the Turks in 1453 and taken to Corfu. Here they were interred in splendour in a new church built for the purpose in the late 16th century. In return he did a fine job of protecting the population of the island — rescuing it from famine, plague, cholera, and an 18th century siege of the capital by the Turks.

St Spyridon relics are paraded around the streets of Corfu Town annually on four occasions — twice over Easter and on 11th August and the first Sunday in November. His church, with its distinctive maroon-topped **campanile** visible for miles around, makes a good pre-agreed meeting place.

the man himself. A 4th-century Bishop of Cyprus, he was buried in Constantinople, then smuggled out to Corfu when that city was captured by the Turks. The present church was built to house his remains in 1596.

Ayios Spiridon is given an airing four times a year (Palm Sunday, the Saturday after Palm Sunday, 11th August and the first Sunday in November), when his remains are paraded around the streets of the capital to celebrate the times when he saved Corfu (from plagues, famine and the Turks). Outside, a stall sells candles to the devoted. His great popularity explains the large numbers of Corfiot males who are called Spiridon – or its diminutive **Spiro**.

Also in the Old Town are the **Museum of Paper Money** (see below) and, a little further west, Corfu Town's second most important church. The **Mitropolis** contains the remains of Ayia Theodora, the wife of a ninth century Emperor, and a wonderful 16th-century icon of St George killing the dragon by Michaelis Damaskinos. Forensic remains and a depiction of violence – you can't go wrong.

Museum of Paper Money
AGE 5 AND ABOVE

Ioniki Trapeza, Plateia Iroon, off Nickiforou Theotoki. 📞 *26 61 04 15 22.*

Just around the corner from Ayios Spiridon, in the Ionian Bank, is the Museum of Paper Money – surely all youngsters are interested in cash? There is a display of Greek money since Independence, together with banknotes from around the world and, upstairs, methods of making banknotes are explained. A quick look around the museum should take no more than half an hour.

Open *9am–1pm Mon–Sat.* **Adm** *Free.*

North of the Esplanade

If you walk through the archway next to the **Palace of Saints Michael and George** (see below) you come first to **Faliraki**, with a lovely view of the church of **Ayios Nicolaou** on its terrace by the sea, with beaches either side, and views across to the Old Fortress and the little basin at Mandraki. A walk west along Arseniou brings you to the **Byzantine Museum** (✆ *26 61 03 83 13)*, housed in the restored church of the Antivouniotissa, whose collection of frescoes, sculptures and mosaic floors are not honestly of much interest to small children, but might give older ones a feel for Byzantine art. It's open Mon-Fri 10am–1pm; admission is €3. Further along is **Solomos's Museum** (✆ *26 61 03 06 74)* with photos and memorabilia devoted to modern Greece's most famous poet. Writer of the lines eventually adopted as the Greek national anthem ('Hymn to Freedom'), Solomos, though a native of Zakynthos, studied in the Ionian Academy (see above), and lived in the house which now contains the museum for much of his life. It's open 9.30am–2pm every day, and costs €2 to get in. Both collections are really only for adults and older teens.

Palace of Saints Michael and George AGE 5 AND ABOVE

Spaniada Square, ✆ *26 61 03 81 24. North of the Esplanade.*

The huge neoclassical Palace of Saints Michael and George was built by the British as a residence for the High Commissioner (the statue at the front is of **Sir Frederick Adam**, the second High Commissioner for the Ionian Islands, 1824–31). It was handed over to the Greek royal family when Corfu ceased to be ruled by Britain in 1864, eventually fell into disrepair, and was finally renovated to house the huge collection of Far Eastern artefacts amassed by Corfiot diplomat **Gregorios Manos** (1850–1929) and others. Whilst it might seem a little bizarre to spend time on a visit to Greece looking at the contents of a **Museum of Asian Art**, the masks, statues, woodcuts, weapons and so on are varied enough to interest almost all children. Also stop in at the Arts Café.

Open 8.30am–3pm Tues–Sun. ***Adm*** *€4.* ***Amenities*** *Café.*

Beyond the Old Town

Further along Arseniou brings you to the **Old Port** (for boat trips out to the little wooded island of **Vidos**), then the **New Port**, where ferries can be caught to nearby islands, Italy, Albania and northern and southern Greece (see 'Visitor Information', p. 43). Watching the boats coming and going, and the locals fishing, is a pleasant way to spend a half-hour. If you take a left at the Old Port you'll immediately be plunged back into the labyrinth that is the Old Town. A left turn at the New Port will take you along Ioannou

Theotoki, past the enormous **New Fortress** (see below), to one of modern Corfu Town's main squares – **Sanrocco**.

New Fortress ★ AGE 5 AND ABOVE

Plateia Solomou, 📞 *26 61 027 370.*

As you walk around Arseniou and along Ioannou Theotoki, you can't avoid being aware of the huge **New Fortress.** Built by the Venetians in the late 16th century – not that much later than the Venetian reconstruction of the Old Fortress, itself preceded by fortifications going back centuries – it is used by the Greek Navy as a training base, so parts aren't open to the public. However, there are **tunnels**, **dungeons** and **battlements** to explore, there's a café and gallery, and the views across the town and out to sea are spectacular. Also, in the wash of medieval buildings and narrow lanes that lap into what was once its moat, you'll come across the stalls of an **open-air market**.

Open *9am–10pm Apr–Oct.* **Adm** €2. **Amenities** *Café.*

Corfu Town's hinterland

Not far out of Corfu Town are several attractions that ooze family potential. South of Corfu Town, between the airport and the sea, is the promontory of **Kanoni** ★★, named after the canon that was stationed there as part of the capital's defences – there's one there still, but opinion as to whether it is original is divided.

The big attraction is Corfu's most famous sight, subject of a million postcards. This is the delightful convent of **Vlacherna**, which sits on an islet at the end of a causeway. Beyond it is the tiny island of **Pondikonisi** ('Mouse Island'), named after the ship that had delivered Odysseus to Ithaca. Unhappy that it had done so (because of bad blood between the god and the hero), Poseidon attacked the ship and turned it into a rock. They did a lot of that kind of thing in ancient times.

The views – of the little harbour, the sea, the convent, the island and the headlands and mountains beyond – are breathtaking, and a couple of cafés with terraces overlooking the bay offer refreshment and plenty of time to enjoy them.

The building of the **airport** next to this idyllic scene has been widely lamented, but for families it's a godsend. Pretty scenery cuts little ice with kids,

TIP ▸ One-way Street to Kanoni ◂

Because it's cut off by the airport runway, Kanoni can't be taken in as part of a tour of southern Corfu – you've got to make a special effort to drive there, or catch a bus (the no. 2 from the blue bus station in Sanrocco Square, every half-hour). And when you have finished, you've got to return to Corfu Town before going anywhere else.

Prince Philippos, Duke of Edinburgh

Prince Philippos of Greece and Denmark was born on 10th June, 1921, on the estate of **Mon Repos** (see below), just south of Corfu Town. He was the son of Prince Andrew, (a younger brother of King Constantine I of Greece) and Princess Alice of Battenburg. As such, he was related to most of Europe's royal families. He was christened in **Agios Georgios church** (see p. 51), within the battlements of Corfu Town's Old Fortress.

The following year, there was a revolution in Greece, and Philippos's uncle was deposed. Things were looking decidedly dodgy for the young prince's family, when King George V of England sent HMS *Calypso* to Corfu to rescue them. Philippos was reputedly carried aboard the Royal Navy ship in an orange box.

From then on, Philippos lived and went to school in France, England, Germany and, eventually, Scotland. He joined the Royal Navy in 1939, and married the heir to the British throne, Princess Elizabeth, in 1947. She was both his third cousin and his second cousin once removed! Not long before the marriage, Philippos was created Duke of Edinburgh, but it wasn't until 10 years later that he became a Prince. He subsequently took his mother's family name, anglicised to Mountbatten.

but watching great jet planes swooping down to land below you, or climbing past you with engines thundering, now that's a different matter...

And once the refreshments and the plane-watching have begun to pall, there's a path down to the little harbour, where you can choose to walk along the causeway to the convent, catch a boat for the five-minute trip out to Pondikonisi (€2–3), or venture out along the right-hand causeway which stretches clear across the bay. If any planes land or take off while you're on it, you can count the rivets on its fuselage.

On the way back from Kanoni you'll come to the **Palaiopolis** archaeological site, with the remains of 5th-century **Agia Kerkyra** on one side of the road and a dig working on a Roman Baths complex on the other. Immediately beyond them is the entrance to the estate of the **Mon Repos** villa ★ (℡ *26 61 020 980*). Built by **Sir Frederick Adam** – the second British High Commissioner of the Ionian Islands – for his Corfiot wife in 1824, the house and its grounds were handed over to the Greek royal family in 1864, and confiscated from King Constantine by the government in 1994. This is where **Prince Philip, Duke of Edinburgh** was born in 1921 (see box above).

The grounds now contain a variety of archaeological remains (including the **Temple of**

Artemis from which the Gorgon pediment in the Archaeological Museum was taken), an outdoor theatre and the **Palaeopolis Museum**. There's an excellent information board just inside the main gate, with a plan of the estate and estimates on how long it will take to walk to each site. But above all, Mon Repos contains miles of traffic-free roads through beautiful parkland – ideal for walks and picnics – and it's absolutely free. The gardens are open daily; admission is free.

Aqualand ★ ★ ★ ALL AGES

Agios Ioannis, 📞 *26 61 05 29 63. www.aqualand-corfu.com.*

As you drive around Corfu, you can't avoid signs drawing your attention to the delights of Aqualand. It's the must-visit place on the island for youngsters. Situated in **Agios Ioannis**, five or six miles west of Corfu Town, it's also accessible from all over the island, well signposted and easy to find. Once you're within range, you can see the great banks of slides poking out above the countryside.

The park has every **water slide** your children could ever need, with something for all ages. **The Caribbean Pirate Adventure** and nearby kiddies' slides, as well as a shallow pool, are aimed at toddlers, whilst the **family rafting** allows everyone to hurl together down an open water slide in rubber dinghies. At the other end of the scale are the monsters that festoon 'The Hill' like an invading giant octopus – the **Black Hole**, the 24m high **Free Fall**, the **Kamikazes,** the **Double Twisters** and many more – enough to keep even demanding teenagers occupied indefinitely.

There are **climbing frames with water canons, mini-cars** and **boats** (for two- to six-year-olds), **a road train**, a carousel, **trampolines, bouncy castle,** and food outlets and shops. Loungers and parasols are free,

Aqualand

so establish a base camp and explore the park in shifts.

Open *10am–6pm daily May–June and Sept–Oct, 10am–7pm daily July–Aug.* **Adm** *€23 (€17 after 3pm) adults, €16 (€12 after 3pm) children 5–12.* **Amenities** *Cafés. Disabled access. English spoken. Parking. Picnic areas. Restaurants. Shops.*

A tour of Northern Corfu

The northern part of the island contains its highest mountain, some of its most beautiful countryside – and certainly its most dramatic coastline – and many of its most attractive towns and villages. On any tour of the north, the best way to make sure that you don't miss anything is to travel in an anti-clockwise direction, taking the road that skirts the bay north of Corfu Town. Drive past the New Port, then follow the road to the right signposted 'Kassiopi'.

Kondokali to Nissaki

The first fifteen kilometres or so – from Kondokali to Nissaki, say – gets a drubbing in most guidebooks for being tatty and touristy. It's true that hotels, bars, restaurants and tourist shops have taken over this stretch of the coast, yet for families it has much to commend it – plenty of accommodation, a good choice of places to eat, a lot to do, and easy access to Corfu Town. It *is* touristy, but I've seen far worse.

Kondokali is the first of the holiday-dominated villages, followed by **Gouvia**. The latter

has the largest marina in Corfu, and its **flying boat** history has recently been revived with seaplane services to Ioannina on the mainland and to other Ionian Island destinations. It also has the remains of a **Venetian arsenal** overlooking the town, and a good selection of water sports.

Dassia continues the heavily touristy theme, with large resort hotels, one of the island's best campsites, a narrow sand-and-shingle, olive tree-fringed beach and wide variety of available watersports.

From **Ipsos to Pirgi** the main road runs along the seashore, with a narrow beach on the right and a strip of restaurants, bars and shops on the left – more likely to attract groups of 20-somethings than families, though a convenient place to stop for refreshment and a swim.

Barbati, the next town along, has one of the best family beaches in Corfu – let's hope that the widespread building activity in the area doesn't ruin it.

It is around **Nissaki** that the holiday sprawl finally starts to peter out, and the real Corfu begins to assert itself. The slopes of Mount Pantokrator drive the coast road upwards and inland.

Mount Pantokrator

For the next 30 odd kilometres or so the coast road circumnavigates **Mount Pantokrator**, at 917m (just under 3000 ft) Corfu's highest mountain. There are several access points all along the coast, but the easiest is off to the left, a couple of hundred metres after leaving Pirgi. Follow the signs for **Spartilas**, a pleasant and surprisingly large mountain village. About one km beyond the village, take a right (signposted Petaleia and Lafki). Keep going until you get to **Strinilas**, perhaps a good place to stop for refreshment. A couple of hundred metres beyond the village, a relatively new road branches off to the summit. There you'll find a monastery, a clutch of antennae, the café-bar Pantokrator, and, depending on weather conditions, terrific views of Corfu, Paxos, the mainland and even Italy. You can then either return the way you came, or go down the other side of the mountain, towards the north coast.

After Nissaki, when you come to a side road to the right (signposted 'Agni') follow it – you're in for a treat.

The northeast coast

Agni consists of a tiny village sitting behind a shingle beach slung between two beautifully wooded headlands. Along the horizon lie the mountains of **Albania** – the straits between Corfu and Albania are here barely a couple of kilometres wide.

You'll need to find a parking space before you get to the village, either on the road or in one of two car parks. The main reason for stopping at Agni, apart from the views, is the three excellent **tavernas** that line the cove (see 'Family-friendly Dining', p. 78) – the Agni, the Toula and the Nikolas – spaced out along a small shingle beach between the two headlands. Each has its own wooden jetty, with customers' boats hitched to them like horses outside a Western saloon, and each provides sun-loungers on the beach

Agni

for that post-prandial nap. The food – a good selection of Greek specialities – is excellent in all three, so each tries to steal a march on its rivals in different ways – Nikolas, for example, has its own free car park in the village (the public car park charges €1.50) – but for entrepreneurship the Agni must take the prize. It has its own fishing boat enticingly moored to its jetty, to draw attention to the freshness of its fish, and will pick customers up by speedboat from several of the little ports along this stretch of coast. It can also arrange speedboat rental, and it runs a travel agency! (for the Agni, see 'Family-friendly Dining', p. 78).

Whichever taverna you choose, Agni is absolutely ideal for families – you can sit out on a terrace or a covered wooden deck whilst the children play on the beach, swim in the translucent water, or jump or dive off the jetty into the sea.

From now on the coast road offers vistas of seemingly endless headlands and bays, with aquamarine seas stretching off to the shores of **Albania** to the right, and the hills rising to the summit of Mount Pantokrator to the left. However tempted, the person driving shouldn't risk trying to take in these views – the road is extremely winding, and local drivers are not known for their patience. A succession of side roads branch off east to meander down to a succession of attractive coastal villages.

The next village off the main road is **Kalami**. Though worth a visit in its own right – it has a pleasant enough pebble beach, lined with tavernas – the main reason for visiting is that this is where Lawrence Durrell lived in the late 1930s, and where he wrote *Prospero's Cell* (see 'Writers on Corfu', p. 43).

Drive all the way through the village and look out for the sign for **The White House**. Now a taverna with rooms to let upstairs ('Prospero Apartment'), it has nice views back across the village and out to sea. Although Kalami has become dominated by new villas and apartments, it is still possible to imagine what the house looked like when Durrell was here – 'set like a dice on a rock already venerable with the scars of wind and water. The hill runs clear up into the sky behind it, so that the cypresses and olives overhang this room in which I sit and write.'

> **INSIDER TIP** ⟩⟩
>
> There are two film versions of Gerald Durrell's *My Family and Other Animals* – one with Brian Blessed and Hannah Gordon (1987), the other starring Imelda Staunton (2005). They are both available on DVD.

Across the headland to the north lies the tiny harbour of **Kouloura**, a simple hook of concrete and stone lined with fishing boats and pleasure craft. The road down to it ends at the impressive wrought-iron gates of a 17th-century mansion, and on the left, just above the harbour, is a taverna.

With a reputation for attracting the middle class and the wealthy, the next village north, **Agios Stefanos** (usually called Agios Stefanos Sinion, to distinguish it from several other villages of the same name) is beautifully unspoilt.

Accessed through **Sinies**, and serving the many local upmarket villas and passing yacht trade, it is a lovely place to pause, especially for lunch. You might stop at the mini-market in Sinies's tiny square to put together a picnic before driving down the serpentine hill, thronged with olive trees and beehives, to the gorgeous horseshoe-shaped village. Or, once you get there, choose one of its water-side tavernas (see 'Family-friendly Dining', p. 78).

Although the locals live mainly off the summer tourist trade (much of it British), and there are a couple of shops selling souvenirs and so on, the village doesn't have the feel of a place that simply shuts down in the winter. Working fishing boats still use the harbour, and you'll see catches being landed and nets being repaired. Just behind the main street there's a small children's playground in the deep cool shade of the trees – a seesaw, some swings and a slide.

From Agios Stefanos you can get access to two small and pretty beach-plus-tavernas villages – **Kerasia** to the south, **Avlaki** to the north. But the next major town along the coast road is the one that appears on all the signposts: Kassiopi.

Kassiopi has had a very mixed history. **The Romans** fortified it, **Tiberius** had a villa here, and it was visited by **Cicero** and **Nero**. Its **Byzantine fortress** was the first to fall to the Franks, and was destroyed by the Venetians – there are atmospheric remains on the hill overlooking the town.

The approach to modern Kassiopi is less than inspiring –

Agios Stefanos

a mish-mash of souvenir shops, cafés, mini-markets and buckets-spades-flippers-and-lilos emporia. But when you get to the port itself, it's all worthwhile. Pretty as a picture, with a cleanly paved quayside and pleasantly sited tavernas, you can dive, hire boats, sign on for local cruises and excursions, use one of its four pebbly beaches, or walk or drive to nearby **Koyevinas**. Renowned too for its nightlife, Kassiopi might well be an ideal base for families with older teenagers.

It is at Kassiopi that the main road strikes west along Corfu's north coast. Though still pleasant, it lacks the jaw-dropping grandeur of the countryside you've just driven through.

The north coast

The first place of note – and of interest to families with children – is the **Hydropolis Water Park** (see p. 63) attached to the **Gelina Village Resort** (see 'Family-friendly Accommodation', p. 72).

Continuing along the north coast, the next major resort is **Sidari**. It gets a battering from other guidebooks, and I can see why. Heavily dominated by the British package holiday industry which moved here after Benitses in the south got a bad name, it seems to consist entirely of a succession of bars and discos, together with a rather scrappy and dusty beach. A lot of British expats live here, too, and some believe that the influx of UK teenage residents has lowered the tone of the place!

Yet Sidari does have its good points. For example, as you approach the town on the coast road, you'll see ads for **Sidari Water Park.** When you finally get to it, just before arriving at Sidari proper, it's hard to believe that you've found the right place. A scruffy gravel lane leads off the main road to a weed-tufted car park. But be of good cheer – the Water Park is a little gem (see p. 63).

The other thing that makes Sidari worth a visit is the extraordinary '**canals**'. Head for 'Kanali' (past a Brit-owned-and-run fishing tackle shop and Internet café) to the west of the main beach and park. Stone-paved paths lead through the broom to the famous canals, a series of inlets where water and wind have carved the soft sandstone cliffs into tortuous shapes, layered like cake. The biggest of these bays has a beach, and if you swim out from it along the '**canal d'amour**' it is said (and depending who you speak to) that you will either find eternal love or, if single, the partner of your dreams. Or maybe it was just dreamed up by the local tourist board!

Whatever the truth, these unearthly formations are really worth seeing. If you have teenagers, though, discourage them from copying local youths who jump into the sea from the cliffs. They know what they're doing, and allow for the swell. Visitors have been known to get

Sidari Canals

quite severe injuries when they mistime their leap and find that the water, so invitingly deep a moment before, has, by the time they arrive, disappeared.

Hydropolis Water Park and Sports Centre ★★★ ALL AGES

Just outside Acharavi, 📞 *26 63 06 40 00.*

Though not advertised as widely as Central Corfu's Aqualand, and not quite as big, it is still worth a full day out, with both children and adults well catered for in a variety of slides, pools and other water features, including a Lazy River, and there's an 'animation' programme for children. There is also the usual support structure of restaurants, cafeterias and bars, and opportunities to play games such as tennis and basketball.

The Gelina Village Resort, next to the Water Park, between the main road and its own private beach, consists of a wide range of accommodation and loads of things for youngsters to do (see 'Family-friendly Accommodation', p. 72).

Open *10.30am–6.30pm.* **Adm** *adults €14, children €10.* **Amenities** *Cafés. Disabled access. English spoken. Parking. Picnic area. Restaurants. Shops.*

Sidari Water Park ★ ALL AGES

📞 *26 63 09 90 66, www.sidariwater park.com.*

Attached to a very pleasant hotel (see 'Family-friendly Accommodation', p. 72), Sidari Water Park consists of three adult and two children's pools, splendid tubular slides (again, some of which are suitable for youngsters), a children's playground, a variety of indoor games such as pool, a restaurant and an open-all-hours bar. Sun-beds and umbrellas are available, and the great thing is that it's all free! The only charge (and then only if you're not staying at the hotel) is for the use of the slides (see below). Should you choose to stay at the hotel, rooms have kitchenette facilities, and there are plenty of shops and a supermarket within easy walking distance without having to venture into the fleshpots of Sidari itself.

Open *8am–11pm.* **Adm** *free, use of slides – adults €8, children €6 per day.* **Amenities** *Café. English spoken. Parking. Restaurant.*

The northwest coast

Beyond Sidari, although the main road heads inland back towards the south, a perfectly adequate road cuts across the extreme northwest corner of Corfu, meandering through pleasant olive groves dotted with private villas, climbing through the hill town of **Avliotes** and heading towards the west coast. It's easy to get lost on this skein of country lanes, but if you're in no hurry, it's very pleasant too.

As the road drops towards the west coast, there's a distinctly British feel, with lots of greenery and nice beaches between low headlands – it reminded me of the Lleyn Peninsula in North Wales. **Agios Stefanos**, the first of the resorts, is spread out around a bay, low-key and family orientated, with a handsome sweep of sandy beach. If you want a traditional British bucket-and-spade holiday, this is the place to come. And since you're now, of course, facing due west, you can also enjoy wonderful sunsets – much is made of them locally.

A kilometre or so south is a new-looking harbour full of boats, from where you can set off for the tiny **Diapondia Islands** – Othoni, Erikousa and Mathraki (there are others in the group, but they're not inhabited). These three are sleepy, pleasant little islands with a few hundred inhabitants (largely women, since the men work in the USA and send money home), the odd taverna and B&B and lots of tranquil views.

You can also get to them from Sidari and Corfu Town.

Continuing south, the villages of **Arillas** and **Afionas** both have sandy beaches which are slowly gaining in popularity. **Agios Giorgios** boasts a spectacular double bay hemmed in by headlands, two long sandy beaches and the beginnings – still in the early stages – of a beach culture. There is windsurfing equipment for hire, tavernas, at least one disco, and rooms to let. Careful as you approach the village, though – the descent is very steep.

A short drive (or a long one if, like me, you get lost) brings you to **Paleokastritsa**, the jewel of Corfu's west coast. A vision of lofty cliffs, spume-flecked rocks and small intricate bays washed by an opalescent sea, the village is clothed densely in olive, cypress and eucalyptus. There's no more beautiful place on Corfu. That said, its beauty does attract dense crowds in the summer.

At the heart of the village lie three bays divided in places by rocks into numerous small coves and beaches. Apart from safe swimming and water sports, Paleokastritsa offers plenty of cafés and tavernas, and there are half-hour boat trips to the Blue Grottoes at a rather steep €8 a head.

At the far end of the village is a car park above which a road, controlled by traffic lights, climbs steeply to the 17th-century monastery of **Theotokou** ★. Open 7am–1pm, then 3pm–8pm

Paleokastritsa

(1st April to 31st Oct), with free admission, it's a haven of peace and tranquillity. It includes a church, whitewashed monks' cells, a museum and museum shop, and a delightfully shady flagged arcade, all decked out in potted flowers and somnolent cats. And the views of the rocky headland are wonderful.

About six kilometres north of the village are the ruins of the 13th-century Byzantine castle of **Angelokastro**. It is possible to walk there, but it's a long hike – far better to drive to the village of **Krini** and walk from there. The remains are atmospheric, and the views spectacular.

From Paleokastritsa it's a fast, easy drive back to Corfu Town. There's a reason for this: Sir Frederick Adam, the Ionian Islands' second High Commissioner, loved to picnic in Paleokastritsa, so he had a road built (as you do) to make the journey from the capital easier.

A tour of southern Corfu

Southern Corfu is gentler and less dramatic than the north. It is served by a single main road off which side roads run down to the east and west coasts.

A 19th Century Princess Diana?

Elisabeth of Bavaria – widely known as Sisi – was the nearest thing 19th-century society came to a **royal celebrity**. She was the wife of the Emperor Franz Joseph of Austria-Hungary and considered a great beauty. Photographs of her confirm that she was pretty – good-looking enough, by the standards of European royalty, to qualify her for the 'absolutely stunning' category. She was particularly proud of her long, dark hair and had it styled every day. If her hairdresser couldn't make the appointment, Sisi would stay out of sight until she could. She married the Emperor when she was 17, hated her mother-in-law, and spent most of her life travelling around Europe, living the high life, taking lovers and generally having a good time.

In 1889 Elisabeth was devastated by the **'Mayerling scandal'**. Her only son, Crown Prince Rudolph, was found dead in his hunting lodge at Mayerling in Austria, together with his mistress Baroness Mary Vetsera. Although there was an attempt to hush things up, it became apparent that the two lovers had a suicide pact – Rudolph shot his lover, then himself, perhaps as a result of his father's attempt to end the liaison. Shortly afterwards Sisi ordered the **Achilleion** (see p. 67) to be built. Elisabeth's eventful life ended controversially in 1898 when she was **assassinated** in Geneva by an anarchist. He said he wanted to kill a royal and it was her bad luck that she was the next one to come along.

The east coast

To begin a tour of the south from Corfu Town, head first for the airport, then follow the signs for the **Achilleion Palace** (see p. 67). This involves driving inland for a couple of miles, then left up a steep, winding hill through woodland, meadows and expensive-looking villas. Arrive early, or you'll get snarled up in intense coach traffic, much of it German. There are lots of cafés, restaurants and souvenir shops outside the palace.

From the Achilleion, the road winds steeply down to the coast, where it joins the main north–south artery. A few hundred metres along it to the right, on the outskirts of Benitses, you come to the **Corfu Shell Museum** (see p. 68).

Benitses used to be synonymous with all that was worst in Corfu holidaying, notorious for youthful mass drunkenness and violence. Indeed, it got so bad that the big holiday companies pulled out. What the locals lost in revenue they have more than made up for in quality of life, and Benitses is now a pleasant little town, with a few Roman remains (just behind the harbour), an atmospheric old quarter, and the **Benitses Waterworks** built by Sir Frederick Adams in the first half of the 19th century to supply Corfu Town.

The road continues to follow the coast, past two huge resort hotels, the Iberostar Regency Beach in Benitses, and the Marbella in Agios Ioannis (see 'Family- friendly Accomodation, p. 72). The next village along, **Moraitika**, is very touristy but has one of the best beaches in Corfu, and the village centre, further inland, is relatively unspoilt. Shortly after Moraitika, the main road turns inland, and continues down the spine of Corfu to its southern tip.

Any continued exploration of the southeast coast should include **Boukari**, either by following the minor road along next to the sea after the main road has swung inland, or by following the main road, then driving down through beautiful farming country to the village. Either way, watch out for donkeys laden with crops, hay or their owners.

Boukari consists of little more than a tiny harbour lined with fishing boats, its quay dotted with nets, and a clutch of tavernas. But the surrounding wooded hills, the locals fishing off a rickety jetty, and the crystal water give it a peaceful, timeless air.

The next place worth visiting (and again watch out for donkeys as you drive down the lanes connecting it to the main road) is in fact the capital of southern Corfu, and the island's second largest town, **Lefkimi**.

Feeling more like a large village than a substantial market town, Lefkimi offers a good idea of what pre-tourism Corfu must have been like. A long main street starts at a field where donkeys are usually tethered, and is lined with houses and the occasional church or shop. At the bottom of the town a bridge carries the road across the pleasant, boat-lined **Himaros** river. You might stop here at the dreadfully named but pleasant Cheeky Face taverna, or put together a picnic at the supermarket across the road. And look out for women in the area's traditional headgear, a rather intricate double headscarf, the outer layer of which is in a fine check.

There is little point in continuing the final four or seven kilometres to **Kavos** – it's Costa del Sol-type Club Med territory, brilliant for the people it's aimed at, which doesn't really include families. Paths beyond Kavos lead to the very tip of Corfu, where the recently inaugurated Corfu Path begins (have a look at *www.travelling.gr/corfutrail*), but there's little there that would justify the family making the long hike.

The Achilleion ★ ★ ALL AGES

Museum Achillio, Gastouri 49100,
☏ *26 61 05 62 45, www.corfu-casino.gr.*

The Achilleion was built for Elisabeth of Bavaria (see box, p. 66) in 1889-91 in memory of her son **Rudolph**, who committed suicide. **Sisi**, as she was known, equated him with the mythical Achilles, and had the house built as a retreat, commemorating him with a statue of the dying heroes which you can still see in the garden.

Sisi was assassinated in 1898, and nearly 10 years later the Achilleion was bought by **Kaiser Wilhelm II** as a summer residence. He stayed at the palace frequently during the years leading up to World War I, and as might be expected it became the scene of a great deal of diplomatic activity.

Kaiser Bill's connections with the building are everywhere in evidence – inside there are several portraits of him and his family, together with his famous swivel saddle, and outside, at the end of the garden, stands a giant (15 m) statue of Achilles which he had erected facing north towards Corfu Town.

With typical grandiosity he had it inscribed 'To the greatest of the Greeks, from the greatest of the Germans', a sentiment with which the Greek government disagreed – they understandably had it removed after the war (you can still see the holes in the plinth from which the metal letters were prised). A spot just up the coast, still called **Kaiser's Bridge**, is where he used to moor his gigantic private yacht *Hohenzollern*.

It seems generally accepted that the Achilleion, both in its architecture and its contents, is a monument to bad taste. It's no coincidence that it was used for the casino scenes in the Bond film 'For Your Eyes Only', and indeed the upper floor actually was a casino during the 1960s and 1970s. The building was used as a hospital (World War I) and as Italian/German HQ (World War II), before finding its present destiny as a fascinating museum. The views from the Achilleion, incidentally, are terrific – the rich really know how to pick sites for their houses – and even with the youngest children, the beautiful gardens alone make a visit worthwhile.

Open *daily 9am–4pm.* **Adm** *€4.* **Amenities** *English spoken. Parking.*

Corfu Shell Museum ★ ★ ★
ALL AGES

Benitses, ☎ 26 6107 22 27.

Signposted as 'the sea museum', the **Corfu Shell Museum** indeed does contain a great deal more than shells. There are sharks galore – both whole stuffed sharks and mounted jawbones – rays, lobsters, crabs, starfish, coral, and, of course, the 10,000 seashells of all shapes and sizes collected over many years by owner Napoleon. Though some of the stuffed sharks are beginning to show wear and tear, the labelling is good (in English, Greek and Latin), the information on the wall charts is excellent, and the shells are just beautiful – you can buy examples in the museum shop. The museum's pamphlet rather endearingly claims, no doubt accurately, that Corfu Shell Museum is 'second best in Europe'.

Open *daily 10am–9pm (last entry 8pm).* **Adm** *Adults €4, children €2. Credit cards not accepted.* **Amenities** *English spoken. Parking. Restaurant. Shop.*

Corfu Shell Museum

The west coast

The return journey north towards Corfu Town provides an opportunity to take a look at the island's southwest coast. Although it has a reputation for wonderful beaches, this coast is actually not very impressive. **Agios Georgios** certainly has miles of sand, backed by scrubby dunes, easily accessible from the road that runs alongside most of it. There's a small modern concrete haven for boats, lots of small hotels and apartment blocks, much of which cater for the UK package trade, and a full excursion programme – Albania, Paxos, Aqualand, Corfu Town, the Blue Lagoon, the Corfu Coast, the Greek mainland – can be accessed through the tiny tourist information office in the centre of the village. Though the variety of trips on offer might just reflect the fact that Agios Georgios itself is a little dusty and dispiriting, with not a lot to do away from beach activities, it still might suit some families, who just want long days on the beach interspersed with the odd boat or coach trip.

The highly-rated **Issos** beach just north of Agios Georgios is pleasant and sandy, but there's little in the way of facilities. Backed by curious shale dunes, it's ideal if all you want is beach and bathing. There's a British-run windsurfing school (*www. mermanwindsurf.com*) and a taverna a couple of hundred metres before you get to the dunes. Issos is much frequented by naturists.

From Issos beach, looking north, you can see standing water between the dunes and a low range of hills. This is **Lake Korission**, a lagoon-like stretch of water much frequented by migratory birds, turtles, tortoises and lizards. The lake and its surrounding countryside is one of the oddest and most appealing areas in the whole of Corfu. The best way to approach it is to follow the signs from the main road for **Gardiki Fortress**.

The 13th-century fortification is the first thing of note you come to. Standing up to its armpits in undergrowth in the middle of the countryside, it consists of an impressive Byzantine gatehouse standing next to an ancient olive tree, and extensive curtain walls enclosing a large bailey full of saplings, grass and wild flowers. Goats with silky-white fleece graze contentedly, bleating occasionally into the insect-loud air. Strange that a place designed for war should be so peaceful.

From the fortress one road leads to the hillside village of **Agios Mattheos**, the verandas of its unspoilt local houses dripping with flowers.

In the other direction, the road swings along through olive groves, vineyards and market gardens growing flowers until it arrives at the edge of Lake Korission. The shallow water of the lake is dotted with clumps of leaves like tiny islands.

The next place up the coast of any size is **Agios Gordis**. It looks a picture when you first glimpse it from the top of the escarpment behind the village. A crescent of golden sand between two wooded headlands, the towering pinnacles of rock behind the village and out to sea, the red roofs of the houses, the green patchwork of gardens and vineyards, the vivid blue of the occasional swimming pool, all laid out like a map far below.

When you drive down the steep and winding hill into the village, you become aware that **Agios Gordis** is given over almost entirely to the holiday industry. Dotted with hotels, villas and apartments, its restaurants, tavernas, cafés, mini-markets, car and bike rental and excursion offices, souvenir and beach shops are all designed to supply visitors, whether in hotels or self-catering apartments and villas.

OK, Agios Gordis isn't the place to come to experience traditional Corfiot life. But all the accommodation, eating places and shops are locally owned and run, and there's a warmth of welcome that you don't get in more commercialised resorts. This family feeling is everywhere – lost children, I was assured, would just be scooped up by locals and reunited with their parents. The beach is delightful and there's plenty to do.

All this, and the position of the village – less than half an hour's drive (or an easy bus ride) away from Corfu Town, central enough to allow excursions to both the north and south of the island, yet isolated by its long steep hill and surrounding countryside from any threatening teen temptations – make it one of the very best bets for family holidays in Corfu. It even has the eccentric but wonderful budget accommodation of the **Pink Palace** (see 'Family-friendly Accommodation', p. 72), which organises a huge variety of activities on the beach.

North of Agios Gordis a little group of villages define an area which is a delight to explore during a day's pottering, or even as a base. **Sinarades** is long and lovely, with picturesquely balconied houses, masses of potted flowers, an imposing church and a really good **folklore museum** ★ ALL AGES (**℡ 26 61 05 49 62**. Open from Tuesday to Sunday from 9.30am to 2.30pm, admission is €2 for adults and €0.60 for children. If you drive through the pretty inland hill town of **Pelekas**, and keep going upwards, you'll get to one of Kaiser Wilhelm II's favourite spots. An iron viewing platform atop a stone column approached along paved paths and stone steps – the **Kaiser's Throne** – offers spectacular 360-degree views across the island. The name of the Sunset Restaurant, next to the Kaiser's Throne, speaks for itself.

Beyond Pelekas, **Glyfada** is dominated by small apartment blocks and the huge Louis Grand Hotel. A good selection of tavernas, a load of loungers and beach umbrellas, all connected up by wooden boardwalks, make this a very pleasant beach indeed, but it can get not only crowded but very noisy at the height of the season.

A little further on, down a steep narrow lane that meanders towards the sea, lies **Myrtiotissa Beach,** which Lawrence Durrell thought 'perhaps the loveliest beach in the world'. Its two tiny bays, like a seagull's wings, at the base of steep wooded cliffs boast beautiful clean sand and clear water lapping around large rocks that look as if they were placed there, just so, by an artist. The first bay is a naturist beach, the second isn't. Above them there's a monastery.

Myrtiotissa Beach

The final stopping place on this brief tour of west-central Corfu is **Ermones,** a little bay with a steep amphitheatre of hotels climbing the hills behind it. A mile or so inland is Corfu's only golf course, the highly rated **Corfu Golf and Country Club**.

For Active Families

There's plenty to do on Corfu – here are some suggestions.

Walking

www.walksworldwide.com
www.exploreworldwide.com
Look out in 'The Corfiot' for announcement of programme of walks – with dates and graded difficulty (€2). Or phone ☏ 26 61 05 28 33.

Horse-riding

www.equitour.co.uk
www.greek-travel.info/adventure.
html

Mountain biking

www.greek-travel.info/adventure.
html (esp. Mount Pantokrator).

Diving

www.divingcorfu.com

Cooking

www.theinvisiblekitchen.co.uk
cooking holidays in north Corfu (Acharavi).

Music

www.chambermusicholidays.com

Shopping With Children

Corfu is good for leather goods, jewellery, ceramics, olive wood ornaments and embroidery.

You'll find all these in abundance in Corfu Town, but also as you drive around the island – in particular look for pottery workshops and places that make and sell things made of olive wood. Prices outside Corfu Old Town are likely to be lower. To make sure what you're getting is authentic, buy from factory shops – I once came across a ceramic pot with Greek writing on the base, which translated as 'Made in China'! Also, look out for shops which are bright orange in colour, because of all the bottles of liqueur and preserves on show – they'll be selling a variety of products made from kumquats. Should you develop a hankering for anything from back home, there's **The British Corner Shop** www.thebritish cornershop.gr (8 km south of Corfu Town on Lefkimi road. Open Mon–Sat 8–9, Sun 10–4. ☏ 26 61 03 00 16), though this is surely aimed at expats going mad because of Marmite deficiency.

FAMILY–FRIENDLY ACCOMMODATION

EXPENSIVE

Corfu Palace Hotel ★★

2 Leoforos Demokratias, 49100, ☏ 26 61 03 94 85, www.corfupalace.com. Five-minute walk south of Esplanade on the coast road.

The great advantage of the Corfu Palace Hotel is its position – it's a large luxury hotel with health club and spa, choice of pools, bars and restaurants, and rooms with all mod cons and either terrace or balcony, yet it's within five minute walk of the heart of Corfu Town. So, if you have exclusively teenage children, and they're lucky enough to have extremely prosperous parents, then this is the place to stay (especially if that prosperity runs to a suite) – all members of the family have the freedom to come and go into town relatively independently, yet there's plenty of activity of the exercising, swimming and lounging variety within the hotel itself. For families with several younger children, however, there are better options further away from the centre of the capital. If you intend to stay at the Corfu Palace, though, book well in advance.

Rooms 115. *Rates* €135– €249 double, suites more, depending on size and season. Rates include buffet breakfast; children up to 12 stay free (without food) in parents' bedroom. *Credit* AmEx, DC, MC, V. *Amenities* Babysitting. Bars (3). Cots (free). Disabled access. Extra bed (€27 to €50, free under 12). Gym. Laundry. Parking. Pools (3) (one indoor, one outdoor, one for children). Restaurants (2). Spa. *In room*: A/C. Internet access. Safe. TV/Satellite.

Dassia Chandris and Corfu Chandris Hotels ★ ★ ★

Dassia, 49100 ☎ 26 61 09 71 00, www.chandris.gr/corfu. In Dassia, on the main road north from Corfu Town towards Kassiopi.

If your family contains both tots and teens, and you therefore want to combine children's stuff

with proximity to Corfu Town, these two hotels, on the same site and sharing facilities, are an excellent choice. There's a kid's club (indoors and out) for 4- to 12-year olds, and children have their own seawater pool. You can order early suppers, high chairs are available and there's a junior buffet in the restaurant. Cots are free. For older children there are all the facilities that will also appeal to adults – a huge variety of games and sports, a lovely beach, water activities, outdoor cinema, fitness centre and spa, and so on, all laid out in beautiful gardens that slope gently down to the beach. Because it's in the centre of Dassia, there are lots of other restaurants within easy reach of the hotel – there's a paintballing centre, for example, directly across the road. And there's a complimentary shuttle bus, four times a day, into Corfu Town – it takes 10–15 minutes, depending on traffic.

Rooms 554 rooms, bungalows and villas. *Rates* €120–€333. Rates include breakfast. *Credit* AmEx, DC, MC, V. *Amenities* Bars (6). Children's club (4–11). Cots (free). Disabled access. Extra bed (small charge). Gym. Non-smoking rooms. Pools (3). Restaurants (3). Spa. *In room* A/C. Internet access. Safe. TV/Satellite.

MODERATE

Hotel Nissaki Beach, Nissaki ★

P.O. BOX 69, 491 00, ☎ 26 63 09 12 32, www.nissakibeach.gr. Between the main coast road and the sea, about two miles north of the village of Nissaki.

Play cars lined up for young guests at the Chandris Hotels

Though 'egg-boxy' in construction this does ensure that all rooms have balconies), the Nissaki Beach stands in pleasant grounds surrounded by countryside. The hotel offers a similar experience to that of the Chandris, but at twice the distance from Corfu Town. There *is* a shuttle into the capital, but it takes twice as long, and the winding coast road won't suite those who suffer from travel sickness. If you want to restrict teenage jaunts, then, the Nissaki Beach is ideal – it's relatively isolated, and therefore easy to police! Provision for children is good – there's a children's club, a team of professionals employed to organise events and activities, playground and swimming pool, the restaurants have high chairs and children's menus and you can order early suppers, there's flexibility regarding accommodation (families of up to four can share a room) and the hotel will provide babysitting on request.

There is usually entertainment available in the evening – shows, dancing and discos.

Rooms *239, including six suites and five family rooms.* **Rates** *€110–€280 double/suite, depending on size and season. Rates are half board, and can be converted to full board for €15 per person per day extra; children aged up to 2 stay free in parents' bedroom, children two to 12: 50% reduction if in parents' room.* **Credit** *AmEx, DC, MC, V.* **Amenities** *Babysitting. Bars (2). Children's club. Cots (free). Disabled access. Extra beds (charge). Gym. Parking. Pools (2). Restaurants (2). Spa.* **In room** *A/C. Safe. TV/Satellite.*

LTI-Gelina Village Resort and Spa, Acharavi ★ ★ ★ FIND

Acharavi, 📞 *26 63 06 40 00,* **www. gelina.gr** *or* **www.lti.de** *Situated on Corfu's north coast just before Acharavi.*

This large, German-owned holiday complex is used chiefly by Germans, Belgians and Dutch – it's relatively little known in the UK. Consisting of Gelina

Village Resort and Spa, the Gelina Apartments and the Gelina Mare Hotel, it offers a hugely flexible combination of rooms, apartments, suites and maisonettes absolutely ideal for families of all sizes. The fact that each of these has a kitchenette, combined with the presence of a mini-market in the complex, means that you have the option of eating 'at home' or preparing your own picnics when everybody's getting fed up with restaurant meals. There's a kid's club and extensive children's playground on site, water and other sports, a theatre, a museum, a small petting zoo, and the magnificent Hydropolis Waterpark, with all the pools, giant slides and lazy rivers you might expect, attached to the site. Guests get one day's admission free, and a concessionary rate thereafter.

Rooms 255. *Rates* €180–220 per night for a family of four. *Credit* AmEx, V. *Amenities* Bars (4). Children's club (age four to 12). Cots (free). Extra beds (free). Gym. Parking. Pools (3: 1 indoor, 1 outdoor, 1 for children). Restaurants. Spa. *In room* A/C. Safe. TV/Satellite.

Sidari Water Park Hotel, Sidari ★★

Sidari, ☎ 26 63 09 90 66, www.sidari waterpark.com. Just as you get to Sidari on the road from Kassiopi.

Like the Gelina Village Resort, above, the Sidari Water Park Hotel has water slides and pools, children's playground and games area, bar and restaurant, but all on a much smaller, more intimate

scale (the hotel has 30 units compared to 255). It has the feel of a locally owned family facility, and provides a beautifully engaging but safe environment for younger children. Teenagers might enjoy it too, because it's on the edge of Sidari, one of the largest holiday towns on Corfu, with all the shops, clubs and discos older children might want, and a substantial expat British population with whom to relate. Kitchenettes and the proximity of one of Sidari's two big supermarkets allows self-catering when you want it, but there are loads of restaurants should you need them, both within walking distance and onsite (the onsite one does English breakfasts, as well as a wide selection of Greek and Italian food). There's even a McDonald's just down the road.

Rooms 30. *Rates* €80 double/suite per night. *Credit* V. *Amenities* Bar. No smoking. Parking. Pools (3 outdoor for adults, 2 for children). Restaurant. *In room* A/C. Internet access. Safe. TV.

Akrotiri Beach Hotel, Paleokastritsa

PO Box 28, 49100, ☎ 26 63 04 12 37. www.akrotiri-beach.com.

Superbly situated on a rocky promontory above the first of Paleokastritsa's three bays, the Akrotiri Beach offers all the basic things you need, but few of the family trimmings. If you want all the kid's club/animation team bells and whistles, then it's probably not for you. And teenagers would probably end up climbing the walls. But for a quiet holiday with very young children in what is probably Corfu's prettiest resort, with access to a sandy beach on one side and a rocky one on the other, with a lovely pool terrace, terrific views from all rooms, and delightful walks into the town, then the Akrotiri Beach is hard to beat. It also uses the hotel minibus to provide a complimentary twice-weekly ride into Corfu Town, so you do get the opportunity for a bit of sightseeing and shopping. Open 1st May to 22nd October.

Rooms 127. **Rates**: €125– €200 for two adjoining rooms suitable for families. Rates include breakfast. **Credit** MC, V. **Amenities** Babysitting. Bars (3). Cots (free). Extra beds (free). Parking. Pools (2). Restaurant. **In room** A/C. TV.

Iberostar Regency Beach, Benitses

PO Box 28, 📞 26 61 07 12 11. **www. iberostar.com.** Between Benitses and Agios Ioannis on the coast road south of Corfu Town.

One of a huge chain of Iberostar hotels which often features in the brochures of the big holiday companies, the Regency Beach offers a comprehensively self-contained holiday, with plenty to do for adults and children. There's a kid's club, a children's swimming pool on the roof, children's buffet available at both breakfast and dinner, and a playground. There's also a wide range of indoor games and outdoor sports, including water sports. Although the hotel and its private beach are separated by the busy main road, this

isn't a problem for families – there's a tunnel underneath. On most evenings there are theme nights, cabarets or discos, and there's also entertainment during the day. The hotel is well placed for exploring the surrounding area – it's only a couple of kilometres from Benitses, and 15 kilometres from Corfu Town. If there is a criticism, it does feel a little soulless.

Rooms 221. **Rates** €110–170 double. Rates are all inclusive, with a minimum of seven nights; children up to 12 pay around 50%, less for subsequent children. Children sometimes go free, subject to availability. **Credit** AmEx, DC, MC, V. **Amenities** Bars (6). Children's mini club. Cots. Extra bed. Laundry service. Parking. Pools, 4 (outdoor). Restaurants (3). **In room** A/C. Safe. TV/Satellite.

Marbella Hotel, Agios Ioannis ★ ★ ★ GREEN

Agios Ioannis Peristeron, 49084 📞 26 61 07 11 83. **www.marbella.gr.**

Another that features in the holiday brochures, the Marbella has, for a big package hotel, absolutely bags of character. It's built interestingly into a steep hillside (though it has to be said that this makes it a bit of trial for those using buggies). The swimming pool terrace has wonderful views up the coast, and paved paths snake here and there to the shops, outdoor theatre, children's playground and chapel. The architecture – faintly Moorish – adds to the 'rightness' of the whole place. The Wellness centre offers a range of treatments (massage, Shiatsu, Feng Shui, reflexology), and there's a sauna and gym. There's an excellent programme of concerts, folklore and beach parties. Add the provision of babysitting, cots, high chairs, baby food, and medical treatment on demand, and you can see that the Marbella goes out of its way to welcome youngsters. Furthermore, it's one of the few hotels that explicitly takes its environmental responsibilities seriously, from re-use of water to energy-saving lightbulbs, use of non-toxic paints to double flush toilets. Oh, and its website is the best by a country mile that I've come across.

Rooms 395. Rates €125–288 double, depending on size, facilities and season. Family rooms which sleep four people: €210–368. Rates are for half-board; first two children up to 13: 50% of pp rates if staying in parents' bedroom. Credit AmEx, DC, MC, V. Amenities Babysitting. Bars (3). Children's club. Cots(free). Gym. Laundry Non-smoking. Pools (3). Restaurants (4). Spa. In room A/C. Safe. TV/Satellite.

INEXPENSIVE

The Pink Palace, Agios Gordis ☆

The Pink Palace Beach Resort, Agios Gordios Beach, Sinarades, 49084, ☏ 26 61 05 31 03. www.thepink palace.com. At the foot of the hill that takes you into Agios Gordios, and it's dotted about elsewhere in the town. You can't miss it – all its parts are painted bright pink!

The Pink Palace in Agios Gordis is a phenomenon. Famous among backpacking island-hoppers the world over, it is archetypal accommodation for young people on a limited budget. Yet it has recently gone very much upmarket in some of its provision, and now offers new rooms with facilities that rival any in far more luxurious tourist hotels. These 'A' class rooms, en suite and with air conditioning and a balcony, can sleep up to four people. Older rooms ('B' class) are for from two to five people, whilst its famous dormitories will sleep up to 10. The hotel has an Internet room, TV room with films and Satellite TV, and games such as ping-pong, pool and table football. There's also private access, via a long, covered staircase, to the beach. The Pink Palace organises a wide range of beach and other activities, the less boozy of which are suitable for families. Don't go to the Pink Palace for a quiet life, or for child-friendly facilities, but if you want budget accommodation in a lively, youth-orientated environment, with lots of young people for your children to relate to, it's a brilliant choice.

Rooms 300 rooms. Rates 'A' class rooms €25–€30 per person; 'B' class rooms €23–27 pp; dorms €18–23 pp. Rates include hot breakfast and three-course evening meal. Credit AmEx, MC, V. Amenities Bar. Extra bed. Laundry. Parking. In 'A' class room A/C.

Dionysus Camping Village

Camping Dionysus, Dassia, Dafnilas Bay, PO Box 185, 49100, ☏ 26 61 09 14 17, www.dionysuscamping.gr. Signposted from the main road about 1 km before getting to Dassia.

Camping Dionysus offers a budget alternative to the big hotels, apartments and villas. Whilst rough and ready, there are many families who swear by the more open-air experience of sites like this. In particular, younger children seem to thrive in this environment. If you've driven across Europe and caught a ferry to Corfu, then you can erect your own tent or set up your own caravan or motor caravan. But even if you've flown from the UK, you can book ready-erected tents or simple wooden bungalows. Don't expect mod cons though – even the bungalows don't have their own plumbing, and consist of simple wooden huts with thatched roofs containing a couple of beds and perhaps a table. But cooking, washing and ironing can all be done in communal facilities, there's a big swimming pool, and the beach is 300m away. Arrangements can be made through reception for excursions, watersports, boat and car rental,

horse riding, etc and the blue bus to and from the centre of Corfu Town runs every half hour.

Rates adult €4.80–€5.40, children (aged four to 10) €2.60–€3.30, car €2.80–€3.30, caravan €4.20–€4.50, motor caravan €6–€6.50, tent €3.30–€3.80, electricity €3.80–€3.80, ready-erected tent rental €8–€ 9 per person, bungalow rental €9–€10 per person. *Credit* AmEx, DC, MC, V. *Amenities* Bar. Parking. Pool. Restaurant.

FAMILY-FRIENDLY DINING

EXPENSIVE

Corfu Palace Hotel ★★

2 Leoforos Demokratias, 49100 Corfu Town, ☎ 26 61 03 94 85. www.corfu palace.com. Five-minute walk south of Esplanade on the coast road.

The Corfu Palace Hotel's Scheria restaurant is not for everyday dining, unless you're well off. But it's ideal for a special occasion – last night of the holiday, good exam results, that sort of

Dionysus Camping Village

thing. You can dine out on the terrace, with a lovely view of Corfu Town.

Open *All year.* **Main course** *€22–45.* **Credit** *AmEx, V.* **Amenities** *Children's menu. High chairs. Reservations recommended.*

Taverna Agni ★ ★ ★ FIND

Agni, 📞 *26 63 09 11 42, www.agni.gr. The Tavera Agni is one of three excellent tavernas that line the beach at Agni, in north-west Corfu.*

The Taverna Agni serves Greek seafood of high quality, with fish caught daily by its own boat. For those who don't like fish, there are always a few meat-based meals on the menu. The relaxed atmosphere, the view across to Albania, the sea lapping onto the beach a few yards away – the ambience is out of this world. Agni, though, is not easy to get to – by car you need to drive down a narrow winding road, and do the last few hundred metres on foot. A really pleasant way of going there for a meal if you're staying in any of the places below is by speedboat taxi – the Taverna Agni operates a service as follows:

● From St Stefanos (NE) –7pm and 8.30pm.

● From Kerasia – 7.05pm and 8.35pm.

● From Kalami – 7.30pm and 8.45pm.

● From Nissaki Village – 8pm.

● From Nissaki Beach Hotel – 8.05pm.

Taverna Agni

The charge is €2– €5 per person.

Open *in the morning for drinks, for lunch from noon to 4pm, for evening meals from 7.30pm, with last orders at 11pm. May 1st to 31st October.* **Main course** *€15–55.* **Amenities** *Children's menu. Reservations recommended.*

MODERATE

Aegli ★ ★

Kapodistriou 23, Corfu Town, 📞 *26 61 03 19 49. One of the row of cafés and restaurants along the Liston.*

You couldn't ask for a more pleasant place to have lunch and watch the world go by than the Aegli. Like all the 'Rue de Tivoli' café/bar/estiatoria that make up the famous 'Liston', it consists of an indoor area (with TV, music and toilets), a halfway house of tables and chairs under the pleasantly shady arcade, and a block of tables across Eleftherios, next to the grass of the Esplanade. It's this last area that you should head for if you've got youngsters. They can play on the grass whilst you're waiting for the food, or on pedestrianised Eleftherios, next to the Liston. Whether you sit next to the grass or the road depends on the direction of the wind. The other tables will be packed with Greeks, all smoking, so choose tables that are up-wind! The food is excellent and consists of a wide variety of Greek snacks and dishes – try the *tiropites* (cheese pastries), *spanakopites* (the same, but with spinach) or the *souvlakia* (pork on skewers).

Open 8am–1am all week. **Main course** €7–12. **Credit** AmEx, MC, V. **Amenities** Highchairs.

Eucalyptus ★ ★ ★ FIND

Agios Stefanos, Corfu, 📞 *26 63 08 20 07. As you arrive in Agios Stefanos, the Eucalyptus is the first restaurant on the left – look out for the large eucalyptus tree with a boat (the 'Irini') beneath it.*

The picturesque, family-run Eucalyptus is in the perfect position, on the beach overlooking the pretty, unspoilt fishing village of Agios Stefanos. Housed in an old building where they once pressed olives (you can still see some of the equipment), it has the three sections common to many tavernas – indoor, outdoor but under cover, with wind barriers which can be wound down when it's breezy, and a narrow terrace on the beach. The food is what might be called adventurous Greek – try the pork with

artichokes, or anything with cheese in it. Whilst you're eating, the children can come and go onto the beach, or use the small playground tucked just behind them main street opposite.

Open 10am–11pm every day. **Main course** €15–20 per person. **Credit** MC, V. **Amenities** Children's menu. High chairs. Reservations recommended for evenings in July and Aug.

Skeloydi Taverna ★ ★ ★ FIND

Paleokastritsa, Corfu, 📞 *26 63 04 16 28. Next to the Theotokou Monastery, and at the top of the steep hill at the end of the town.*

The Skeloydi has one of the most spectacular settings of any taverna in Corfu. Next to Paleokastritsa's famous Theotokou Monastery (they share both the car park and outlook), it is perched above glorious vistas of wooded cliffs and foam-fringed rocks. The service is good, the menu offers traditional Greek and Corfiot specialities, and the terrace induces a great feeling of well-being as you watch the Adriatic surging around the jagged rocks at the foot of the cliff, or the swallows banking and swooping above the trees. Handy for the children too – the toilet block is at the end of the terrace, so they don't have to keep fighting their way through the restaurant to get to the loo. Since the monastery's shut from 1pm to 3pm, it would be a good idea to visit the monastery then eat, or eat then visit the monastery.

Open 9am–10pm daily. **Main course** €7–12. **Amenities** Highchairs. Play area. Reservations.

Taverna Sebastian, Agios Gordios

Taverna Sebastian, Agios Gordios Sinarades, 49084, ☎ 26 61 05 32 56. www.sebastians-taverna.gr. As you turn into the village, Sebastian is high on the left, with a view down the main street towards the sea.

Very much a hands-on family business, Sebastian offers a Greek menu with a cosmopolitan spin. Although Sebastian himself (and his mum Vassiliki, who also works in the restaurant) are Greek, his wife Teresa is English, so the taverna's approach has been tweaked to suit British tastes and preferences. For example, on the dessert menu you'll get baklava, but also apple crumble and chocolate brownies.

Open *9am to midnight, all week* **Main course** *€7.50–15.* **Credit** *MC, V.* **Amenities** *Children's menu. Entertainment: bouzouki nights, toys, games and colouring in. High chairs. Reservations not necessary, but recommended in high season.*

INEXPENSIVE

The Farm ★★★ FIND

☎ 26 61 07 70 97. On the road between Gardiki Fortress and Lake Korission.

Sometimes you come across a place that's just perfect. The Farm is one of these. It *is* a farm, with beautiful grounds running down to the country road upon which it stands. But it also sells food at the roadside – no great gourmet menu, but just one standard main course: Kleftiko. Lamb or pork cooked (for eight hours!) in clay crocks in traditional wood-fired ovens. The ovens are there for you to see – two of them. Both have smoke-blackened domes surrounded by stacks of wood, bellows and long rods for edging out the steaming pots. It's living history. You can sit at stepped brick-and-timber benches and tables next to the drive or on a more conventional terrace, you can listen to the birds singing in the olive groves and watch the farm vehicles trundle by. The children can play in the garden whilst you eat your appetisers and then, when it arrives, you can eat unbelievably tender meat with herb-flavoured fried potatoes, break fresh home-made bread, drink chilled beer from the big fridge next to the road, and sigh. Contentment!

Open *12.30pm–9 or 10pm.* **Main course** *€7–10.* **Credit** *MC, V.* **Amenities** *Children's menu. Reservations required in Aug.*

Mic Mac/Goody's/ McDonald's

If the children are getting bored with Greek food, and want something a bit more familiar, then these three fast food restaurants are within a two-minute walk of each other. **Mic Mac** (my personal choice) and **McDonald's** are both on Kapodistriou, just behind the southern end of the Liston. Mic Mac does a good range of burgers, pizzas and other stalwarts of western cuisine, all served with excellent chips. McDonald's does what it always does, though in a

Kleftiko at The Farm

very pleasant old mansion looking out across the Esplanade, and with nice outdoor tables and chairs. **Goody's**, one of a chain that you'll come across all over Greece, is on Evyeniou Voulgareos, the main alley that travels east from the end of the Liston. Prices in all three are a little more than you'll pay in similar establishments in the UK, but not outrageously so.

Kalleon's Sandwich Corner FIND

Agios Gordios, 49084, 📞 *26 61 05 38 39. Directly across the road from Taverna Sebastian.*

If you're in a hotel, B&B, or in self-catering villa or apartment, you sometimes get sick and tired of eating out, yet can't be bothered to buy food and cook.

That's where Kalleon's Sandwich Corner and places like it come in. Its selection of sandwiches, filled pitas, hot dogs and burgers, together with a variety of 'and chips' children's meals (chicken nuggets, sausage, fish fingers, pizzas), all freshly made or cooked, offers a brilliant and flexible budget alternative to the pocket-hammering family meal out. So before setting off on an excursion, having a day on the beach, or settling in for an evening playing cards or watching telly, take the orders and phone them through.

Open noon to 11.30pm every day.
Main course €3–7.50. Amenities Children's menu. Some items on the menu require 20 minutes' notice if you don't want to wait. Or just have a beer.

4 Rhodes

RHODES

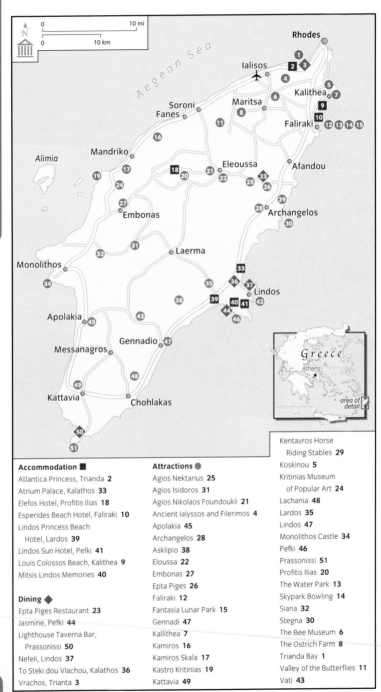

Rhodes is the easternmost of Greece's major islands. It is also the furthest from the Greek mainland, and the closest to Turkey. Slung beneath the belly of Asia Minor, and shaped like a cartoon whale, with flippers halfway down and a tiny tail, it is heavily imprinted with its past. In particular, you'll see evidence of its occupation by the Crusader Knights St John (1309–1522), the Turks (1522–1912) and the Italians (1912–1948), all overlying the continuity of its Greek history. The Italians particularly have exerted an influence out of all proportion to the length of time that they occupied the island, both through enthusiastic renovation of buildings from earlier eras, and energetic development of its infrastructure.

Like Corfu, Rhodes has committed itself wholeheartedly to tourism. Consequently it has a well-developed infrastructure, with a wide range of accommodation types, attractions, activities and places to eat. It is also in the throes of a property boom; the range of hotels, villas and apartments available to families on holiday is second to none. Add that it is one of the most easily accessible Greek islands from the UK, with flights from a host of regional airports, and you can see why Rhodes is a premier destination for parents.

Some of the things that make Rhodes ideal for family holidays are common to most other Greek islands – good weather, a laid-back approach to life and an enviably relaxed, even enthusiastic, attitude to children. Others are unique to the island. Rhodes Town, astride its very northernmost tip, with its medieval buildings, narrow lanes, hidden gardens, boat-thronged harbour and colourful beach, is its number one tourist draw. The island's other hotspots are less than an hour's drive from the airport, along the northwest and northeast coasts. Inland, mountains and monasteries, vineyards and villages, beauty spots and butterfly valleys provide the impetus to get away from the coastal crowds. And the southern half of the island, quiet and rural, offers a glimpse of what Rhodes was like before it became the EU's playground.

The contrast between Rhodes's west and east coast is marked. The west is relatively green and verdant, the east bare and rocky. The west is cool and breezy, the east much hotter – there's often a 5 °C difference between the two coasts. The west coast road sticks much closer to the sea, so that development tends to be in a continuous ribbon, especially as you approach Rhodes Town. The east coast road lies further inland, with spurs running down to villages or beaches.

So, which bits of Rhodes are most suited to families? As far as exploring and visiting attractions is concerned, it doesn't much matter. There are excellent family hotels all over the island, and it's small enough for everything to be reasonably accessible wherever you stay. As a rule of thumb, choose the southern half for peace and quiet, the north for lots to do. But the further south you choose, the longer it'll take to get to Rhodes Town – and you really must visit for at least a day-trip.

If you plump for the northern half – for shorter transfer times and easier access to the capital – the west coast, particularly the stretch from the airport to Rhodes Town, is more family friendly than the east with big resort hotels, sandy/pebbly beaches and some attempt to provide low-key attractions. The east (particularly Faliraki) has some wonderful family-friendly hotels, nice beaches and an awful lot to do. It has, too, begun to shed its 'lager-lads' reputation, but it can still be very noisy at night, and its attractions are all available as days out from elsewhere. Look further south – the resorts around Lindos, for example, are particularly suitable for families, though Lindos itself becomes unbearably crowded at the height of the season.

ESSENTIALS

Getting There

By plane Rhodes is one of the most popular destinations for flights from British regional airports. The best choice of routes is from Thomsonfly and Flythomas Cook. **Thomsonfly,** for example, (☎ *0870 190 0737 www.thomsonfly. com*) flies from Gatwick, Luton, Bristol, Cardiff, Birmingham, East Midlands, Liverpool, Manchester, Doncaster, Newcastle and Glasgow. Thomas Cook (☎ *0870 516 8242 www.flythomas cook.com*) offers a similar number of routes from regional airports.

In addition, the two big national carriers – British Airways and Olympic Airlines – offer a range of scheduled flights. Flight time is around four hours, depending on which airport you're flying from. It is also easy to get to Rhodes by air from a number of other Greek islands, and from the mainland – Olympic Airlines (☎ *0870 606 0460 www.olympicairlines.com*) and Aegean Airlines (☎ *21 06 26 10 00 www.aegeanair.com*) from Athens and most Greek islands. **Rhodes Diagoras Airport** (☎ *22 41 08 32 00*) is about 16 km south of Rhodes Town, on the coast. There's a regular public shuttle-bus into the capital, Olympic Airlines also runs a service that coincides with their own arrivals, and taxis can be hailed at the airport rank and, at €16, are a reasonable alternative for a family. If you've arranged to hire a car, turn right after leaving the airport, then drive straight on (keeping the sea on your left) for the main holiday areas of the northwest coast and Rhodes Town, or bear right at the lights to cut across to the northeast coast.

By sea It is possible to visit Rhodes by boat – either on a cruise, or directly by ferry from Athens, the other Dodecanese islands and Crete, or indirectly from some of the Cyclades. Have a browse through what the cruise companies have to offer (try *www.pocruises.com*), or consult one of the agents representing the Greek ferry lines (*www.viamare.com* for example).

Rhodes Town

VISITOR INFORMATION

There are several websites that are worth a look – try *www. rhodestravels.com, www.rhodes. gr, www.tourist-information.biz/ Rhodes.htm, www.rhodesguide. com, www.GoToRhodes.com*

Also get hold of a copy of '*All about Rhodes – the Island Guide*', a free magazine with masses of useful information – phone numbers, maps of the main towns, ads for attractions, restaurants, apartments and so on. It is widely available in more than 200 outlets across the island – hotels, petrol stations, tourist offices, restaurants.

The **Rhodes Municipal Tourist Office** is on Rimini Square, in the same area of Rhodes Town as the bus station, taxi rank and New Market. It's only open during the season, though, and the services it offers are limited. There's also an office dealing with the Dodecanese islands as a whole – **South Aegean Tourist Office**, Makariou Papagou (*www.ando.gr/eot*).

Getting Around

Tourist trains If you're fed up with hoofing it, look out for the little tourist trains that operate in several of the island's towns. The one in Rhodes Town takes in many of the sights – certainly, it's a pleasantly outdoorish way of getting about. The starting point is outside the Town Hall, just north of Mandraki harbour. It departs on the hour, and takes in the town walls, the Acropolis of Rhodes, Monte Smith and the Aquarium (€5, children up to 3 years free). There are also tourist trains in Kalithea and Afandou.

By bus The island's bus services are efficient and cheap. Buses leave for the rest of the island from just behind the New Market – you can get timetables from the nearby Tourist Office. Fares range from less than €1 for destinations in the capital to €10 for more remote parts of the island like Kattavia or Prassonissi.

By taxi Taxis shouldn't be dismissed as a means of getting around – for a family of four it can work out little more than the bus. The main taxi rank is in the Rimini Square/Alexandrias Square area, where there's a huge sign giving fares to all the main towns, villages, tourist attractions and beaches: Ialyssos €9, Faliraki €13, and the resorts around Lindos around €40, for example.

By boat If you expect your holiday to be spent largely in one resort, but would like hassle-free excursions (especially to the capital), look out for boat trips. A boat plies regularly from Lindos to Rhodes Town, for example, and there are excursions out of Mandraki to Lindos (€23), Symi (€22), with children 5–10 half price, and under 5s free) and the Turkish mainland (€57), and around the smaller ports of Rhodes island. All the above prices are for the round trip. They are also illustrative – shop around down at the port. (For excursions by sea, try *www.seadreams.gr*).

By car Great-value car rental is widely available throughout Rhodes. **Rodos Cars** (*www.rodoscars.gr*) were offering cars at €17 per day, all-inclusive, the last time I was there. The business is now so well organised

that you don't even have to book much in advance – the bigger companies can usually provide a car with 24 hours' notice, though they can't guarantee that you'll get exactly the class you want. Most large hotels can also arrange car rental for you but it makes sense to surf the net for the best deals, and book before you go. Pay extra for the **collision damage waiver** – it saves a lot of faffing and expense if you have a bump. **Parking** is colour-coded – a white line means it's unrestricted, a blue line that you need to get a ticket from a machine, and yellow that you mustn't park there at all.

By moped, motorbike or quad-bike As with all of Greece's holiday islands, there are rental places for mopeds, motorbikes and quad-bikes everywhere in Rhodes. But, though I have seen families out on motorbikes, and roads are not at all bad, it still doesn't seem sensible to put family members at risk – it only takes one pothole to bring disaster.

Planning Your Outings

For visits to Rhodes Town under your own steam, the best advice is to **get there early**. Before 9am there's plenty of space to park, and the tour buses, excursion boats and cruise ships have yet to disgorge their multitudes. For the best places to park, and the best family mustering point, see 'Rhodes Town and its hinterland', below.

The same advice (get there early to beat the crowds) applies to all the most popular tourist attractions – they are busiest from mid-morning to mid-afternoon. Outside the capital, especially in the south, you may find that many businesses still observe the traditional Greek siesta, and close at lunchtime, re-opening for the evening. Try it yourselves – an afternoon nap lets you avoid the heat of the day, and freshens you up for the long, cool evenings.

When you're out and about, by all means take water, but even if you buy it as you go, you shouldn't be charged more than €0.50 per bottle. Wherever you are in Rhodes, you never seem to be very far from a café or taverna.

FAST FACTS: RHODES

American Express Local agents are **Rodos Tours**, Ammochostou 29, open Mon-Sat 8.30am–1.30pm and 5pm–8.30pm. 📞 22 41 02 10 10.

Banks and ATMs Most of the banks and cash machines are in Averof, behind the New Market.

British Vice Consulate 29 Gr. Lambraki Street, 851 00, Open to the public Mon–Fri 8.30am–1.30pm. 📞 22 41 02 20 05.

Buses The bus stations in Rhodes Town are just behind the New Market, in Platia Rimini

(largely for the east coast) and Averof (for the west coast and the east coast as far as Faliraki).

Business hours Tourist shops stay open for long hours, tavernas and restaurants often close when the last customers have left; see also Chapter 2.

Credit cards As in the rest of Greece, all larger establishments (hotels, restaurants, shops) accept the main credit cards, but a lot of smaller ones don't. And even when they have the technology to accept them, it's very common to encounter a reluctance to do so. When you're paying for petrol, for example, there are usually pump attendants, and they prefer taking cash – they carry great wads of change.

Hospital 📞 22 41 08 00 00.

Internet access Big hotels usually offer Internet access, either in-room or in a dedicated 'Internet corner'. Internet cafés and bars are common in most towns visited by tourists, often with just two or three machines. In Rhodes Town, Internet facilities are available at Cosmonet Internet Café, in the Place of Martyrs and opposite the Casino, and at Minerva Travel – also near Argirokastrou Square.

Police 📞 22 41 02 32 94 or just dial 📞 100.

Post Office on Mandraki harbour. Open Mon–Fri 7am–8pm, 📞 22 41 02 22 12.

Top 10 Family Experiences

1. Climbing up the Valley of the Butterflies, the sunlight streaming through the trees, the air alive with the red, brown and yellow Jersey Tiger Moths. Then calling in at the Ostrich Farm further down the mountain. See p. 112.

2. Flying kites on the broad sandy spit of Prassonissi, or windsurfing on the calm waters of the east, or choppy waters of the west. See p. 117.

3. Exploring the rills and rivulets of Epta Piges. See p. 111.

4. Riding a donkey up the steep approaches to the Acropolis at Lindos, then enjoying terrific views from the top. See p. 103.

5. Screaming through the Black Hole in Faliraki's Water Park, or pootling along its Lazy River. See p. 102.

6. Swinging into the sky on the Big Wheel at Lunar Park in Faliraki. See p. 102.

7. Wandering the narrow lanes of Rhodes' Old Town, up towards the medieval splendour of the Palace of the Grand Masters. See p. 95.

8. Fighting for space on Rhodes Town's Elli Beach, then eyeballing the fish in the Aquarium. See p. 98.

9. Walking in the cool air of Profitis Ilias, before taking tea, or spending the night, at the Elafos Hotel. See p. 93.

10. Having a Turkish bath at Mustafa Hamam. See p. 11.

EXPLORING RHODES

Rhodes is an easy island to explore. In a determined week, or a relaxed fortnight, you can visit everything worth visiting, and come away with a reasonably comprehensive mental picture of the place.

The island is circumnavigated by a good-quality main highway – take no notice of maps, which indicate that the northern coast road is better – and the roads that cut across from one coast to the other are often surprisingly good. Indeed some, courtesy of the EU, are brand new, and a delight to drive upon. Whilst bus services between the main towns are fast and efficient, the best way to explore the island with your family is to hire a car (see 'Getting Around', above) for some or all of your stay.

Rhodes Town & Its Hinterland

Not many towns and cities can pinpoint the exact year of their birth. Rhodes can. In 408 BC, the island's dominant city triumvirate of Lindos, Ialysos and Kamiros, in a rare display of cooperation, decided to establish a new capital city on its northern tip – at the top of the whale's head, if you will. Since it had no natural harbour, a series of bays on the eastern side of the new city were adapted to form havens for ships – you can still see the effects of this decision today, in the commercial harbour, the small fishing boat dock and the large yacht basin of **Mandraki**. These provide the secret to getting yourself oriented when planning the family assault on Rhodes Town – the **Old Town** is directly west of the commercial port, the **New Town** directly west of Mandraki.

The best place to **park** is along the outside walls of the Old Town facing the commercial port, along the road (Papagou) which separates the Old and New Towns, or in the side streets of the New Town. An excellent mustering point and rendezvous are the gardens of Rimini and Alexandrias Squares, outside the walls in the northeast corner of the Old Town – there are lots of benches in plenty of shade and you can buy drinks, ice-creams and snacks nearby; this is the location of the main taxi rank, bus station and tourist information office, and you can even get your portrait painted while you wait. It's also very easy to find: if you come out of the Old Town on to the commercial port, walk north; if you come out of the New Town on to Mandraki, walk south.

The Sulleyman Mosque

RHODES TOWN

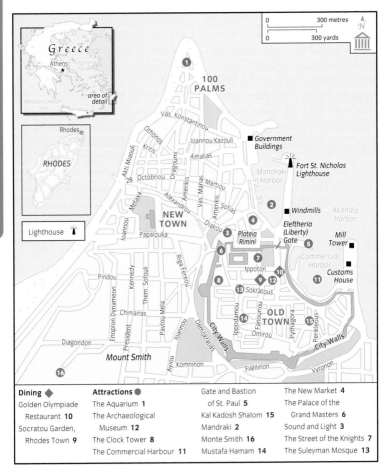

Dining ◆	Attractions ●	Gate and Bastion	The New Market **4**
Golden Olympiade	The Aquarium **1**	of St. Paul **5**	The Palace of the
Restaurant **10**	The Archaeological	Kal Kadosh Shalom **15**	Grand Masters **6**
Socratou Garden,	Museum **12**	Mandraki **2**	Sound and Light **3**
Rhodes Town **9**	The Clock Tower **8**	Monte Smith **16**	The Street of the Knights **7**
	The Commercial Harbour **11**	Mustafa Hamam **14**	The Suleyman Mosque **13**

The Old Town

Without any doubt the star turns of the Old Town are the great buildings erected by the **Knights of St John** (see p. 94). Yet it's not just these medieval set pieces that attract the crowds, but the whole unity of the town, with its principal shopping streets joined by lanes flying-buttressed against earthquakes, its Turkish and Jewish buildings, its hidden gardens and colourful street cafés, all ranged around the commercial harbour. Dominating the whole scene, the **Suleyman Mosque**, recently refurbished and with striking pink waterproofing, looks like a giant wedding cake. It cannot claim any great antiquity, though – it dates from the late 19th century.

Behind the Suleyman Mosque, the **Clock Tower** offers one of the best **viewing points** in Rhodes, with terrific vistas across the Old Town to the commercial harbour, the New Town and Mandraki to the east and north, and the suburbs rising to Monte Smith to the west. Run as a commercial enterprise, the entrance fee of €6 seems excessive, even if you do get a free drink from the café. But since children get in free, the average cost gets less the more youngsters you have.

Thronged with tourists throughout the holiday season, **Sokratous** climbs down from the Suleyman Mosque towards the fishing boats and cruise ships of the commercial harbour. Here are all the leather, jewellery and tourist shops you could wish for, together with fur emporia, cafés, exchange offices and travel agents. Keep a tight hold on toddlers, though – it really does get packed, and it only takes a second to lose a child.

At the bottom of the hill the crowds thin out into pretty **Platia Ippogratous**, dominated by the crenellations of the city wall and by its fountain. Bearing right along **Aristotelous**, parallel to the wall and often as busy as Sokratous, you come to café-dotted **Platia ton Evreon Martyron** – the Place of Martyrs. Named to commemorate the 1604 Jewish residents of Rhodes and Kos transported to Nazi death camps on 23rd July, 1944, it has at its hub a polished black granite memorial which is often the focus of tour groups paying their respects. Beyond it lies the synagogue of **Kal Kadosh Shalom** ★ (Dossiadou Street *www.rhodesjewishmuseum.org/ kahal.htm*), the only one of the Jewish Quarter's six to survive. It contains a small museum to the area's holocaust victims, and is open from 1st April–1st Nov, 10am–4pm. There's a small gift shop, and admission to the synagogue and museum is free, though donations are welcome.

Don't leave the Old Town without taking a look at the **Mustafa Hamam** ★★, the still-working **Turkish Bathhouse**. Indeed, it offers a wonderfully peaceful hour or two's relaxation, not to mention a unique experience that the children are unlikely to come across elsewhere in Greece. There are separate men's and women's rooms, and the further in you go, the hotter the rooms become. The entrance fee of €1.50 includes use of a locker, but you need to take your own towel. The baths are open from 10am to 5pm Monday to Friday, 8am to 5pm Saturday. A visit usually takes between one and two hours.

When you tire of the heat and clamour of the Old Town, head for one of the gates in the east wall, and have a wander around the **commercial harbour** and the **fishing dock**. There's a wooden walkway which helps to distance pedestrians from the stream of traffic that swirls around the port, where the throng of fishing boats, pleasure craft and palatial cruise ships are a never-ending source of fascination. Look out for the boat

The Knights Of St John Of Jerusalem

It's impossible to understand what you see in Rhodes without a basic knowledge of the Knights of St John of Jerusalem (often called, among other things, the **Knights Hospitallers**).

The Knights of St John of Jerusalem started as a hospital founded in Jerusalem, with the permission of the Muslim authorities, in the second half of the 11th century. Financed by Italian merchants and run by monks, it was charged with the care of sick and poor Christian pilgrims visiting the Holy Land.

Jerusalem was captured from the Muslims by the armies of the First Crusade in 1099, and from then the Knights of St John started to widen their role to the care and protection, not only of the sick and poor in the region, but of *all* Christians. To do so, they became increasingly militaristic, a cross between an army and a police force – an example of muscular Christianity, or the Church Militant.

When the Muslims reconquered Jerusalem in 1187, the Hospitallers withdrew, moving from pillar to post to keep ahead of Muslim expansion, finally arriving on Rhodes in 1306. They immediately demanded that control of the island be handed over to them, and when the Byzantine authorities refused, began a two-year military campaign which ended in victory in 1309. For the next 200 years, on their fortified island, they became a major force in the eastern Mediterranean, heavily armed and with a powerful navy, fighting off repeated attempts by the Turks to flush them out, and attacking Muslim forces whenever they encountered them.

On Rhodes, the Knights were organised into 'tongues' or languages, according to their origins – France, England, Germany, Italy, Spain (later divided into Castile and Aragon), Provence and Auvergne – under the leadership of a **Grand Master**. Each tongue had an inn, governed by a bailiff, and the seven (later eight) bailiffs elected the overall ruler of the order, the Grand Master.

The rule of the **Knights of St John** ended on 1st January, 1523, after a long siege by **Suleiman the Magnificent**. In recognition of their bravery, the surviving Knights and their entourages were allowed to leave the island. After seven years in Crete, they settled in **Malta**. Rhodes, meanwhile, began almost 400 years of Turkish rule.

in the fishing dock that sells a huge variety of **sponges** and shells: ask the owner for his advice and he'll be happy to explain why some of the sponges are white and some brown, and help you choose a good one.

Sound and Light ★★★
AGE 5 AND ABOVE

Municipal Garden of Rhodes. ☏ *22 41 02 19 22.*

Before even getting into the Old Town, have a look in Rimini

Square (through the gates, which are likely to be locked during the day) at the beautiful **Municipal Garden** behind the Palace of the Grand Masters but outside the town walls. This is where, on all evenings except Sunday, a *son et lumière* (sound and light show) is held. It tells the history of the town in a dramatic and accessible way.

Open Performances in English 9.15pm Mon, Wed, Fri, May–Aug (8.15pm Sept and Oct) and 11.15pm Tues,Thurs, May–Aug (10.15pm, Sept and Oct). *Adm* €7, €3 concessions (including members of multi-children families), under nines free. *Amenities* English spoken. Shop.

The Archaeological Museum ★ AGE 5 AND ABOVE

☏ 22 41 02 76 57. 2 Symis Square, 851 00 Rhodes. On the corner of Apellou and Ippoton.

Housed in what was the **Hospital of the Knights**, The Archaeological Museum is, for the non-specialist at least, as interesting for the architecture of the building as for the contents of the galleries. The grand arcades, on two storeys built around a courtyard, can be a welcome oasis of cool on a hot summer's day. There is no English guidebook to the collections, but exhibits are labelled in English. The upper floor is accessed via a grand open flight of steps (careful with young children – there's no banister), and the secret of making the seemingly endless displays of pottery interesting is to concentrate on the pictures that decorate the

pots. There's no better introduction to the life of the ancient Greeks. Look out too for piles of cannonballs, the eroded statue of the Marine Venus much loved by Lawrence Durrell, and for a display of lenses used by engravers in the 5th century BC – they look brand new!

Open 8am–7pm 1st April–31st Oct; 8.30am–3pm 1st Nov–31st March, closed Mon. *Adm* €3. Children under 18 free. *Amenities* English spoken. Shop.

The Street of the Knights ★

Striking west immediately before the Archaeological Museum, the Street of the Knights (prosaically known as **Odos Ippoton**) climbs up to the Palace of the Grand Masters. This is the medieval street, heavily restored by the Italians, which contained the 'inns' of the **Knights of St John** (see p. 94). The Knights came from all over Europe, and each nationality (or 'tongue') had its own inn. It is these inns (with their relevant coats of arms) that you can see as you climb up towards the Palace of the Grand Masters.

The Palace of the Grand Masters ★ OVERRATED
AGE 5 AND ABOVE

Kleovoulou Square, 85100 Rhodes. ☏ 22 41 07 56 74.

The Palace of the Grand Masters was originally the centrepiece of medieval Rhodes, a great fortress built to repel invaders and withstand sieges. It was an effective emblem of the military might of the **Knights Hospitallers of**

The Palace of the Grand Masters

St John, and was adapted for use by the Turks after they conquered the island in 1522. Virtually wiped out in the 19th century, first by an earthquake, then by a fireball caused by a lightning strike on an ammunition dump, it was reconstructed by the Italians in the 1930s as a residence for Mussolini and King Victor Emmanuel.

The Palace of the Grand Masters as it now stands is imposing from the outside, and gives a good idea of what a medieval castle looked like. Inside, however, the concessions made to modernity (electricity, lifts) give it a peculiarly inauthentic air which is a little disappointing. Still, children might be diverted by the sombre scale of the building, by the mosaics, and by the excellent ground-floor exhibitions on the history of Rhodes. As in the Archaeological Museum, look out for staircases with no balustrade.

There is a café, but it was derelict when I was there, and I could discover no plans for its resurrection. Incidentally, neither Il Duce nor the King ever visited Rhodes.

Open 12.30pm–7pm Mon, 8.30am–7pm Tues–Sun (1st Nov–31st Mar closes 3pm). *Adm* €6 Children under 12 free, 13 to 18 half price. *Amenities* Shop.

The New Town

The New Town is built on a narrowing spit of land that lies north of the Old Town. Though, as its name implies, most of the New Town is relatively modern, much of it has a stateliness which, when added to the quirkiness of many of its buildings, makes for a pleasant walking tour which older children will enjoy.

To the north of the commercial harbour lies the Gate and Bastion of St Paul. From here you'll get wonderful **views** of the harbour and the Old Town, and also of picturesque **Mandraki Harbour** and the New Town. As you push through onto Mandraki's quayside, look out for a tiny **shingle beach** where you can stop for a dip.

Yachts, launches, excursion boats and hydrofoils, even a floating restaurant built on a raft (the Kon Tiki!) crowd the edges of Mandraki, dominated by the **Agios Nikolaos lighthouse** at the end of the sea wall, the three **windmills** (minus their sails) grouped along it, and the twin columns, topped by statues of a male and female deer, that guard the harbour entrance. The deep blue of the water, the domes and towers of the New Town, the quality of the light, create a harmonious picture reminiscent of Venice. This is where you can buy tickets for excursions along the coast to **Lindos**, to the nearby (and very beautiful)

island of **Symi**, or to **Marmaris** on the Turkish mainland. Excursions to Lindos can take anything from 90 minutes to many hours, depending on whether they are direct or include stops for swims, barbecues, and so on. The price varies accordingly – you could even try haggling with the captain. Rhodes–Symi takes an hour by hydrofoil, and just under two hours by ferry, and costs around €14 return for adults on the ferry, €28 on the hydrofoil (under-fours free). The trip to Marmaris takes 50 minutes by hydrofoil and two hours by ferry, and for a day return costs around €60 adults, €45 children aged seven to 12, and a nominal €1 for under-sixes.

A fine place to stop for refreshment, use the toilets and do a bit of shopping, the **New Market** is a rather splendid pink building with domes, archways and arcades designed to fit in

Windmills, Mandraki Harbour

The Colossus of Rhodes

The Colossus of Rhodes was a (very large, as you'd expect from the name) statue of the god of the sun **Helios**, designed by sculptor Chares of Lyndus to commemorate the lifting of a long siege of Rhodes in 305 BC. Financed, it's said, by the sale of siege engines left over from an earlier war, it took 12 years to build, starting in 294 BC. Standing over 32m (100 ft) high, it was, during its relatively brief lifespan, one of the **Seven Wonders of the World**. The modern fad for compiling lists isn't so modern – they were doing it during ancient times!

Although there is a lot of disagreement about how it was built, it is agreed that bronze, iron and stone came into it somewhere – perhaps with a core made up of stone columns, cross braces of iron, and an outer skin of bronze. One thing everybody agrees upon: it did *not* straddle the harbour entrance, but stood somewhere nearby.

The statue was toppled by an earthquake in 225 BC, having stood for only 57 years. It's said that its remains could be seen for 800 years afterwards, when Arabian forces broke up what was left and sold it for scrap in AD 654 (taking over 900 camels to shift it).

There has been some talk of rebuilding the Colossus of Rhodes as a tourist attraction, but the phenomenal cost of such an undertaking is likely to keep it as just that – talk.

---

with Rhodes Town's architectural style. Built around an open courtyard, but with its main arcade facing the harbour, there are cafés, restaurants and shops, together with a shady bandstand-come-gazebo in the middle.

As you make your way north, with the sea to your right, you pass a series of impressive public buildings – the **Post Office, Evagelismos Church**, the **Town Hall** and the **National Theatre**. The domes of the **Nautical Club**, and of the **Elli nightclub**, add quirkiness to the prevailing stateliness. The **Mourat Reis Mosque** is worth a look, with its peaceful burial ground full of oddly shaped gravestones inscribed in Arabic script.

You now come to the great scimitar of sand known as **Elli**

Beach, not that you can usually see much sand under the mass of loungers, parasols and bodies that usually crowd it. Halfway along towers the huge bulk of the **Casino of Rhodes**, and in the distance, right on the tip of the peninsula, seeming to float above the mass of humanity that lines the beach, stands the Aquarium.

The Aquarium ★ ALL AGES

Kos Street. ☎ *22 41 02 73 08.*

Even if it contained no fish, the Aquarium would be worth a visit. Built by the Italians in the 1930s, it is a wonderful example of the **Art Deco** style of architecture, a cross between a cinema of the period and somewhere that Flash Gordon would feel comfortable. Inside, sea-water tanks set into rock-like walls along meandering passageways contain a cross-section of the sea life of this part of the Mediterranean. There are also stuffed examples of some – one or two, it has to be said, now looking a little tired. The Aquarium doesn't exist just for its visitors, though. Rather, their admission charges help to finance the serious work of the **Hydrological Institute**, which is the Aquarium's more formal name.

Open Apr–Oct 9am–9pm, Nov–Mar 9am–4.30pm. **Adm** *€4.50. Children under 18 free.*

Monte Smith ALL AGES

South of the New Town, and West of the Old, Monte Smith rises up from the coast. Its rather risible name replaced a more appropriate Greek one in 1802 in honour of the Admiral of the British Fleet – Sir Sidney Smith – during the Napoleonic Wars. On a 112m hill overlooking the capital, it was once the city's **acropolis**, and has the partially restored remains of a theatre, together with bits of a stadium. To enjoy the views from Monte Smith, you'll need to take a half-hour walk from the Old Town, catch a bus from the harbourside at Mandraki (you can buy tickets at the kiosk next to the bus stop (€1) then validate them using the machine on the bus). Or look out for the **Municipality of Rhodes tourist train** which regularly visits the summit – it sets off every hour, on the hour, from the Town Hall, follows the city walls, climbs to the Acropolis on Monte Smith and returns via the

Aquarium (€5, children up to 3 years free). The one-way trip takes about 15 minutes.

The Northeast Coast

Just as there's only one way to go when you're on the top of a mountain – down – there's only one direction you can take from Rhodes Town – south. But there are, of course, two coasts to choose from. To explore the east coast, follow the main road towards Lindos. This road runs just a little inland, so to explore the coast you'll need to make frequent diversions off it.

The first is a loop, off to the east, which takes in Koskinou and Kallithea, before returning to the main road at Faliraki. To take it, after Rodini Park and immediately after Asgorou, turn left off the coast road towards Koskinou.

The old part of **Koskinou**, perched on a hill, is worth a few minutes exploration because, unlikely as it seems so close to Rhodes Town, it is completely **untouched by tourism**. If you park near the big church in the centre, you can wander the narrow lanes and admire typically Rhodian houses, their courtyards and balconies dripping with flowers.

Some 5km on (drive down to the coast road and turn right) you come to **Kallithea**, known for the **Thermes Kalitheas** (turn down the small road opposite a domed ruin on the right). Built by the Italians in the 1920s to exploit the warm spring waters that rise here, the spa is a riot of Moorish domes

Fantasia Lunar Park

and archways built around a small bay, its tropical atmosphere emphasised by the many palm trees. There are sunbathing terraces, a couple of small beaches and the sea which, famous for its clarity, attracts snorkellers. Admission is free and you can park near the café at the entrance.

The reputation of **Faliraki**, the next town south, as a brash destination favoured by gangs of British youths, was well-deserved. But its worst excesses lie firmly in its past – we've all, no doubt, done things in our younger days of which we're now a little ashamed! So, although Faliraki can still be very noisy at night, it should not be overlooked as a destination for a family holiday. It has a great deal going for it: not only a long, sandy beach and some wonderful family

hotels (see 'Family-friendly Accommodation', p. 119) but a range of amusements second to none. Chief among these is the enormous **Water Park** – it claims to be the largest in Europe – **Fantasia Lunar Park** and **Skypark Bowling** (see p. 103).

Other attractions include the **Family Fun Centre** (📞 *22 41 08 51 92)*, a 'play barn' facility similar to many to be found in the UK, together with a variety of watersports on the beach, and, up near the main coast road, a **go-kart track**. There are also numerous **supermarkets** (cheekily named after UK ones like Safeway and Asda – they're not connected to the real ones in any way!).

Beyond Faliraki, travelling south, is a succession of coves and beaches to explore, from rocky **Anthony Quinn Bay** (where some scenes of 'The Guns of Navarone' were filmed) to little **Ladiko Bay** to **Afandou**. The island's only **golf course** lies between the main road and the sea (don't expect English-style verdure, though – it's rather dry and dusty looking, despite constant watering), and you'll also see a lot more jewellery and ceramic workshops and outlets which might be worth a look.

Tsambika Bay has possibly the best sand of any beach on Rhodes. It has four tavernas, a restaurant, a beach shop, a mini-market, a couple of toilet blocks, a watersports centre and lots of wooden duckboards, all scattered along a crescent of sand. The tiny white monastery, perched on the headland, is said to miraculously cure infertility. If the number of people on Rhodes named Tsambikos, or Tsambika, is anything to go by, it really works!

With plenty of space to park, Tsambika Bay makes an ideal place to stop off, have a swim and something to eat.

The next turning on the Rhodes to Lindos highway brings you to **Archangelos**. A long, straggly village overlooked by the remains of an imposing medieval castle, it is famous for its **ceramics** (there are still several workshops in the village), for making **carpets** and **music**, and for speaking their own **dialect**.

Beyond the village, the road snakes down through rugged countryside to the village of **Stegna**. Beyond a functional boat marina and a small children's playground, the attractive beach curves around to a rocky headland. There are numerous tavernas and cafés, even some fishermen's cottages, and, on the beach, sand to enjoy, rock-pools to explore, and 'Water Sport Nikos' where you can arrange to paraglide, wakeboard, ride on a banana or, for the less active, sign up for one of several boat trips.

Rodos Gold   AGE 5 AND ABOVE

85100, 📞 *22 41 08 66 70, www. rodos-gold.gr. On the Rhodes-Lindos road, just before you get to Faliraki.*

A factory that not only manufactures gold jewellery, but also has a huge range on sale, Rodos Gold has an area where you can see goldsmiths at work making

Archangelos

Archangelos is in many ways like being plunged into the traditional Rhodes of old. Men sit in the cafés, playing *tavli* (backgammon), flicking their worry beads and putting the world to rights. Working donkeys, being led by women, patiently carry their loads. The old part of the town, around the tiered wedding-cake-style church, is full of winding lanes and old, flower-decked houses. Look out too for Archangelos's characteristic leather anti-snakebite boots.

Stegna

14-, 18- and 22-carat jewellery, a fascinating museum of exact copies of famous pieces from history, and a pleasant café with Internet access.

Open *9am–8pm all week (all year).* **Adm** *free.* **Amenities** *Café. English spoken. Parking. Shop.*

The Water Park ★ ★ ★ ALL AGES

📞 *22 41 08 44 03, www.water-park.gr*

Set on a hillside with views across the town to the sea, Faliraki's Water Park has every ride known to man – giant slides, black holes, a wave pool, rafting slides, a lazy river, a pirate ship, children's slides, a tipping bucket – you get the idea... The range of food outlets is vast and the facilities family-friendly. There are children's toilets, a mini-train, a lost-and-found, and so on. The suitability of all rides is marked – some are for those aged 13 and up, some for eight and up, the rest for everyone. If there is one feature that, whilst no doubt appealing to teenagers, can be a bit of a trial for adults (i.e. me), it's the deafeningly loud rock music in some parts of the park. Look out, though, for the two old cars mounted outside the entrance – they're lovely. There's a free bus service from Mandraki in Rhodes, and during high season, from six of Faliraki's hotels.

Open *9.30am–7pm June–Aug, 9.30am–6pm May, Sept, Oct.* **Adm** *€20 adults, €15 children 3–12; free infants 0–3.* **Amenities** *Café. English spoken. Parking. Picnic area. Restaurants. Shops.*

Fantasia Luna Park ★
AGE 3 AND ABOVE

www.water-park.gr

Run by the Water Park company, and dotted with palm trees, this huge funfair is easy to find because the ferris wheel dominates the town. It has all the rides you'd expect – the Big Wheel, Roller Coasters, 'Bumper

Cars', even a Rodeo Bull and aircraft simulation ride.

Open *7pm–1am May to Oct.* **Adm** *€1–3 per ride. Cafes. English spoken.*

Skypark Bowling

AGE 3 AND ABOVE

📞 *22 41 08 75 08.*

A couple of hundred metres away is Skypark Bowling, a 12-lane 10-pin bowling alley. You can't miss it – it has a giant bowling pin outside. In addition to the bowling alleys, there's a snack bar, bouncy castles, lots of coin-in-the-slot games and Internet access.

Open *2.30pm till 'late'.* **Adm** *€4 adult, €3.50 child.* **Amenities** *Café.*

Kentavros Horse Riding Stables ★★ AGE 3 AND ABOVE

Tsambika Beach 📞 *69 45 80 26 28). In the angle between the main coast road and the one down to Tsambika Bay, and with access by dirt road from both.*

The Kentavros Horse Riding stables, widely advertised in this part of the island, turn out to be a surprisingly homely outfit. However, its 15 horses look in fine condition, and they are clearly its young owner Gianni's passion – in winter he works on building sites to pay their fodder bills. A basic session of 1 hour 20 minutes costs €30 for adults, €25 for children. Helmets are provided. Longer rides can be negotiated – a popular one is to Epta Piges (see below), which takes 6 hours – 2 to get there, 2 to enjoy the springs and 2 to get back. If you don't have a car,

incidentally, they will pick you up from, and deliver you back to, your hotel.

Lindos Town and the Marmari Peninsula

Second only to Rhodes Town as a tourist attraction, Lindos suffers the same fate as the capital – heaving crowds during the high season.

And you can see why everybody wants to come here. Picturesquely set on a rocky promontory, its white, cuboid houses scattered in an arc around the imposing ruins of the fortified Acropolis, the village itself a mass of cobbled lanes dotted with examples of the traditional Lindian **archondiko** or mansion, it looks a picture against the deep blue of the Mediterranean. Its prettiness is safe for posterity – it has been designated an archaeological site, and is therefore subject to stringent planning controls.

It's not just a place to enjoy for its looks, either. The heights upon which it is set are flanked by three **beaches** – the sandy Main and Small beaches on one side, and a short shingle strand at St Paul's Bay (where St Paul made landfall in AD 58) on the other.

So there's plenty of swimming and watersports and boating, and, the piece de resistance – an absolute must for children – **donkey rides** ★★★ AGE 3 AND ABOVE from the village up the hill to the Acropolis. The

TIP **Parking**

There is no parking in the village itself, so either park at the top of the hill, where the road down to the village branches off the main road, or down by the Main Beach (there's a charge, which I found to my cost when I was fined €20 – the ticket machines should have been a clue! Taxis are allowed to drop off in the centre of the village, so that might be the way to go.

path for pedestrians is more direct, and therefore steeper – follow the signs. Once at the top, you can explore the remains of the **castle**, the **governor's palace**, a **sanctuary** and a **temple**. Perhaps the biggest bonus, though, is the wonderful **views** across the village, the surrounding countryside and the sea. On the way back to the village, look out for the **lace** and **embroidery** for which the town is famous. Eating and drinking in Lindos are no problem – there are loads of lovely courtyard and rooftop restaurants, or lunch can be combined with a swim down on the beach (see 'Family-friendly Dining', p. 123).

The whole of the peninsula upon which Lindos stands, from Vliha Bay to Lardos Bay, together with the villages of Kalathos, Pefki and Lardos, is developing into one large, family-friendly holiday area which is well worth considering when choosing a base on the island. It is handily placed halfway down the east coast, so there's nowhere on the island that's too far to visit. It has a large stock of good-quality hotels and restaurants to suit most pockets and some of the best beaches on the island. You'll notice, incidentally that, such is the cachet of the name 'Lindos', many of the hotels in the area include the word in their title, even when

Lindos

they're miles away from the actual village!

Pefki's beach, accessed by a loop of road off the main street, is a sheltered curve of lovely golden sand with lots of parasols and sun-loungers. There are lots of child-friendly cafés and restaurants, offering a variety of different sorts of food (Greek, international, Chinese, fast), snack bars with swimming pools at which a pleasant afternoon can be whiled away, supermarkets, bakeries and tourist shops. Nightlife is lively without being raucous. Though not perhaps the place to experience traditional Greek life, it's certainly an understated resort that has absolutely everything that most families need to make their stay a success.

A much better place to sample ordinary Greek life lies just down the road from Pefki. Although in many ways similar to it, **Lardos** has the advantage that it is separated into two sections, with a beach-side development on Lardos Bay, and a traditional village centre several kilometres inland. It's here, around the attractive town square, that you'll come across ordinary Greeks going about their everyday business.

The Northwest Coast

The road down the northwest coast, from Rhodes Town to Monolithos, sticks much closer to the sea. There are far fewer beaches than on the northeast coast, and those that there are tend to be gravel or shingle, and rather windy. This can be an advantage if you have youngsters, though – the whole coast is cooler and greener.

Almost immediately, still within sight of Rhodes Aquarium, you're travelling through one of the most family-friendly holiday areas on the island. Not only does it boast some exceptional hotels, a scattering of facilities specifically for children and proximity to some of Rhodes' most famous attractions, it is just down the road from an airport which is one of the main charter-flight destinations for many of the UK's numerous regional airports.

Around **Trianda Bay**, from Rhodes Town through **Kritika** to

The Mansions of Lindos

Many of the mansions for which Lindos is famous were built from the 15th to the 17th centuries by prosperous ship owners, and around windows and doors you may find cables carved into the stonework. The number of cables tells you how many ships he owned. If you manage to peek inside, you'll see that they are usually built around a courtyard (often containing the type of pebble mosaic common on the island).

Ialyssos then on to **Kremasti**, a succession of beaches is backed by a series of hotels, among them some of the biggest and most palatial on the island. Because it's so windy (a boon to windsurfers), most of the hotels have their own pools. Check out Trianda Beach itself, for example – the whole area is very child-friendly, with a nice hotel, the Atlantica Princess (see 'Family-friendly Accommodation', p. 119) at one end, an excellent and extensive **children's playground** with its own snack bar at the other, and some first-rate cafés and restaurants in between, not to mention, again with its own snack bar, **Planet Z**, an indoor 'fun factory' children's play facility with ball pools, climbing frames, slides, rides and so on. The beach itself is rather gritty, but has colourfully skimming windsurfers and an enticingly milky sea.

Beyond the airport, the road heads south along the narrow coastal plain. If you're into ruins there are some important ones at **Kamiros** which it's worth diverting off the coastal highway to see. Splendidly laid out on a hillside, Kamiros was one of the original three Ionian cities on Rhodes (the others were Lindos (see p. 103) and Ialyssos (see p. 115), who cooperated in building a new capital for the island at Rhodes in 408 BC. For Kamiros, this appeared to be like a turkey voting for Christmas, since, as the new city flourished, ancient Kamiros went into decline. Having disappeared in the early Christian period, it was rediscovered by archaeologists in 1859, after which they, and later the Italians, uncovered the ground plan of the whole city.

About 18km south along the coast road is **Kamiros Skala**, said to have been the port for Ancient Kamiros, though it seems rather far away to have been much used. A little harbour with a clutch of tavernas, Kamiros Skala is now the only link with the outside world of tiny offshore island of Halki.

Though just a waterless limestone speck, **Halki** is counted as a fully fledged member of the Dodecanese, and consists of a small village and nothing much else. The population is only a few hundred. Since there is only one boat a day, which leaves at 2.30pm and returns the next morning, any visit to Halki has to involve at least a one-night stopover on the island, though at the time of writing a day trip on a Sunday was possible. But it's rather a long way for very little reward, and can't really be recommended for families.

The next place worth stopping is at **Kastro Kritinias**, one of the island's many castles attributable to the Knights of St John. Perched atop a 130m crag overlooking the coast, it's hugely impressive from a distance, but a bit more dilapidated on closer inspection. Although there are signs of renovation, there seems to be little sense of urgency about it. The main entrance is up a steep climb from the car park, but there's an easier side entrance, though it involves bouncing up a distinctly rickety set of planks. The castle gives an impression of what medieval life must have been like, and the views are terrific. It's an open site, and entrance is free – don't be conned into paying anybody.

Back on the main road at Kritinias, the local **Museum of Popular Art** is a good place to stop for refreshment (see below).

Continuing south, you come to **Siana**. Built on the side of a hill, Siana is famous for two things – **honey** and **souma**, the Greek version of moonshine. The flavour of the honey depends on the season, and therefore what plants were flowering, at the time it was made.

Souma (it's called tsipouro on the mainland) is a spirit made from what's left after the wine has been produced, and is manufactured illegally in many parts of the island. However, Siana was given a licence to produce it by the Italians, and this was never revoked. So Siana is one, if not

the only, place you can legally buy it.

Kritinias Museum of Popular Art ★ AGE 3 AND ABOVE

Back on the main coast road, the little Kritinias Museum of Popular Art, housed in an attractive porticoed building, is well worth stopping for, especially as it sits in the grounds of a very pleasant café. Entrance to the museum is free, the exhibits are interesting (look out for a tripod cradle used to park the baby whilst the mother was working), and few enough not to be overwhelming, and you can stock up with ice-cold bottled water at the kiosk. A good place for a drink-and-toilet break, with something for the youngsters to do.

Monolithos Castle
AGE 5 AND ABOVE

There's no real explanation as to why Monolithos Castle has become firmly established on the coach tour itineraries of the island. Similar in pedigree to

Monolithos Castle

Kastro Kritinias, it has the same impressiveness at a distance, but again there's little to see when you get up to it. Balanced on a 235m pinnacle of rock, access is gained up a steep flight of steps from the car park. Inside is the white Agios Panteleimon church, and the views are, as ever, spectacular. Five kilometres down a bendy road beyond the castle is Fourni, a pleasant pebble beach.

Inland in Northern Rhodes

Tours inland from the two northern coasts bring a totally different picture of what the island is like. The quality of the roads is surprisingly high – indeed, some of them are brand new, courtesy of European Union funding. And all the places mentioned below are accessible from both the east and west coasts – I've covered them from east to west, but they can be done in the opposite direction. Rhodes is small enough, too, for you to create your own tours by dismantling the three below and rebuilding them to include only what your family is likely to be interested in.

Tour 1: Epta Piges – Eloussa – Profitis Ilias – Emponas – Agios Isidoros

Just off the main east coast road, halfway between Rhodes Town and Lindos, lies one of the island's main tourist attractions. The rushing streams and deep verdant shade of **Epta Piges** (Seven Springs) contrasts so strongly with most of this hot, sunny island that it attracts visitors, both Greek and foreign, in large numbers. But the network of trails and pathways that follow its rills and mini-waterfalls is so extensive that it rarely seems too crowded. With its restaurant, toilet block, children's playground, coin-in-the-slot rides, enclosures of geese and ducks, and free admission and parking, it's the perfect excursion destination for families, either on its own or as part of a day's tour. It's clearly signposted and therefore easy to find (see below).

Back to the main road, turn left and head towards Archipolis. Look out for the low concrete **aqueducts** – part of the Italian irrigation scheme – that stride along under the pines beside the road. Within minutes you'll arrive at the impressive **Agios Nektarius's** church, high on a knoll to the left of the road. Park in the spacious car park opposite.

If you didn't stop at Epta Piges, this would make an ideal journey break. There's a **taverna** (the Taverna Krioneri), a **spring** with three spouts ('Krioneri' means 'cold water') and the impressive **church** and **bell tower**. You can have a look inside the church – but women whose shoulders are bare will need to borrow a shawl from the lady sitting at the entrance. Beyond the church a beautiful footpath climbs up to viewpoints high above it, and across the road, below the car park, is a really nice picnic area above the River Loutanis.

Four kilometres into the hills beyond Archipolis is the pleasant village of **Eloussa**. Above the village, on the road to Profitis Ilias, are further reminders of the Italian occupation of Rhodes. A whole piazza is surrounded by the unmistakeable architecture of the 1930s' rationalist movement. Designed as a residence for the governor, and as the centrepiece for an agricultural colony, it is now, sadly, crumbling and dilapidated. It is nonetheless atmospheric, and merits a wander. You may find yourself sharing it with Greek soldiers or firefighters – they still use part of the complex.

Further along the road is a large **Art Deco** pool belonging to the same period, this is really worth seeing, and not just for its beautiful setting and architectural purity. It is part of an EU-supported conservation project, aimed at the survival of one of Europe's most endangered freshwater fish – the **gizani** (*www.life gizani.gr*). Found in several parts of Rhodes, its numbers are declining alarmingly. If the project isn't a success, this may be your last chance to see these little fish.

Beyond Eloussa, a couple of kilometres brings you to one of the most perfect places for a picnic in the whole of Rhodes. Its focus is the ancient-looking (though, having been built in the 15th century, there are many older) church of **Agios Nikolaos Foundoukli**. Inside it are some important **frescoes**, beside it is a **playground** and toilet block, and across the road a lovely **terrace** with benches, a **water fountain** and plenty of room to park. Below the terrace, picnic tables and benches nestle in the deep shade of the trees. With the church standing against the hillside behind, butterflies and wild birds everywhere, it's a truly magical spot.

Agios Nektarius

The road now climbs towards the summit of **Mount Profitis Ilias**. Near the top stands the **monastery of Profitis Ilias**, surrounded by the tiny village of the same name. Yet another part of the Italian legacy, the two large Alpine-chalet-type hotels – the **Elafos** (Stag) and **Elafina** (Doe) – were opened in 1929. After World War II they fell into disrepair. However, a group of local villages decided to renovate them, and the Elafos is now open for business (see 'Family-friendly Accommodation', p. 119), whilst the Elafina rings to the sound of hammering and sawing.

The Elafos is a delight, inside and out. With its overhanging timber eaves and balconies, its high, cool vaulted rooms and wooden panelling, a day or two here would be a blessed relief from the heat and hurry of the coast. There's not much to do, though – a small **children's playground**, lots of **walks** in the surrounding countryside (there's a map at the entrance to the hotel car park, but all the labelling is in Greek), and the small monastery of Profitis Ilias, next to the hotel, to spend a minute or two exploring, and that's about it. If you decide on a ramble, be aware that there are many areas, including the summit of the mountain, that are occupied by the army, and are therefore closed to civilians.

Continuing southwest, the road swoops and plunges through beautiful pine-forested hills, the 1215m grey bulk of Rhodes' highest mountain, **Attavyros**, rearing to dominate the skyline ahead. On the mountain's northern slopes, vineyards start to dominate the landscape, and you arrive at **Embona**, the capital of Rhodes' premier wine-producing area. The village seems to have far more tavernas and cafés than you might expect, a result no doubt of the pull during the season not only of its several wineries (see p. 112), but also as host to numerous folk-dancing tours.

Going back the way you came, take a right turn in about 2km. Keeping Mount Attavyros on your right – the road circumnavigates it – head for **Agios Isidoros**.

And what a road it is! Marked on the map simply as 'a paved road', it is in fact brand new, an exhilarating roller-coaster ride through woodland and across the foothills of the mountain, with extensive views across central Rhodes. You couldn't feel further from the holiday ballyhoo of the coasts. The superb tarmac stops dead as you enter the Agios Isidoros, though it's still perfectly adequate thereafter. If you're up for a pretty energetic walk, look out for the placard marking the beginning of the path to the summit of Attavyros – it's well marked, but takes five or six hours for the return trip, so is suitable only for fit families with no young children.

The village of Agios Isidoros itself is stacked steeply on the slope of the mountain, with the road sometimes passing opposite the chimneys of down-slope houses. With its vine-covered tavernas, Agios Isidoros is a pleasant place to stop.

Epta Piges ★ ★ ★ ALL AGES

The hub of Epta Piges is the pleasant **café-restaurant** (see 'Family-friendly Dining', p. 123), its extensive terraces meandering off under the trees. There's the sound of rushing water everywhere, and the unearthly cry of the many **peacocks** which strut between the tables. Have a look at the information boards, then either cross the wooden bridge and walk up into the wood to the left of the restaurant, or follow the path to the right, past various concrete constructions designed to control and channel the water, to a path that drops down to the main road.

Epta Piges owes its present form to the Italians. They built the channels and sluices, together with the reservoir over the hill, to irrigate the surrounding area. You can get to the reservoir either by following a trail, or through the dark, narrow **tunnel** that burrows its way for nearly 200m through the intervening hill. It is possible to get through this tunnel, but you'll need to take your shoes and socks off – water streams along the tunnel floor – and if you have one handy, take a torch. Not for small children, the faint-hearted or claustrophobes.

Beyond the entrance to the tunnel the path winds its way through woods and rocky outcrops above the river. It only takes about 15 minutes to get to the main road (where there are often coaches waiting for their parties), and it's a pleasant walk, but hold on to young children – parts of the path are high above the river, with unprotected drops into the ravine. If you're lucky you'll glimpse half metre-long lizards that look like miniature dinosaurs, sunning themselves on the rocks.

Café at Epta Piges

The Emery Winery

☎ 22 41 04 12 08, www.emery.gr

On the right just as you enter the village of Embona, stands the Emery Winery, where you can enjoy some highly reckoned red and white wines. Park in front of the winery, and enter the tasting area on the right – several pleasant blue-and-white outdoor areas, with counters, tables and benches, lead to a large indoor bar lined with bottles. There are tours of the works with free wine-tasting as well, and it can get very busy with coach parties during late morning and early afternoon.

Open 9.30am to 3.30–4.30pm. **Adm** free. **Amenities** Café. Parking. Shop.

Tour 2: Valley of the Butterflies – The Ostrich Farm – Ancient Ialyssos – Filerimos – the Bee Museum

From the east coast road, follow signs for 'Butterfly Valley', through **Afandou** and **Psinthos**. The road is another of the island's excellent inland highways, again courtesy of the EU – it climbs up to a pass. As the road snakes down towards the west coast, look out for the **Moni Kalopetra** monastery on the left. This marks the top of the **Valley of the Butterflies** – you need to drive several kilometres further down a serpentine hill to arrive at the entrance. Incidentally, the monastery serves refreshments on its beautiful terrace, and the views are amazing!

The Valley of the Butterflies is, quite understandably, one of Rhodes' biggest tourist attractions. It's lovely – a beautiful steep vale with paved or cobbled walkways, rustic fences and bridges, deep and mossy shade, and the constant sound, sometimes a trickle, sometimes a roar, of running water (see below).

Continuing west beyond the Valley of the Butterflies, a couple of minutes brings you to **Rhodes Ostrich Farm and Park** (see p. 113) where, oddly enough, the star turns are not the ostriches but the camels.

Arriving at the west coast highway and driving north, a short diversion will bring you to the **Bee Museum** (see p. 114), that is not only fascinating in itself but has lots of honey-related merchandise on sale.

Finally, back on the coast road, head towards Rhodes Town and, at Ialyssos, follow the signs for the Ancient Acropolis of Ialyssos. The road winds upwards onto the top of an escarpment, ending at a large car park. Here you have not only the **Ancient Acropolis of Ialyssos**, but also the medieval monastery of **Our Lady of Filerimos** and an Italian-built avenue lined with the Roman Catholic **stations of the cross**, ending at an enormous cross from which there are magnificent views (see p. 115).

Valley of the Butterflies ★★★
ALL AGES

The insects after which the Valley of the Butterflies is named are not butterflies at all, but Jersey tiger moths (*Euplagia quadripunctaria,* according to those who know). Found in the Channel Islands (hence the name) and in parts of southern England, they are not, like most moths, nocturnal. They flock to the valley from June until September, attracted perhaps by its moist coolness, or by the gum exuded by the trees found here – nobody is really sure. What is certain is that there are thousands, flashing their red rear wings in flight, looking like brown-and-yellow Art Deco guitar plectrums when motionless, flat, on the tree trunks.

The entrance to the valley has two free car parks – one 200m before you get to it, the other right next to it. Cafés and shops line the road under the trees, and a taverna occupies a shady site over a pool just below the road. The butterfly motif is everywhere. Information boards tell you all about the Jersey tiger moth, and warn you not to disturb the

insects with loud noise, or by smoking or deviating off the path. You pay at the kiosk (€5, children up to 12 half-price), and start the long climb upwards. (Keep your ticket – there's a payment kiosk at the top as well, and you'll need it to begin the descent). There are benches for you to catch your breath, and little observation platforms over pools or beside waterfalls. It is all very well planned.

At the top, the path comes out onto open grassland, where there's a café. Just a short distance above this, the path comes out onto the main road, just below Moni Kalopetra monastery.

Open *May–Sept 8am–6pm (upper path open all year).* **Adm** *€5*

Rhodes Ostrich Farm and Park ★ ★ ALL AGES

📞 *69 45 32 71 42, www.rhodos-info. de/rhodos-ostrich-park*

In addition to the extensive enclosures of ostriches (and what

The Ostrich Farm

Organise Your Trip

There are several ways of organising your visit. If all family members are reasonably fit:

- Park at the entrance at the bottom, climb to the top, then back down again.
- Park at Moni Kalopetra monastery, walk down through the valley, then back up.

If you have young children that you don't want to over-tire:

- Park at the entrance, climb up through the valley, then the children with one parent can have something to eat or drink at the café at the top, or at the monastery, whilst the other parent climbs back down to the entrance, retrieves the car, and joins the rest at the top.
- The same, only in reverse – park at the monastery, climb down through the valley, then the parent who picks the short straw climbs back up the valley and retrieves the car, joining the family at one of the cafés near the entrance.

strange and intimidating birds they are!), there are lots of other species on show, from rabbits to foxes, llamas to kangaroos, goats to deer to monkeys to ponies to ferrets and a variety of fowl. Our own favourites were the camels, belying their reputation for bad temper by looking lugubriously contented in the sunshine. The German for skunk also raised a laugh – *das Stinktier.*

The farm has a snack bar/restaurant, a children's play area (though with no shade, so it could only be recommended in the early morning or late afternoon), and a gift shop. And yes, you can order ostrich-egg omelettes and ostrich steaks in the restaurant!

Open *9am–7.30pm all week.* **Adm** *Adults €4, children 3 to 12 €2 , under 3s free. Camel rides: adults €6, under–12s €4.* **Amenities** *Café.*

English spoken. Parking. Restaurant. Shop.

The Bee Museum ★ ALL AGES

☏ *22 41 04 82 00, www.mel.gr On the road that cuts across from the east to the west coast, just south of Rhodes Town. It's well signposted.*

A terrific little museum which tells you all you'll ever need to know about bees, bee-keeping and honey production. There's a short introductory video, lots of interesting artefacts, and a couple of transparent hives in which you can see thousands of bees in all their teeming glory. The shop stocks not only honey and honey-based products, but some nice toys.

Open *8.30am–3pm Mon–Sat.* **Adm** *€2 adults; €1 children 6 to 18, children under–6 free.* **Amenities** *English spoken. Parking. Shop.*

Ancient Ialyssos and Filerimos ★ ★ ALL AGES

It was on this hilltop that Suleiman the Magnificent made his base during the assault on the Rhodes of the Knights of St John, in 1522, that ended in their defeat and expulsion, and ushered in almost four centuries of Ottoman rule.

Here you have today what is, in fact, three separate attractions – the remains of Ancient Ialyssos (the foundations of 13th-century twin temples to Zeus and Athena), the monastery of Our Lady of Filerimos, built (or rather converted from an earlier church) by the Knights of St John and restored by the Italians (it looks fake, but apparently isn't), and a long avenue, again built by the Italians, lined by 14 stone monuments bearing bronze reliefs of the Stations of the Cross. It ends in a massive concrete cross (a recent replacement of an earlier Italian one, which they themselves destroyed during the World War II defence of the hilltop) which contains a spiral staircase, allowing you to climb up inside, and out onto one of the cross arms. Not for vertigo sufferers, but the view, needless to say, is amazing.

Southern Rhodes

There is no doubt that it is the northern part of the island that the vast majority of holidaymakers are likely to experience – the head of the whale, from the flippers upwards. However, the southern part, from the flippers down to the tail, is well worth exploring – it gives a good idea of what the whole of rural Rhodes must have been like before the arrival of tourism. The figures for the Municipality of Southern Rhodes speak for themselves – the total population of the region is only just over 4000 (about the same as my home town of Pwllheli in North Wales!), representing less than 4% of the island's total, with a population density of about an eighth of that of the north.

Southern Rhodes is farming country. You'll see tiny villages, fields of wheat, barley, oats or melons, vineyards, and olive and citrus groves. In the extreme south you'll see sheep and cattle. Look out too for the remains of Italian attempts to increase the productivity of the land – in particular, many of their metal wind pumps (the same sort you'll have seen in pictures of midwestern American cattle ranches and Australian sheep stations). You might even end up staying on the southeast or southwest coast, since isolated hotels are beginning to spring up there as well. And when you get to the whale's tail, you'll find a place that's worth a day of any family's time.

All the places are accessible from both coasts, and you can pick'n'mix what you wish to see. With one exception (see 'Prassonissi', p. 117), none of them are likely to be worth a special visit, but taken together they give a good impression of the whole region. Most are made up of white, cuboid houses (if you get the chance to peep inside, you'll see embroidery and ceramic plates used as decoration), and many have the old outside ovens – look for a blackened dome and stacks of fuel.

Askipio is a lively village, with a fine **Byzantine church**, a rather good **folk museum** next door in what was once an olive press owned by the church, and the remains of a **12th-century fortress** from which there are excellent views. **Gennadi**, a rather scattered village just inland off the main road has a dark gravel beach beyond it, might be worth a quick wander, and supermarkets if you want to make up a picnic. Look out for an unmistakeably **Italian police station** and a verdant oasis fed by a fountain. A scattering of houses, surrounded by forests and olive groves, **Vati** has a pleasant **village square**, a couple of tavernas, a ruined **windmill**, and an air of having been bypassed by modern life – until the weekend, when many Greeks arrive from elsewhere on the island. Though the main church is fairly recent, the one in the cemetery dates from as early as the 14th century.

Beyond Vati, a number of villages, recognised by the Rhodes authorities as typical of the area, are worth a look: **Profilia** (extensive views, a central café and a scattering of white houses), **Istrios** (surrounded by olive groves and vineyards, with a particularly large platia), **Arnitha** (set into a hillside, with a natural spring from which to drink at the entrance to the village).

Apolakia is worth a visit not only for itself (it has an interesting Italian-built school, now a cultural centre, in the village *platia*), but for the surrounding olive and citrus groves and, 2 kilometres away, the **Apolakia Dam**, built in 1989 to irrigate the region and now an ideal place to walk – look out for wildlife, or have a picnic.

Olive Groves

If you're in the area in July, you might want to take part in the village's **Watermelon Feast** – it's on the first Saturday after the Feast of Agia Marina (17th July). To celebrate the village's main crop, there are tastings of all sorts of dishes made from watermelons, together with games, music and dancing. Stretching along the southernmost reach of the main coast road, the **Kattavia** region is heavily agricultural, with sheep and cattle as well as the usual crops. The village itself is pretty standard, but a couple of kilometres east the ruined model agricultural community – called **Agios Pavlos** – built by the Italians can be seen. There's a **church with a barrel roof** and a squat **clocktower**, an old **silk factory, a prison** and several farmhouses. The whole area is dotted, too, with **old windmills** – some renovated traditional ones, others the metal ones erected by the Italians.

A road strikes off due south between Kattavia village and Agios Pavlos to **Prassonissi** (see below). This is the one place in the south that is worth a whole day's family visit to itself.

Beyond the turn-off to Prassonissi, the coast road continues, turning north and heading for distant Rhodes Town, this time along the east coast. A couple of kilometres off to the west, **Lachania** has been called the most beautiful village on the island. Tiled white houses with blue-painted windows and doors, a pretty platia shaded by a couple of plane trees and stone water troughs – it really is a

picture. However, all is not quite as it seems. Most of the houses have been renovated by outsiders (mainly Germans, with some Brits) since the village was abandoned following a devastating earthquake after World War II. Still, it's very pretty, and the taverna in the square (the Platanos) does a mean meze.

Prassonissi ★ ★ ★ ALL AGES

As you approach along a good road that dips and soars, you feel that you're approaching the end of the known world. But then, coming over the rise above Prassonissi, prepare for a treat.

This is where the east and west coasts collide. An almost-island attached to the mainland by a wide sandbar with twin curving beaches on either side, this southernmost tip of Rhodes is breathtaking. A steady wind blows across the sandbar, funnelled by the island and the mainland. The sea on one side (usually the west) is choppy, that on the other is calm.

What lifts the view out of the ordinary into the wonderful is the vigorous human activity. The sea on both sides of the strand is full of surfers – the **windsurfers** with their colourful sails, the **parasurfers** with their billowing chutes – all skimming along on the waves at what seems like supersonic speeds. On the strand itself, tyre-tracks weave across the sand in intricate patterns, and everywhere banners snap in the breeze – on equipment hire shacks, on lifeguard towers, on refreshment cabins. This is what a medieval joust must have looked like.

As you drive onto the beach there are several café/bar/restaurants (the Light House is particularly inviting (see 'Family-friendly Dining', below), and next to them is a well-stocked mini-market. So Prassonissi has all you need for a family day on the beach – watersports with equipment-hire for the adults and older children, two beaches for swimming, guaranteed wind if you want to fly kites and the means either to have lunch or to make up a picnic. You could even let teenagers drive the car across the sand!

For Active Families

Most places in Rhodes have a selection of activities to keep the family occupied, and many are advertised on roadside hoardings, in hotel lobbies and in tourist literature. In addition to the ones already mentioned, here are a few others to check out:

Cycling www.2wheeltreks.co.uk This site offers a boat and cycle trip which includes Rhodes.

Jeep safaris www.faliraki-info.com A variety of jeep safaris on the island.

Water sports
Pefkos Water Fun: ℓ 69 32 43 34 98 (boat hire); Pefkos Main Beach
Big Blue Water Sports: ℓ 69 32 38 33 23. Vliha Bay (jet skiing et al); **Yacht Agency Rhodes** ℓ 22 41 02 29 27 (yachting); **Dive Med**

ℓ 22 41 06 11 15, www.rodos.com (scuba diving).

Golf Rhodes Afandu Golf Club ℓ 22 41 05 12 25.

Tennis Rhodes Tennis Club ℓ 22 41 02 57 05.

Gym Fitness Factory ℓ 22 41 03 76 67.

Shopping With Children

The main shopping streets of Rhodes Town are in the New Town – **Grivas Street** (near the Aquarium) has a vast array of traditional Greek shops, and **Amerikis Street** has many upmarket international outlets. Look out in Rhodes Town and elsewhere on the island for carpets and rugs – there's a workshop (**Kleopatra**), off the east coast road at **Afandou**, though how you get them home is another matter. There are also lots of jewellery and ceramic workshops along this road; the biggest and best is **Rodos Gold** (see p. 101). Rhodes is known for the quality of its wine (buy it at the **Emery Winery**, see p. 112) and honey (similarly, at the **Bee Museum**, see p. 114). In **Sokratou Street** there are shops selling fur coats, mostly from Kastoria in northern Greece – the anti-fur movement seems to have made little headway in Greece. Prices are usually very reasonable, largely because the coats are made up from imported scraps rather than whole pelts.

FAMILY-FRIENDLY ACCOMMODATION

EXPENSIVE

Atrium Palace ★★

85102, ☎ *22 44 03 16 01, www. atrium.gr Between the main coast road and Kalathos Beach.*

For high luxury, the Atrium Palace is hard to beat. Everything in it oozes class. On first acquaintance it looks like the sort of hotel that's for adults only; further investigation shows that, though surely aimed at grown-ups looking for a bit of pampering, a great deal is put on to keep the children happy as well. The hotel, festooned in trees and flowers, looks lovely, a range of sports is available, there are restaurants nearby in Kalathos, and golf-carts can be provided to help you get around. Accommodation is luxurious, with all double rooms and villas suitable for up to three people. An ideal hotel for young couples with a young child.

Rooms *300, plus villas from deluxe to presidential.* **Rates** *€125–280 triple; €360–3000 villa depending on size, level of luxury and season; includes B&B.* **Credit** *AmEx, MC, V.* **Amenities** *Babysitting. Bars (2) Cots (free). Children's club (age 4 to 12). Gym. Parking. Pools (4). Restaurants (3). Spa.* **In room** *A/C. Safe. TV.*

Esperides Beach Hotel ★★

85100, ☎ *22 41 08 42 00, www. esperia-hotels.gr At the northern end of Faliraki.*

The Esperides Beach Hotel bills itself as a **family resort**, and you can see why. It has everything you could want, in spades. The swimming pools (with slides and all sorts of interactive stuff), playgrounds (with bumper cars, carousel, bouncy castle) and indoor play areas are so extensive that you'll find it difficult to lure children away for even one day's excursion. There's a kid's miniclub for 3 to 12-year olds all day, every day, a full animation programme, and regular children's

Atrium Palace

films. There's also a range of sports available to encourage healthy family rivalry – volleyball, tennis, billiards – and evening entertainment.

Accommodation is in **family rooms** for four or five, which consist of a main bedroom plus children's room separated by room dividers.

The **blue-flag beach** has everything you need in the way of changing cabins, sun-beds, parasols and showers, and there's a range of watersports available. Also, of course, being in Faliraki, the hotel has resort facilities on the doorstep.

Rooms 575 **Rates** €248 family room; includes breakfast. **Credit** AmEx, MC, V. **Amenities** Babysitting. Bars (4) Children's club (age 3 to 12); Cots. Extra bed. Laundry service. Parking. Pools (6). Restaurants(2). **In room** A/C. Fridge. Safe. Satellite TV.

Lindos Princess Beach Hotel, Lardos ★ ★ ★ VALUE

Pefka/Lardos, 85109, 📞 *22 44 02 92 30, www.lindosprincess.com On Lardos Beach.*

For families with younger children who qualify for concessionary rates, the Lindos Princess is terrific value for money, especially offpeak, and especially when you consider that the rates quoted are inclusive. If your children are in their teens, though, it can get a bit pricey. On site, apart from the beach, a wide range of games, sports and entertainment (with its own band in its 500-seat amphitheatre) are available, and children are well catered for – there's a

kid's club, a full animation programme, a mini-disco, a children's amusement park (with a charge) and two swimming pools. Children's meals are available on request, as are high chairs, buggies and cots. The Lindos Princess is well placed near very pleasant village of Lardos, just outside the hugely popular Lindos peninsula.

Rooms 416 (238 double, 160 family room, 18 suites). **Rates** €52–89 per person, per night for family rooms (two adults, two children). Rates all inclusive; first child up to 5 free, 6 to 11 –50%, second child 0 to 1 free, 2 to 11 –50%, third person –30%. **Credit** AmEx, DC, MC, V. **Amenities** Babysitting (charge). Bars (2). Children's club. Cots. Gym. Laundry service. Parking. Pools (5): 1 indoor, 2 outdoor, 2 for children. Restaurants (4) Spa. **In room** A/C. Fridge. TV/ DVD/Satellite.

MODERATE

Louis Colossos Beach, Kalithea ★ ★

85100, Kalithea, 📞 *22 41 08 55 02, www.louishotels.com On the beach just north of Faliraki.*

One of the Louis chain of hotels to be found on many Greek islands, as well as Cyprus and Egypt, the Colossos Beach has everything a family is likely to need – an almost infinite flexibility of accommodation, from double rooms through specially designed family studios to bungalows (in all of which extra cots or beds can be requested), supervised kid's club and animation programmes, several playgrounds and babysitting facilities. Children's menus and highchairs are available in the restaurants. Games and sports facilities are first class – apart from the excellent sandy beach, two swimming pools and children's paddling pool, there are billiards, tennis, table tennis, mini-golf and electronic games. Sun-beds and parasols around the pools are free. Evening entertainment is organised, including Greek evenings. And although there would be no need to set foot outside the hotel, just down the road all the facilities of Faliraki are available, including the spectacular water park and funfair.

*Rooms 742 (616 doubles, 114 family studios, 12 bungalows. **Rates** €37–78 per person per night, depending on view and season. Rates include half board; first child staying in parents' room – free low and mid season, second child and first child high season –50%. **Credit** AmEx, DC, MC, V. **Amenities** Babysitting. Bars (3). Children's club. Cots. Extra beds. Gym. Laundry service. Parking. Pools (outdoor, 1 for children). Restaurants (3). Spa. **In room** A/C. Fridge. Internet access. Safe. TV/DVD/Satellite.*

Atlantica Princess, Trianda ★★

Trianda, ☎ 22 41 09 61 00, www.atlanticahotels.com At the northern end of Trianda beach.

A good family hotel with a nice pool, free sun-beds and parasols, daily entertainment and flexible, comfortable rooms – try to get one of the family rooms suitable for two adults and two children. They have got either bunk beds or sofa beds, and a kitchenette, cooker and fridge. There's a separate children's swimming pool, outdoor playground and indoor play room, and daytime entertainment, and the restaurant can provide children's menus and early suppers by arrangement. Cots are available on request, and are free. Although most family hotels provide all this and more, the great advantage of the Atlanta Princess is its position right on Trianda beach. Immediately outside the hotel entrance is Planet Z, an indoor children's playbarn, and just along the beach, the best-equipped children's playground I saw during my whole stay on Rhodes. Trianda is, too, only a stone's throw from Rhodes Town.

*Rooms 216. **Rates** €108–156 for family room suitable for two adults and two children. **Credit** AmEx, DC, MC, V. **Amenities** Babysitting. Bars (2). Children's club. Cots (free). Parking. Pools (1 for children). Restaurants (3). Spa. **In room** A/C (summer only). Internet access. Safe. Sat–TV.*

Mitsis Lindos Memories

85107 Psaitos, Lindos, ☎ 22 44 03 50 00, www.mitsishotels.com Just off the main road from Lindos to Lardos.

A small though relatively palatial hotel on a spur off the main Lindos to Lardos road, the Mitsis Lindos Memories would be a good choice if your children are relatively young. Cots, cribs and highchairs are available free on request, and babysitting services can be arranged for an extra charge. There are board games in the games room, and there's a small children's pool next to the hotel's main pool, together with a selection of children's outdoor toys. The hotel is happy to provide a junior menu on request, and you also get the peace of mind knowing that the hotel will arrange a doctor's visit, should the need arise. Greek evenings, with local food and dancing, are put on in the Lindia Tavern. Families with older children might feel that there isn't enough to do in the hotel itself to keep them occupied for a whole holiday, and although lively Lindos is not far away, transport would be necessary. There is a really nice sandy beach – created, presumably, for the hotel – but the rest of the surroundings are rather bleak and arid.

Rooms 70 standard doubles, maisonettes and suites. **Rates** €190–290 for junior suite consisting of double and two singles. **Credit** AmEx, DC, MC, V. **Amenities** Babysitting. Bar (2). Cots (free). Disabled access. Extra bed. Gym. Laundry service. Parking. Pools (1 outdoor, 1 for children). Spa. **In room** A/C. Internet access. Safe. TV/DVD/Satellite.

Lindos Sun Hotel, Pefki VALUE

Lindos, 85102, ☎ 22 44 04 82 70, www.hotellindossun.com Just off the main road between Lindos and Pefki.

If you want to stay near the pretty town of Lindos without paying premium prices, then the Lindos Sun Hotel is a good choice. Since tariffs are per room rather than per person, infants are free throughout the year, and older children are free outside the busiest periods – this really is a very viable budget choice. As you would expect, the hotel lacks the range of facilities you'd get in the big hotels, but rooms are clean and pleasant, all have their own terrace or balcony, there's a hotel swimming pool with free parasols and sun-beds, and a pool bar that supplies drinks, ice-creams and snacks all day. And the area – Lindos/Pefki/Lardos – is one of the most family friendly on the island, with everything you could need, from restaurants to café/bars, beaches to playgrounds, and a range of watersports. Excursions all over the island and outside can be arranged through reception.

Rooms 42. **Rates** €30–150 per room per night, for two adults and one or two children. Rates include B&B; children up to 2 stay free, and children from 3 to 12 are free outside high and peak periods. There's a 10% discount for booking online. **Credit** AmEx, DC, MC, V. **Amenities** bars (2). Cots (free). Parking. Pool. Restaurant. **In room** A/C.

Elafos Hotel, Profitis Ilias ★★
FIND

Profitis Ilias, ☎ 22 46 02 24 02, www.elafoshotel.gr On the right as you enter the village, right next to the little monastery.

Built in 1929 by the Italians as Albergo del Cervo (the Hotel of the Deer), the Elafos offers old-fashioned interwar comfort at a

Elafos Hotel, Profitis Ilias

very reasonable cost. With a fixed rate per room and free cots and beds, the hotel really is a bargain. And, although the Elafos's provision is somewhat basic compared to the big coastal resort hotels – no kid's clubs, pools or even air-conditioning (you don't need it at this altitude) – there is a sauna and a small children's playground. There's not a lot to do – walking in the fresh mountain air, eating and drinking, resting – and you're as far away from discos and amusement arcades as you possibly could be on Rhodes. So if you want a day or two's peace and quiet with the family, and perhaps to get in some serious walking, book your room(s) and head for the hills.

Rooms *23 (20 rooms and three suites).* **Rates** *€75 per double room, flat rate.* **Amenities** *Bar. Cots (free). Extra beds (free). Parking.* **In room** *TV.*

FAMILY-FRIENDLY DINING

EXPENSIVE

Golden Olympiade Restaurant ★★

Apellou and Evdimou, Old Town, 85100, ☎ 22 41 02 01 19. In Evdimou, where it intersects with Apellou, between Socratous and the commercial harbour.

Well-known for its meat, fish and vegetarian dishes, traditional Greek and pasta dishes, all with fresh ingredients locally sourced, and with homemade bread and **organic** olive oil, the Golden Olympiade is a pleasure during the day or in the evening. And it's a grand place to watch the world go by.

Open *11am–midnight (April to Oct).* **Mains** *€10–30.* **Credit** *AmEx, MC, V.* **Amenities** *Highchairs. Reservations accepted.*

Lighthouse Taverna Bar

Lighthouse Taverna Bar ★

Prassonissi Kattavia. 📞 *22 44 09 10 30/45.*

The Lighthouse café/bar is right on the beach at Prassonissi, and ideal for snacks, pastries and ice-cream, as well as more substantial meals. The menu consists largely of traditional Greek food, and serves also as the dining room for the **surfer hotels** Lighthouse I and Lighthouse II. There's a large, cool interior, together with tables on the terrace at the front. As you climb the steps into the building, you'll be met by a cabinet with the most enticing sweets. Try the **chocolate pudding** in a red earthenware pot – it's delicious. Otherwise, snacks start at around €4 and meals at €7.

Open *9am–11pm. Mains €15–36.* **Credit** *MC, V.* **Amenities** *Children's menu. Highchairs.*

MODERATE

Socratou Garden ★ ★ ★ FIND

Socratou, Rhodes Town. Halfway up Socratou Street, towards the top on the right as you walk up the hill, through an arch between a tourist shop and one selling skincare products.

The Socratou Garden has it all. In a large, cool **secluded garden** just off Rhodes Town's busiest shopping street, close against the medieval town walls, in the shade of banana and palm trees, and with the sound of running water all around, it's an absolute delight. The food – traditional Greek – is excellent and reasonably priced, and the service attentive. With features which make it child-friendly – a parrot at the entrance, room to move around, pristine outside toilets, the rear entrance to a large tourist shop (Harri's Market) in which to browse – it's the perfect place to get away from the crowds. Note: it's not easy to find.

Open *10am–late May–Oct.* **Mains** *€6.50–12* **Entertainment** *Parrot.*

Vrachos

☏ 22 41 09 22 20. On Trianta Beach.

One of the string of restaurants that line Trianta Beach, the Vrachos has an extensive menu of Greek and continental dishes, with a more experimental and adventurous spin than most. It's a pleasant setting right on the beach, and its proximity to the excellent playground at one end of the beach and Planet Z at the other, make it a convenient stopping-off or meeting place for families.

Open *11am–2am.* **Mains** *€5–24.50.* **Credit** *AmEx, MC, V.* **Amenities** *Children's menu. Highchairs. Play area. Reservations accepted.*

Nefeli ★

☏ 22 44 03 18 22. On the big beach at Lindos.

If ever there was a restaurant with a perfect **location**, it's the Nefeli. Right on Lindos's main beach, it has steps down onto the sand (so older children can play on the sand whilst parents refresh themselves), a large, shaded open terrace with ranks of fans suspended from the roof, at the end of which is a small clutch of children's toys. The food is the usual range of holiday fare, and ordering is made easy by pictures of all the dishes on offer – a way of circumventing language barriers. The food's OK, the coffee is excellent, and the music's Greek. And, though there are no highchairs, there's plenty of room between tables for buggies.

Socratou Garden

Open *11am–10pm Apr–Oct.* **Mains**
€8–16.50. **Amenities** *Play area.
Reservations accepted.*

Epta Piges Restaurant ★ ★ ★

*Archangelos-Rhodes, ☎ 22 41 05 62
59. At the hub of the Seven Springs
attraction.*

You wouldn't expect the Epta
Piges Restaurant to be much
good – it's the only one for
miles, with thousands of visitors
to the Seven Springs as captive
customers. Yet it is, in fact,
excellent. The setting, with terraces under the trees on both
sides of the stream joined by a
wooden bridge, couldn't be better. It has a good range of snacks
and drinks all day, and the food,
served from noon till 8pm, is
first rate. Look out in particular
for the specials board – if there's
lamb *stifado* (€11), snap it up.
There's a small children's playground, and they will love the
tame peacocks that wander
imperiously between the tables,
and the ducks that quack and
splash in the little waterfalls.

Open *all day, food served noon–
8pm.* **Mains** *€8–14.* **Amenities** *Play
area.*

INEXPENSIVE

To Steki tou Vlachou

*☎ 22 44 03 12 02. On the left as you
drive south along the coast road
through Kalathos.*

One of the many excellent **take-
away restaurants** that you'll
find all over Rhodes, To Steki
tou Vlachou provides excellent

food at rock-bottom prices
which you can eat either in the
restaurant (indoors or out on the
pavement), order by phone and
pick up, or have delivered. Main
meals range from €1.50 (meat
and salad wrapped in a pitta) to
€7 (a full mixed grill). As seems
common now throughout
Greece, the practice of putting
chips in the pitta wrap (the most
popular take-away), introduced
to satisfy the tastes of tourists,
has now been embraced by
locals. If, like me, you prefer
them without chips, say '*choris
patates*'. Like all the best places,
To Steki tou Vlachou has a
charcoal grill, which is usually
fired up in the evenings only.

Open *8am–10pm.* **Mains** *€1.50–7.*

Jasmine

*On the corner of Main Road and Boat
Trip Road, in the centre of Pefki.*

A pleasant bar/café/creperie, the
Jasmine's great attraction for families with young children is its
excellent play area. Attractively
astro-turfed, it is well stocked
with colourful play equipment –
slides, climbing frames, Wendy-
houses, rocking horses, riding
toys – all safely fenced, and accessible down a shallow flight of
steps. The speciality of the house
is crepes, savoury and sweet, and
a huge range of cocktails. So the
whole family can eat, then the
adults can have a drink whilst the
children play.

Open *9am–late May–Oct.* **Mains**
€3–5. **Amenities** *Play area.*

5 Western Crete

CRETE

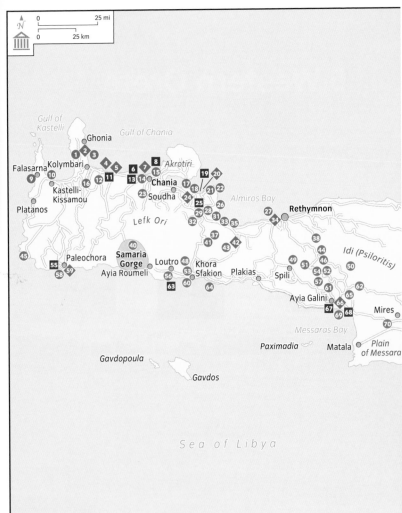

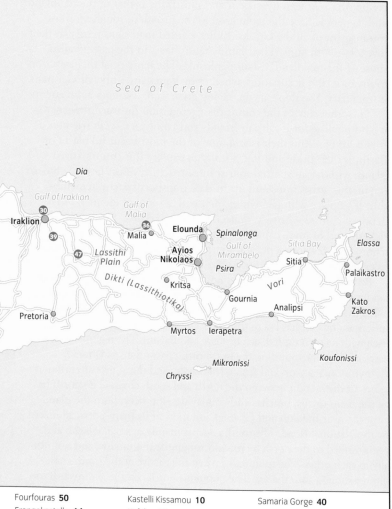

Sea of Crete

Dia

Gulf of Iraklion

Gulf of Malia

Iraklion ㉚
㊴
㊼ Lassithi Plain
Malia Elounda Spinalonga
Ayios Nikolaos Sitia Bay Elassa
Dikti (Lassithiotika) Gulf of Mirambelo Psira Sitia
Kritsa Vori Palaikastro
Gournia
Pretoria Analipsi Kato Zakros
Myrtos Ierapetra
Koufonissi
Mikronissi
Chryssi

Crete is defined by its extremes. It's the biggest Greek island. The furthest south. The hottest. It has the longest summers. Its civilisation is at least as ancient and illustrious as that of the mainland and its people have the reputation as the proudest, toughest, most intransigent of all the Greeks. Bullet-riddled road signs testify to their love affair with guns. Their family feuds have, in the past, rivalled those of the mainland's Mani peninsula. The ferocity of their reaction to invasion and occupation, whether by Venetians, Turks or Germans, is legendary. You don't, as the saying goes, want a Cretan as an enemy.

The other side of the coin is their reputation for warmth, generosity, hospitality; for loyalty to friends and family: a Cretan friend is a friend for life. And their island, one of the most beautiful places on Earth, is their pride and joy. So, as you explore this country-sized island, with its substantial tourist infrastructure, resort hotels, modern restaurants, attractions and up-to-date transport system, remember this: it's a place with its own history, with a sense of identity and a depth of culture – history, dialect, music and dance. Crete has the richest fund of myths and legends of any of the Greek islands. For all its modern development, you don't have to get far off the beaten track to experience the **authentic**, unchanging spirit of Crete.

Because of its size, Crete does not follow the usual 'capital plus hinterland' pattern of other Greek islands. Its length (260km, east to west), allied to its relatively narrow width (50km, north to south) and its great mountain ranges, has led to the development of four distinct regions, each with its own capital, atmosphere and flavour. The regions, west to east, are those surrounding the four north-coast towns of **Chania, Rethymnon, Iraklion** and **Agios Nikolaos**. And this draws attention to a clear-cut distinction between the north and south coasts. The north has all the main towns, beaches and holiday development, both the island's airports (near Iraklion and Chania) and most of its main ports, all linked by the National Road. The south consists mainly of small villages and ports, linked to the north by roads through the mountains, and not usually to each other. The mountains when they arrive at the south coast plunge straight into the sea. The populous north coast looks inwards to the rest of Greece and Europe, the south, at the very edge of the continent, looks across the Libyan sea to Africa.

This whole rich and diverse island has the potential for wonderful family holidays. But the **western** half (dominated by Chania and Rethymnon) offers the best mix of countryside, villages, resorts, hotels, restaurants, attractions and history, with a good balance of towns and tours. It also has some excellent **walking**. The central region – dominated by the capital, Iraklion – is where the major **Minoan** sites are situated. Excursions visit from all over Crete. It's on these main areas, western and Minoan Crete, that the rest of this chapter focuses.

ESSENTIALS

Getting There

By plane Crete has two international airports which can give you access to western Crete – Daskalogiannis Airport, on the Akrotiri peninsula just outside Chania, is the most convenient, but Kazantzakis Airport, just to the east of Iraklion, is also perfectly viable – it's a 2-hour drive along the National Road to Chania. British Airways and Olympic Airlines both run scheduled flights from the UK to Iraklion from London and Manchester, and Olympic Airlines also has a route to Chania. A variety of no-frills airlines fly to both airports – Thomsonfly, for example, have seasonal routes to Iraklion from 10 regional airports (and to Chania from Gatwick and Manchester), and Flythomascook from 11.

By boat As with most Greek islands, it's not feasible to get to Crete from the UK by sea. However, it is possible to visit it by boat – either on a cruise, or by ferry from Athens or from other islands. Take a look at *www.pocruises.com* or *www.viamare.com*.

VISITOR INFORMATION

The main tourist offices are:

Iraklion 1 Xanthoudidou ☏ 28 10 22 82 25, Mon–Fri 8am–2.30pm.

Chania National Tourist Office 1866 Square ☏ 28 21 09 29 43, Mon–Fri 9am–2.30pm.

Municipal Tourist Office Kidonias 29 ☏ 28 21 03 61 55, Mon–Fri 9am–2.30pm.

Chania

Rethymnon Venizelou ☎ 28 31 02 91 48, Mon–Fri 8am–2.30pm. Some useful websites: **www.greekisland.co.uk/wcrete/creteinfo.htm; www.explorecrete.com.**

You might try to get hold of the Cretan holiday magazine 'Frappe' as well (**www.frappe-magazine.com**).

Getting Around

On foot and by taxi You can explore each of the Cretan towns covered in this chapter on foot – even in the capital Iraklion, everywhere you're likely to want to see is within walking distance, and the centres of Chania and Rethymnon are very compact. If you do want to explore a little further afield, grab a cab (Radio Taxis ☎ 28 21 09 87 00). It's wise to negotiate a fare before you get in.

By bus Crete's bus system is excellent – it's well-organised, efficient and cheap. Most fares fall into the €3–6.50 range (for example, Chania to Kastelli is €3.90, Chania to Rethymnon is €6, Rethymnon to Iraklion €6.50). If you intend to use the buses a lot, do visit KTEL's excellent website and run off the routes and timetables you need. (**www.bus-service-crete-ktel.com**).

By car In Crete, as in other parts of Greece, a rented car is by far the best way of seeing the island. Car rental provision is widespread and easy to arrange. The roads are far better than you might expect, especially as many routes have been upgraded and resurfaced,

courtesy of EU grants. The National Road that runs along the north coast of the island is fast and well engineered, but apart from the odd section, is not dual carriageway. This can make turning across the traffic flow a little hairy, though a central lane is usually provided. Signposting is clear, and in most places is in both Greek and Latin lettering. Main roads from north to south are also in excellent condition. Secondary roads are sometimes subject to rashes of potholes, though they too can be surprisingly good.

> **INSIDER TIP** ⟫
>
> When facing what is marked on the map as a dirt track, check with locals – in many places they have been resurfaced since the maps were drawn. If you are determined to use a dirt track, check your insurance: many rental companies don't cover use on unsurfaced roads.

By moped, motorbike or quad-bike Not recommended unless you're an expert – don't be tempted by the low rental rates. Lots of Brits end up in hospital because of unwise and unsuitable rental.

By boat Most coastal towns offer boat excursions, and this can be a pleasant way of seeing more of the area. They are invariably advertised at the quayside. On the south coast, they or the coastal ferry are the only way of getting to many of the prettiest beaches and villages if you don't want to walk.

Planning Your Outings

The main rule of thumb when planning outings in Crete is to start early. Crete is the furthest south of Greece's main islands, and is therefore the hottest. So it's a good plan to emulate the Greeks themselves, and divide your day's activities into two sessions – morning and evening – separated by a siesta from about 2–6 pm. So whether visiting the beach, driving to see attractions or going shopping, it's best to do so in the morning or evening. And you'll find that the Cretan day is organised accordingly, with many shops and attractions closing down in the afternoon, to open again in the evening.

As for getting into the main towns (Chania, Rethymnon, Iraklion), again an early start is recommended to make sure you can find somewhere to park.

Wherever you're going in Crete, remember the big three – hats, sunscreen and lots and lots of water.

FAST FACTS: CRETE

Airport See 'Getting there by plane'.

American Express Adamis Travel Bureau, 23 25th Augusto Street, Iraklion, ☎ 28 10 34 62 02.

Banks and ATMs There are cash machines throughout western Crete.

British Vice Consulate 16 Papa-Alexandrou Street, 712 02

Iraklion, ☎ 28 10 22 40 12. Open to the public Mon–Fri 8am–1pm.

Buses KTEL information numbers are: Chania, ☎ 28 21 09 33 06; Rethymnon, ☎ 28 31 02 22 12; Iraklion, ☎ 28 10 24 50 20.

Business hours See Chapter 2. Tourist shops stay open for long hours, tavernas and restaurants often close when the last customers have left.

Credit cards All larger establishments (hotels, restaurants, shops) accept the main credit cards, but a lot of smaller ones don't. And even when they have the technology to accept them, you may find a reluctance to do so. In service stations, for example, there are usually pump attendants, and they'd far prefer taking cash – they always seem to have enough money on them to give change – than return to the office to process a credit card.

Internet access Big hotels usually offer Internet access, either in-room or in a dedicated 'Internet corner' on the premises. Internet cafés and bars, often with just two or three machines, are common in most towns visited by tourists. Internet cafés come and go – try Vranas Studio Café ☎ 28 21 05 86 18, just behind the Cathedral (Chania); Galero ☎ 28 31 02 13 24, Plateia Rimini (Rethymnon) or the Konsova Internet Café on Dikeossinas (Iraklion). But there are lots of others.

Police If you need the police, your best bet is to contact the tourist police in the first instance – they are specially trained, and are more likely to speak English than their mainstream colleagues. Dial 171, or Chania ☎ 28 21 02 59 31, Rethymnon ☎ 28 31 02 81 56, Iraklion ☎ 28 10 28 31 90.

Post Office Chania: Tzanakaki 3 (near Municipal Market) Mon–Fri 8am–8pm, Sat 8am–noon. Rethymnon: 37 Moatsu (east of the Public Gardens) Mon–Fri 8am–8pm, Sat 8am–noon. Iraklion: Plateia Daskaloyiannis (due south of the Archaeological Museum) Mon–Fri 7.30am–8pm, daily.

EXPLORING WESTERN CRETE

When visiting western Crete, you're most likely to be staying on the **north coast**, in one of the two stretches dominated by Chania or Rethymnon – this is where most of the holiday accommodation is situated. The small resorts and intimate hotels of the **south coast** are also worth considering if you want a peaceful family break. You are likely to want to visit other parts of Crete – the mountains, rural valleys, coastline, or the great Minoan sites around Iraklion –

either on excursions or under your own steam.

This chapter is organised accordingly, with walking tours of the two principal towns, Chania and Rethymnon, driving tours along the north and west coasts, excursions across the mountains to the south coast, with a quick look at the Minoan sites of central Crete.

Chania

Chania, the capital of Crete's westernmost *nomos* (province), is one of the island's, and Europe's, finest looking towns. It's sometimes called the **Venice of Greece** (for its architecture and light, not for canals – there aren't any). With a glorious harbour, its mixture of Greek, Venetian and Turkish architecture, narrow alleys and imposing walls, it's an absolute gem. And although tourism is now very obvious during the summer, you never get the feeling that Chania lives just for visitors, hibernating in the winter. It has a life that's all its own. It is, indeed, a large, modern regional capital (until 1971 the capital of Crete) but it is the old part around the harbour that is of greatest interest to the visitor.

 Your Own Wheels

Whatever type of holiday you're going for, I recommend hiring a car, at least for a few days – it's the only way of doing justice to this beautiful and fascinating island.

CHANIA

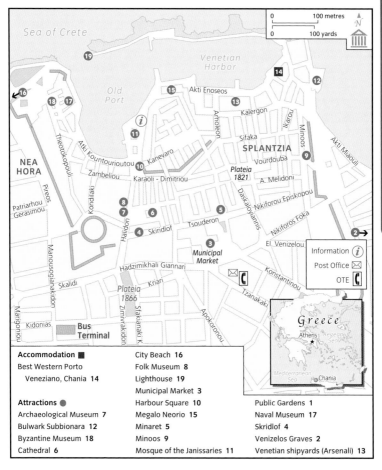

0	100 metres	
0	100 yards	N

Sea of Crete

Venetian Harbor

19

Old Port

14

12

16

18 **17**

15 Akti Enoseos

13

Arholeon

Kalergon

Sifaka

Theotokopouli

Akti Kountourioutou

Kanevaro

11

i

10

Zambeliou

Karaoli - Dimitriou

SPLANTZIA

Vourdouba

9

Minoos

Akti Miaouli

Katou

Plateia 1821

A. Melidoni

NEA HORA

Pireos

Patriarhou Gerasimou

Kondilaki

8

7

6

4 Skiridlof

Halidon

Tsouderon

Nikiforou Episkopou

Daskalojannis

5

Nikiforos Foka

El. Venizelou

3
Municipal Market

Hadzimikhali Giannari

Manousogianakidon

Skalidi

Krian

Plateia 1866

Tzanakaki

Konstantinou

Apokoronou

Marigoniou

Kidonias

Zimivrakidon

Sfakianaki k.

Bus Terminal

Information **i**
Post Office ✉
OTE **(**

Greece
Athens ★
Aegean Sea
Mediterranean Sea
Chania

Accommodation ■	City Beach **16**	
Best Western Porto Veneziano, Chania **14**	Folk Museum **8**	
	Lighthouse **19**	
	Municipal Market **3**	
Attractions ●	Harbour Square **10**	Public Gardens **1**
Archaeological Museum **7**	Megalo Neorio **15**	Naval Museum **17**
Bulwark Subbionara **12**	Minaret **5**	Skridlof **4**
Byzantine Museum **18**	Minoos **9**	Venizelos Graves **2**
Cathedral **6**	Mosque of the Janissaries **11**	Venetian shipyards (Arsenali) **13**

INSIDER TIP 》

To see Chania at its best, get in **early** (before 9am), preferably on a **Sunday**. The best place to park for an exploration of the Old Town is at either end of the harbour – behind the medieval bastion at the western end, or in the streets around the Arsenali to the east. Everything you want to see lies within walking distance of these two points.

The town centre

The centre of Chania's Old Town is flagstoned **Harbour Square** (once Platia Sindrivani, now officially Eleftherios Venizelos Square), with its central fountain, shops and cafés on three sides and, instead of a northern side, the great shimmering blue width of the harbour. Here you can hop on a cruise boat, for anything from a half-hour spin in a

Top 10 Family Experiences

1. Enjoying the exhibits in Chania's **Naval Museum**, and the views out of its windows (see p. 139).
2. Competing with each other at the **Golden Fun Park**'s eight-lane bowling alley, pool tables, go-karts or mini-golf (see p. 142).
3. Feeding the animals at '**The Ark**' against the stunning backdrop of the White Mountains (see p. 147).
4. Pedalo-ing on **Lake Kournas** (see p. 148).
5. Eating under the shade of the trees at **Argiroupolis** while water cascades around you (see p. 149).
6. Walking the rugged **Imbros Gorge** (see p. 151).
7. Taking the ferry along the coast from **Hora Sfakion** to Loutro (see p. 152).
8. Absorbing one of modern Greece's most heroic episodes at the **Monastery of Arkadi** (see p. 157).
9. Sitting on the beach at **Maleme**, watching the sun go down over the Rodopou Peninsula (see p. 141).
10. Rafting, riding or mountain biking at the **Diadromes Centre** outside Chania (www.diadromes-chania.gr).

glass-bottomed boat (€5) to a three-hour trip to the quaint little islands of **Thodorou** and **Lazaretta** (€15).

Just to the right of Harbour Square stands Chania's talismanic building – the **Mosque of the Janissaries**. With its large, central buttressed dome, and the surrounding smaller secondary domes, it looks like a spider with its young. One of the first buildings erected by the conquering Turks in 1645, it used to have a minaret, subsequently demolished between the two World Wars. It's now used as an event and exhibition hall.

East of the centre

Continuing eastwards around the harbour to the right, past the port police building, you come to the **Venetian shipyards** ★. When Venice ruled Crete, shipyards were needed to maintain and repair its ships during the winter. So a large shipyard was built in Chania. The first building of the complex you come to is the '**Megalo Neorio**' (the Great Shipyard). It's a large, red-tiled building, with two arched windows flanked by two smaller ones in the side facing the harbour, and a row of small windows on the top floor, just under the roof, on the longer side facing east. Started in 1585, this is one of the earliest buildings of the complex.

Just beyond it, also facing the water, are the seven distinctive '**Arsenali**' ★ – long buildings designed to house the ships

The Naval Museum

while they were being repaired (there's a display explaining all this in the **Naval Museum**; see p. 139). Each one could handle a single ship at a time, and the ends were originally open – they have since been bricked up and fitted with windows and doors. Of a total of 17 completed in 1599, these are the only seven to have survived. The remains of a further two can be seen at the eastern end of the harbour.

Beyond the Arsenali, the quay, all jostling boats and floating docks, curves around to the Venetian walls at the eastern extremity of the harbour.

Here you can see the only remaining gate of the Venetian walls, though all that remains is the **Bulwark Subbionara**, which actually stands in the water.

Carved on it you can see a **Lion of St Mark** (the emblem of Venice) and a coat of arms. The walls themselves are festooned in flowers, and, beside them, there's a nice **children's playground** in a small public park. Curving across to form the northern edge of the harbour is a long sea wall, usually dotted with fishermen, which leads out to the **lighthouse**, looking very much like a minaret, marking the harbour entrance.

Returning towards the centre of town from the end of Minoos, along Tsouderon, you'll pass a romantic-looking **minaret** peeping out above the trees, and the town's large, cross-shaped covered **Municipal Market**. Built in 1913 to celebrate Crete's unification with Greece, the market was opened by Eleftherios Venizelos,

---

TIP ▶ **Shop Local** ◀

If, instead of following the sea wall, you continue to follow the town walls south, you'll come to Minoos, where an excellent **farmers' market** ★ is held on Saturdays.

the locally-born Cretan patriot and eventual Prime Minister of Greece.

Beyond it, the narrow lane called **Skridlof** is chock-a-block with shops selling handbags, purses, shoes and anything made from leather. A right turn at the end takes you down Chania's main street, **Halidon**, passing the relatively modern **Cathedral** on the right, and the **Folk Museum** on the left. Beyond it, and well worth a visit, is the town's **Archaeological Museum** (see below).

A few paces beyond the museum, and you're back in Harbour Square.

Archaeological Museum ★

AGE 5 AND ABOVE

Halidon, 73131 Chania. ☎ *28 21 09 18 75.*

The building that houses Chania's Archaeological Museum is almost as interesting as the collections. Originally the Venetian church of the monastery of St Francis, it became a **mosque** after the Turkish conquest, then more recently a cinema and a military storehouse. The permanent collections trace the history of Chania – look out particularly for the Minoan pottery and tablets inscribed in the **Linear A** and **Linear B** script – and the garden contains a beautiful Turkish fountain.

Open 8.30am–3pm Tues–Sun, but call ahead as times vary (sometimes closed Sun not Mon). Adm €3, €2 concessions. Amenities English spoken.

West of the centre

The western part of the Old Town is wedged between the Outer Harbour and the Venetian walls. To explore it, walk along the quayside towards the harbour entrance opposite the lighthouse. Here are all the restaurants, tavernas and shops you could wish for. Check out the **Mourello**, which has a children's play room, and free cartoons and ice cream. There's an Internet café and a bookshop with a good English-language section. Above street level, the buildings are all beautiful – balconied and shuttered, all in different pastel shades. Even the scruffy ones somehow look right. You can see where that 'Venice of Greece' tag came from.

Just before getting to the harbour entrance spot a huge ship's propeller and a massive anchor. They mark the flag-bedecked entrance to the **Naval Museum of Crete**, housed in a square, brownish building (see p. 139).

Immediately beyond the museum, directly opposite the lighthouse, stands the massive Venetian fortress, the **Firkas** (Turkish for 'barracks'). This held the military garrison – with a commander's quarters and the arsenal – and had a tank which collected rainwater from the roof. In times of siege, a chain would be slung across from it to the lighthouse to close off the harbour. It was here, on the corner tower in 1913, that the Greek flag was first raised when Crete unified with Greece.

Crete, 1944

Beyond the Renieri Gate was Chania's old Jewish Quarter – you can still see the Synagogue. In a tragic story common to many places in Greece and Europe, the Jewish population of Chania was shipped off to the death camps in 1944. For more on the history of wartime Greece, see Chapter 8.

From the quayside beyond the Firkas, the half-hourly tourist train ('**The Little Train**') departs for Chania's main sights – a nice way of seeing things it if you don't want to walk. Adults pay €4, children €2.

Returning to Harbour Square along Theotokopoulou, stopping perhaps for a quick look at the **Byzantine Museum**, enjoy the crowded alleys, quaint houses and overhanging wooden balconies of one of the most unspoilt parts of the Old Town.

Away from the harbour, the rest of Chania is a modern city, with all the facilities (and traffic problems) that entails. The **Public Gardens** are worth a visit

for the cafés under the trees, the play area, the few caged animals (look out for the kri-kri, a species of indigenous goat) and an open-air auditorium sometimes used as a cinema and for folklore productions. You'll find details at Chania's Tourist Information Office (see Visitor Information p. 131).

The Naval Museum ★★★
AGE 5 AND ABOVE

Akti Koundourioti, 73136 Chania. www.tuc.gr/marmuseum. At the western entrance to the Venetian harbour.

Much bigger than it looks on the outside, the Naval Museum is a must. Inside you'll find careful

The 'Little' Tourist Train

reconstructions of Chania in days gone by: beautiful model ships, explanations of how the Venetian Arsenali (see p. 136) worked, what Minoan ships looked like and how they were built, a whole gallery devoted to the World War II Battle of Crete (see p. 141) and much more. It all offers an insight into a Chania (and Crete) that's now firmly in the past.

As a bonus, there are also wonderful **views** ★★ from the museum's windows – north across the mighty Firkas battlements, south and east to Chania's delightful harbour.

Open *9am–2pm daily (Nov–March), 9am–4pm (April–October). Closed public holidays.* **Adm** *€3, €2 students/children, 5s and under free.* **Amenities** *English spoken. Shop.*

Away from the centre

To the west of the harbour, beyond an open-air swimming pool and a small dock, the **City Beach** offers Chania's closest bathing, though it gets very crowded in season, at weekends and on public holidays. Further west you get to a string of beaches – Kalamaki, Platanias and Maleme – lined with hotels, restaurants and tavernas (see p. 141). To the east, a visit to the **Venizelos Graves** (of Eleftherios and his son) is a worthwhile side-trip: the views across Chania are wonderful, and there's a statue to commemorate the events of 1897, when a Greek flag was raised in defiance of the combined Turkish and European powers. The flagpole

was hit by a naval shell, so the Greeks raised the flag manually, with one of their number acting as a flagpole – hence the statue of a man heroically bearing the streaming banner. It's a popular place for Greeks to visit at weekends, and there are several excellent cafés in the vicinity. On returning towards the city, you might want to swing around towards **Souda**, Chania's ferry harbour, to look at the warships moored in the naval base or visit the **Allied War Cemetery**.

Limnoupolis Water Park ★
ALL AGES

☎ *28 21 03 32 46.* **www.limnoupolis. gr.** *8km southwest of Chania, near Varypetro.*

This water park staple has all the usual features: kamikaze slides, the Black Hole, the Crazy River and a variety of multi-slides and tubes, some of them suitable for very small children, together with cafés, shops, a restaurant and lots of child-friendly activities. It does exactly what it says on the tin – and does it well and in a safe environment for families.

Open *10am–6pm May–Sept.* **Adm** *€17, €12 children 6–12 (after 3pm €12/€9), Over 65s and 5s and under go free.* **Amenities** *Cafés. English spoken. Parking. Picnic areas. Restaurants. Shops.*

The Northwest Coast

The western end of Crete, west and south of Chania not only contains some of the best children's attractions, but is also, as you travel towards the west and

The Battle of Crete

The Battle of Crete was one of the bloodiest of World War II. Having been defeated by the German army in mainland Greece, Greek and Allied (largely Australian and New Zealand) forces withdrew to Crete, where they hoped to make a stand. The Nazi onslaught started on 20th May, 1941, and to begin with the Germans suffered horrendous casualties – the first wave of paratroopers and gliders were cut to ribbons even before they reached the ground. But the successful establishment of a bridgehead around Maleme airport allowed more and more German troops and materials to be brought onto the island, until the allies were forced to retreat southwards towards Hora Sfakion on the south coast. From there most of them were successfully evacuated to Egypt. Those who were left simply had to take to the mountains and fend for themselves. The large numbers of Cretans who helped the allies suffered vicious reprisals, though this didn't stop the Resistance continuing to harry the Germans and help to get allied soldiers out of Greece to safety. The greatest coup of the Resistance (with the help of Britons Patrick Leigh-Fermor and Stanley Moss) was the abduction to Egypt of the German commander General Kreipe in 1944. The ferocity of the German response (they wiped out a whole series of villages in the Amari Valley) was a measure of the humiliation they felt at this audacious kidnapping.

south coasts, the most **unspoilt** part of the island.

From Chania to Maleme

It doesn't take long to find stuff for the whole family to do. Before you've even left the outskirts of town, heading along the coast road towards Kastelli Kissamou, on the right next to a branch of the Lidl supermarket, is the brand new **Golden Fun Park** (see p. 142) – an excellent day out.

Continuing along the coast road, you'll come to lots more for the children to do. In **Kalamaki** there's a full-on go-kart track (☎ *28 21 03 30 72,* open 9.15am–3pm and 5.30pm–11pm, for anyone 6 and up, including adults), with snack bar and coin-in-slot rides for younger children. There are also three snack bars, with mini-golf, go-karts other rides, between Kalamaki and Platanias – **Alaoum, Golf Land** and **Fun Park Pantou**, whose prices and terms are all similar – open May to September, with mini-golf at €5 a round for adults, €4 for children, and go-karts €3 for 5 minutes; the children's playgrounds are €6 for as long as you can stick it.

After Platanias, the hotels, restaurants and play areas start to thin out. A short diversion towards the sea at **Maleme** brings a long sandy **beach** ★ with lots of family-friendly bars,

Older Than the Hills

In the pretty little village of **Vouves** stands (what is claimed to be) the oldest olive tree in the world. With a circumference of 12.5m and a diameter of 4.6m, its estimated age is 3000 years. In other words, it was already 1000 years old when Christ was alive. A branch from the tree was sent to the 2004 Olympic Committee, as a symbol of world peace.

cafés and restaurants, whilst inland is the **German War Cemetery ★**, beautifully set on the hill that played a big part in the **Battle of Crete** (see p. 141). This was where German paratroopers seized Maleme airfield on 20th May, 1941, ensuring a German victory – until then far from a foregone conclusion. It was also the first successful invasion by paratroopers in history. A cemetery might seem an odd place to visit with youngsters, but the battle was a crucial event in World War II, and you'll encounter references to it all over the island. The rows of headstones stretching into the distance, laid flat in beds of red flowers, each bearing the names of the two German soldiers buried beneath, will bring home to children the scale of the battle – around 4500 men are buried here. Their ages too might give pause for thought: most were between 19 and 26.

Golden Fun Park ★

Kato Daratso, Chania, ☎ *28 21 03 21 32, www.goldenfunpark.gr.*

A well-thought-out entertainment complex specifically aimed at families, the first thing you'll notice at Golden Fun Park is the huge outdoor inflatables –

bouncy castle, slides, and so on – together with a playground, bumper boats, mini-golf, go-karts (€1 extra) and trampolines. The children won't be able to wait to get at them. Inside there's an indoor play area, large computer-games room, café and snack-bar (pizzas, sandwiches, toasties and other snacks, costing from €3.50–7.50), five pool tables and an eight-lane 10-pin bowling alley. Something for everybody.

Open 10am–1am daily. **Adm** *€7 child.* **Amenities** *Café. Internet access.*

The Rodopou Peninsula and beyond

Back on the coast road, **Kolimbari** is worth a look – unspoiled, with a shingle beach, concrete harbour and attractive tavernas – on the way through to the base of the **Rodopou Peninsula**.

Most of the peninsula is completely road-free, and therefore a walker's paradise (check out the excellent website created by a British expat who lives in the area, *www.cretanvista.gr*). The best place to stop, since it's the last village on the peninsula, is **Afrata ★** – there are several tavernas (see 'Family-friendly Dining', p. 174), and the pretty pebble beach, stretched between two rocky headlands down a winding hill to the right, is a lovely place to spend an hour or two. There are a few sun-beds and a seasonal cantina selling drinks and snacks.

On the way back to the coast road, the monastery at Gonia is open to the public (mornings and late afternoon – dress code applies, see p. 26), and is very proud of the Turkish cannonball still stuck in one of its walls.

Continuing westwards, the town of Kastelli Kissamou is an unpretentious working port that provides a good example of the sort of hidden gems you come across in the unlikeliest of places on Crete. Following the signs for the beach ★, behind low dunes with marram grass and sea holly, you arrive at a perfect crescent of sand with a smart taverna, a patch of sun-beds and parasols, and a little children's playground, all immaculately clean and tidy. It's an ideal place to let the children out of the car for a swim and something to eat. In the

town itself there's a museum and some Roman mosaics; ferries depart the port for Kythira and the Peloponnese.

A Tour of Crete's Western End

Crete's west and southwest coasts are delightfully unspoiled, with some of the island's best beaches.

From Kastelli Kissamou to Elafonisi

Travelling south from Kastelli Kissamou the road climbs and swoops and curls through mountainous countryside, with terrific sea views. Even the pockets of market gardening in the valleys don't spoil the tranquillity of the area. Two wonderful beaches are along this western coast – at Falasarna ★ at the base of the Gramvousa peninsula, and at Elafonisi, much further south. Each requires a detour off the main coast road. Elafonisi, an

Falasarna

uninhabited islet, is famous for its lagoon of pink-tinged sand and aquamarine water. With fame, of course, comes the crowds. Pick your times to visit carefully.

Paleochora

Arriving at the south coast, the main town in the west is Paleochora. The view from the hill above the town gives a clear idea of its layout – it's built on a narrow spit of land that widens at the end to accommodate rather untidy docks and the remains of a 13th-century Venetian castle destroyed by Holy Roman Emperor Barbarossa in 1539. It was never properly restored. Because its grid-planned streets span the narrow base of the peninsula, Paleochora has two beaches looking in opposite directions – a sandy one facing west and a stony one to the east. It takes about 5 minutes to walk from one to the other.

There's little specifically to do in Paleochora – but like so many places in Crete, it's perfect for pottering, having a swim and something to eat (see 'Family-friendly Dining', p. 174). Several of the town's streets are closed off in the evenings after 7pm, so you can walk about in safety. The town makes a good temporary base if you're touring the countryside at this western tip of Crete.

Along the main road back north, you pass two sites remembered for Nazi atrocities during World War II. At Kandanos the village's heroic resistance fighters held up for two days German forces despatched south after their victory at Maleme. Following the inevitable defeat of the Greek irregulars, the Germans completely destroyed the village. There are now German and Greek commemorative plaques in the town square – the German one translates as, 'Here stood Kandanos, destroyed as punishment for the murder of 25 German soldiers, never to be rebuilt'. It was rebuilt (and is now a pleasant village of shops and tavernas), which is presumably why the Greeks let the plaque remain.

North of Kandanos is Floria, where another pair of memorials face each other across the main road, to commemorate civilians gunned down by the invading forces.

East of Chania

East of Chania you'll find some of the most intriguing parts of western Crete.

The Drapano Peninsula

One of my favourite parts of Crete, the Drapano Peninsula is very much off the tour-bus mainstream, yet has a good range of first-rate beaches and off-beat attractions that make it a delight to visit. Several scenes for the film 'Zorba the Greek' were filmed here. From Chania, drive east along the National Road past the Souda Interchange, and come off

The Stone Garden

On the outskirts of Kalives is one of the oddest attractions you'll ever come across – the '**Stone Garden**' ★ of Taverna Koumos. You'll know you've arrived when you spot a huge carving of a man apparently emerging from a block of white stone, and a no-less-massive slab of rock carved with a portrait of a young man and a poem. Behind this tableau stretch the grounds of the taverna, with all sorts of structures and ornaments, built by the owner Giorgos Havaledakis from rocks gathered in the foothills of the White Mountains (see p.150). (To find the Garden, as you enter the village, turn right at the IN.KA supermarket, drive under the National Road, then turn left and left again).

Georgios was born in 1939 – he says that his favourite school subject was break! Since 1990 he spent time fetching stones from nearby hills to build and decorate his Stone Garden. There's a cave, a chapel, a house with a balcony, a museum, tables and chairs, some soldiers, all created out of rough stones. Interspersed are pieces of archaic agricultural machinery. The centrepiece is a re-created *koumos*, or shepherd's hut. There are also sheep and goats (real ones this time), and extensive views across to the White Mountains. There's no charge for wandering around, though you are asked at least to buy food or a drink – it is, after all, a taverna (see 'Family-friendly Dining', p. 174). Some might call the whole thing a folly, but the children will be enchanted.

at **Kalami**. You are now on the old coast road. Head for Kalives. The castle on the right as you drive through Kalami was used by the Colonels during the years of the Junta (see p. 227) to imprison political opponents.

Although there are ever more villas being built in the region, **Kalives** ★ is still unspoilt, with a good range of shops and a really pleasant beach. A nice place to stop for a coffee (or even for a few nights) is the **Kalives Beach Hotel**, where the local river flows into the sea. There's a terrace pleasantly sited next to the river, with two or three fishing boats moored next to it, and a footbridge from the rear terrace out

onto the beach (see 'Family-friendly Accommodation', p. 169).

Next stop on this tour of the Drapano Peninsula is the town of **Almyrida**, with its beautiful Blue-Flag **beach** ★ and row of excellent tavernas. The sea here is shallow and safe for young children. There are lots of family-friendly bars and cafés – try the Irish-run **Sirocco** (see 'Family-friendly Dining', p. 174) – and the restaurants provide wonderful fresh food, since most grow their own vegetables and catch their fish. **Psaros**, for example, comes highly recommended. Most of these establishments are stretched out along the beach, so the adults

A Taste of Authentic Crete

Vamos is at the very forefront of Cretan Agritourism – the movement to replace the young people leaving rural areas in large numbers with sustainable tourism. In 1995 local people formed a cooperative (**Vamos S.A.**) to develop and market a range of traditional products and establishments. It has successfully renovated a variety of houses in the village for letting to visitors, and now runs a taverna (To Sterna dou Bloumosifi), a travel agency which handles the renovated houses, the Arts Café (To Liakoto) and a shop (Mirovolon) selling a range of revived local products – cheeses, wine and spirits, honey, herbs, soap and local crafts. A variety of activities is also on offer, from walking to cooking lessons to participation in the olive and wheat harvests, wine and raki production, and cheese-making. If this sort of holiday appeals – and it's ideal for families with children – check out **www.vamossa.gr**. See also 'Family-friendly Accommodation', p. 169.

can get refreshments whilst the children play in the sand. If you've not already stopped for a break, this is an excellent place to do it. Elsewhere in the village you can hire boats and windsurfers (pre-book on ☎ *28 25 03 4 43*). From Almyrida, climb up through Plaka towards **Kokkino Horio** ('Red Village', which may refer to its geology or its politics). Just before the village is the **glass-blowing factory**. Set up in 1986 to recycle glass, it's open from 8am to 8pm, though you can only see the two glass-blowers at work between 8am and noon, then again from 1pm to 3pm. Outside is a huge mound of broken bottles – the raw materials for the factory – and a display area for the finished glassware. The owner, Andreas Tzompanakis, can arrange for anything you buy to be transported home.

Now travelling south, you come first to the lovely unspoilt village of **Kefalas** ★, all whitewashed walls, winding streets and stately eucalyptus trees, with the usual busts of fierce Cretan fighting men and a charming *kafenio*. There's also a rather nice **children's playground** under the trees.

Bearing right in the square at Kefalas will bring you, five kilometres later, to the district's capital, **Vamos**. It's a small market town with a slow village atmosphere. A couple of kilometres outside Vamos is **The Ark** (see p. 147).

The first village on the road from Vamos towards Georgioupolis is **Kalamitsi Amygdali**, where you'll notice that every house seems to have its own mulberry trees. This is because the women of the village formed a **silk-workers collective**, to weave and sell silk. They buy eggs from Japan, hatch them, feed the worms with

The Ark

is wooded, with a delightful playground, a quasi-religious grotto (St John's Cave), and (bizarrely) a monument to Hippocrates.

The stars of the Ark (they've appeared on American television) are a monkey and a dog. The dog lost its vision in a car accident; the monkey had lost her little brother, so began feeding the dog instead – they're now firm friends and share an enclosure.

Open hours vary – phone ahead. **Adm** €2, €1 children. **Amenities** Café/restaurant. Parking. Picnic area. Playground. Shop.

mulberry leaves from their gardens, then spin the resulting cocoon silk into yarn. There *is* a **shop**, but it's not marked in any way – just ask. Opening hours can be erratic, too.

The Ark ★★ FIND ALL AGES

Kivotos, Vamos, 📞 *69 79 10 68 86.*

Set on a hilltop against the magnificent backdrop of the White Mountains, the Ark **ostrich farm** consists of large enclosures of different varieties of these huge, rather strange birds. Each is carefully labelled, so you know which you're looking at. Other enclosures contain deer, ponies, cows, llamas, pigs and poultry.

If you spend more than €10 in the park, you get your modest entry fee refunded – adventurous little eaters might fancy a crack at the restaurant's inevitable specialities, ostrich-egg omelettes and ostrich sausages! The whole park

Georgioupolis

Continuing south from Vamos, you come eventually to the large river-and-seaside village of **Georgioupolis**. A bridge crosses a boat-lined estuary, just before the village. Immediately after the bridge on the left is the **fishing harbour**, with a booth where you can hire **canoes** and **pedaloes**. This is worth doing if you have the time, because you might see **loggerhead turtles** and **terrapins** in the river, especially in the morning.

Up a short hill after the bridge, and you're in the town's main square. Lined with tavernas, a small supermarket, a post office, an Internet café and a pharmacy, it's a good place to stop if you need to do a bit of shopping. It also contains the **Tourist Information Office**, which offers the usual rather limited range of services that Greek Tourist Offices often do. Just down the road that heads towards the church and the beach from the square, **Children's World** offers a wide range of play equipment in a large, astro-turfed, securely fenced enclosure – swings, ball-pools, slides and rockers (€3 for the day, with an extra €3 for the mini-golf). There's also a taverna on-site with a range of Greek dishes.

From just outside the play area, a tourist train – the **Talos Express** – makes the trip to many of the highlights east of Chania – Lake Kournas (see below), the Ark (see p. 147) and the glass-blowing factory (see p. 146). The beach itself is long and sandy, and the hotels and restaurants that line it will deliver food and drink to you as you sunbathe. Be aware that it's not a good beach for swimming: there are powerful currents and undertows, and the warning flags are often out. Indeed, if you want a swim, go back out of the village the way you came, and just after crossing the bridge, turn right. This brings you to a

much safer and more sheltered beach – **Kalivaki** – with a nice view of tiny **St Nicholas's chapel** at the end of the rocky break-water, and, outside the Taverna Arkadi, a cluster of **model buildings** ★ (including the Parthenon and Arkadi Monastery), which children will love.

Lake Kournas ALL AGES

South of the National Road from Georgioupolos.

Crete's only freshwater lake, **Lake Kournas**, is about 1½ km across, and is in places over 40m deep. The little street running down to it from the main road, and the lakeside either side of it, are lined with tavernas and shops selling ceramic wares. You can hire **pedaloes** (€7), and posters show pictures of the wide range of wildlife you can spot on the lake – including freshwater turtles.

Noticeboards, adorned with lurid pictures of a glamorous blonde, also fill you in on the 'Myth of the Lake' – a sinful

Lake Kournas

Argiroupolis Church

village (now under the lake) was drowned by a vengeful god, the only inhabitant spared being the virtuous daughter of the local priest. She was turned into a water-sprite, who rises each night to feed the lake's wildlife.

Open *Always.* **Admission** *free.* **Amenities** *Cafes. Parking. Restaurants. Shops.*

Argiroupolis

Argiroupolis ★★ is a delightful hill village just over the border in Rethymnon's bailiwick. Clearly signposted, the road climbs up into the hills beyond Kournas through leafy valleys beside rushing streams. Watch out for potholes – they loosen your fillings when you least expect them.

On this route, you'll come first to the **lower village**, where five tavernas spread up a narrow valley beside rushing streams in the shade of huge and leafy chestnut, walnut and plane trees. All the tavernas have a good reputation for their meat and fish, but even if they didn't, you'd want to stop. There's the roar of water everywhere, and the tavernas have all built water-features into their terraces – waterfalls, water bells, water wheels. One, the **Taverna Afivoles**, also has a wooden slide and a couple of swings, so is ideal for youngsters (see 'Family-friendly Dining', p. 174). At night, the whole area is magical.

A short drive up the hill brings you to the **upper village**. Now a sleepy little town with wonderful views out across the mountains, it was once the important Dorian settlement of **Lappa** – you can see its remains in the town square next to the church. Destroyed and rebuilt several times, it acquired its present name in 1822. This chequered history has

TIP

Some Real Local Knowledge

The best way to see everything in Argiroupolis and have it explained is to park up and walk through the archway on the right as you enter the village. Just inside the arch, on the left-hand side, is a herb shop – **Lapa Avocado Beauty Products** – run by Stelios Mannousakis. One-time mayor and owner of one of the tavernas by the waterfalls, Stelios and his Canadian wife Joanna are experts on every aspect of Argiroupolis's history. They will give you a sketch-map of the village with everything worth seeing marked on it – free! You might feel that it would be polite to buy something in their shop, to say thanks.

left a great deal of interest that you might not expect on first entering the village. Check out the small **museum** just past the town square.

A circular tour of the village takes in the doorway of a **Venetian villa** (with the philosophical inscription, 'All things in the world are smoke and shadow'), a church **(Agia Paraskevi)** whose step consists of a baby's sarcophagus from Minoan times, and a magnificent **Roman mosaic** under a protective roof. Elsewhere in the village are extensive pre-Roman and Roman remains, including a **reservoir** said to have been built by the Emperor Octavian in 27 BC which is still in use today.

> **INSIDER TIP**
>
> Doing the whole tour on foot can be exhausting, especially on a hot day. A far better alternative, and one which will be popular with the children, is to do it by **donkey** ★ – ask at the herb shop, or ring Stelios or Joanna (☎ 28 31 08 10 70) who will book it for you. You need to book at least a couple of days in advance. Go for the earliest you can get there, or late in the afternoon – it can still be hot, even with the donkey doing all the work.

The Imbros Gorge and Crete's South Coast

This tour includes some of Crete's most spectacular **scenery**, and its loveliest and most remote south-coast towns.

Crossing the White Mountains

From the National Road, take the turning off to Vrisses/Sfakia. When you get to the very pleasant, shady village of **Vrisses** (in about two kilometres) turn left. The road almost immediately starts to climb up into the foothills of the **White Mountains** (named either after the covering of snow they display in the winter, or the dazzling white colour of their limestone summits, or both), which loom over the road to the right. This is the region of **Sfakia**, famous for the ferocity of its warriors – neither the Turks nor the Germans ever really subdued it. After an exhilarating climb, the road tops a rise and drops down into the **Askifou Plateau** ★★.

And what a sight it is. Overlooked by the remains of a Turkish fortress, the plateau is a

The Samaria Gorge

Crete is renowned for its quality walking, and the most famous walk of all is the Samaria Gorge. But in my opinion it isn't the best option for families. It's too long (the whole route comes to 16 km, a very long way on a hot Cretan day), and because of its fame it's too congested. Forget 'I wandered lonely as a cloud' – you're likely to be one of hordes of tourists who arrive, by car and coach and even taxi to do the walk, shuffling downwards towards the Libyan sea. And it's not as if it's even convenient – you have to get to the head of the Gorge early (and, because of the length of the walk, everybody seems to be starting at the same time), do the walk, get a boat from the village at the bottom, and then a bus back to where you came from. It's a gruelling test for even the very fit – the helicopters and donkeys kept in reserve for rescues bear witness to the frequency of broken legs, heat stroke and heart attacks.

If your children are older, and you're a rambling family, then ignore the warning and give it a go – there are coach trips to the Gorge from all over the island. And check out **www.west-crete.com/samaria-gorge. htm** – not only does it contain all you need to know from an authoritative source, but it corrects several common errors about the Gorge – a sobering warning to guidebook writers about the perils of taking information from other guidebooks unchecked!

patchwork of fields cupped by the surrounding mountains. It looks like some sort of lost kingdom, a Cretan Shangri-La. Thought once to have been a lake, the contrast between the richly cultivated farmland of the plateau and the aridity of the surrounding mountains takes the breath away.

At the bottom of the hill is the village of **Askifou**. If you follow signs off to the left ('War Museum Original 1941–1946') you'll come to the house of Giorgos Hatzidakis, with a private, wonderfully impromptu collection of **World War II memorabilia**. Opening times vary, and there's no admission charge, but donations for upkeep are welcome.

The Imbros Gorge

From Askifou, the road climbs once more into the mountains. After about 6 kilometres you'll come to a taverna on the left – the **Café-Taverna Porofarango**. This sits above the clearly signed entrance to the **Imbros Gorge ★**, which is a better bet for a family ramble than its more famous brother to the west, the Samaria Gorge (see above). It's half the length (8km rather than 16km), it's less crowded, there's no torrent to dodge, and its cheaper – €2. It's also far more accessible,

This way to Imbros Gorge

it's greener, with more flowers, yet in places just as dramatic. The downside is that there are far fewer facilities (there is a drinks kiosk about halfway down, but don't rely on it – opening hours are erratic). The track's also rather rough so wear sensible shoes, don a hat (and make the children wear one, however much they moan), take plenty of water and lather everybody in sunscreen.

Assuming you'd rather walk downhill, there are two ways of negotiating the gorge. Park opposite the Taverna Porofarango, do the walk (2–3 hours), then get a taxi (€25 from the village at the mouth of the gorge – **Komitades** – back up to Imbros) to fetch the car. Alternatively, drive to Komitades, get a taxi to the entrance of the gorge at Imbros, do the walk, and your car will be waiting for you at the bottom. Of course, if you think the family's up to a much longer walk then by all means have a crack at the **Samaria Gorge** (see p. 151).

The south coast

When the road from Imbros hits the coast, it snakes down the hillside in a series of hairpin bends, through clumps of heather-like plants that turn the hillside into a multi-coloured rockery, then allows you a choice of turning west or east.

To the west lies the pretty little port of **Hora Sfakion**. Look out for the ferry kiosk just north of the harbour, and park – it's free. The only way of exploring the coast to the west is by coastal ferry, or if you're feeling particularly intrepid, on foot. So choose your destination, check the times, pay for your ticket, and if you've got time, have a look around the village or stop for a coffee.

Hora Sfakion played a major role in the Battle of Crete; it was the Cretan Dunkirk: 10 000 Allied troops were evacuated to Egypt under attack from Luftwaffe Stukas. It was achieved with heroic help from the local people, many of whom were subsequently executed in Nazi reprisals. There are monuments to both events – to the evacuation near the harbour and to the reprisals above the town.

The ferry from Hora Sfakion travels west along the coast, calling in at **Loutro**, **Agia Roumeli**, **Sougia** and **Paleochora**. Agia Roumeli is the village at the mouth of the Samaria Gorge, and is not worth stopping at – though if you're on the evening boat back to Hora Sfakion, you'll be among hundreds of weary walkers going to rejoin their tour buses. **Sougia** is a little village which, though pleasant enough, is barely worth the stopover. Paleochora is certainly worth visiting if you haven't already done so (see p. 144). Pretty-as-a-picture **Loutro** ★★ really is worth the €4 per person it'll cost you for a return ticket. There are ferries from Hora Sfakion at 10.30am, 1pm, 4.55pm and 7pm. The trip takes about 15 minutes (time for a drink and snack on the boat), costs €4 per person, and you get a good view of the rugged and arid coastline. It's no wonder there's no coast road. Little cave-riddled coves pass by, and the one beach with a taverna at Sweetwater Bay. You can see skeins of footpaths on the mountainsides, a tiny white church, but otherwise it's just rocks and the deep blue sea.

As the ferry approaches **Loutro**, it looks just as a Greek village should. The dazzling white cubes of houses, their windows and doors painted blue, curve around an emerald bay beneath craggy red-tinted rocks. Cafés, tavernas, umbrellas, sunbeds, pedaloes and canoes line the little pebble beach; boats bob in the bay. As you walk down the ramp of the ferry, you'll be accompanied by supplies for the village, carried on wheelbarrows

Loutro

Each year, on the anniversary of the bloody battle at Frangokastello (and for 12 days afterwards), the **ghosts** of the Greek dead, wreathed in mist, march from the local church to the ruined fort. They're known as the Drossoulites, or 'dew men'. According to the myths, anyway. Spooky.

or little motorised carts. Everything needed by the village has to be brought in this way – there's no road.

Though there's nothing specifically to keep the children amused in Loutro, they're bound to love the ferry ride, and you can have a swim, or hire pedaloes or kayaks. There's an Internet café too – at the Daskalogiannis Hotel (named after a local Cretan hero who died at the hands of the Turks; the ferry's named after him as well). It might even be worth a stay – the hotel is very pleasant and not at all expensive (see 'Family-friendly Accommodation', p. 169).

INSIDER TIP ⟫

In Loutro, be ready to go when the return ferry arrives. From when it appears from around the headland to when it drops its ramp is a matter of minutes, and it doesn't hang about.

Frangokastello

East from Hora Sfakion, past the road from Imbros and the bottom of the Imbros Gorge in Komitades, you'll spot signs for **Frangokastello ★**. The castle appears long before you reach the village; park in its grounds.

The castle, and the beach it overlooks, are on a very human

scale – nowhere near as overpowering as they look in photographs. The castle itself is just a shell, though youngsters will enjoy exploring it. Look out for the **Lion of St Mark** carved by the Venetians above the main gate. The beach is beautiful – golden sand, warm shallow sea, rocks to the left, a nice taverna.

There are several more tavernas just behind the castle.

Built in the 14th century by the Venetians, the castle is famous largely for the ferocious battle that took place here on 18th May, 1828. An Epirot called Hatzimichaelis Dalianis led a rebellion against the Turks and took the castle. Greatly outnumbered by the soldiers sent to retake it, Dalianis and a large number of Cretans were killed. There's a memorial to Dalianis and to Nik Deligiannakis (leader of the Cretans involved in the uprising) next to the castle.

On your way back north to the National Road, you could stop at one of several cafés that overlook the Imbros Gorge – the café/taverna **Thea ★** is a good choice.

Rethymnon

Rethymnon sees itself as the intellectual and cultural capital

RETHYMNON

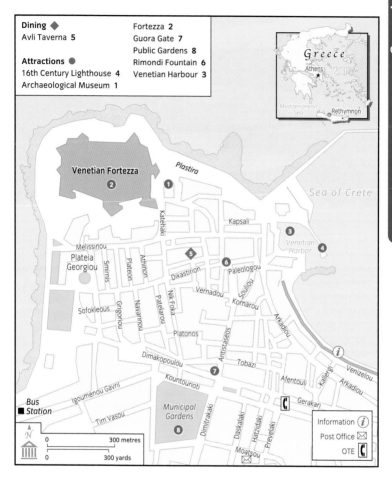

Dining ◆
Avli Taverna **5**

Attractions ●
16th Century Lighthouse **4**
Archaeological Museum **1**

Fortezza **2**
Guora Gate **7**
Public Gardens **8**
Rimondi Fountain **6**
Venetian Harbour **3**

Greece
Athens ★ *Aegean Sea*
Mediterranean Sea Rethymnon

Venetian Fortezza ②
① Plastira
Sea of Crete
Katehaki
Kapsali
③ Venetian Harbor ④
Melissinou
Plateia Georgiou
Smirnis
Plateon
Athinon
⑤
⑥
Dikastirion
Paleologou
Vernadou
Souliou
Kornarou
Sofokleous
Grigoriou
Navarinou
Patelarou
Nik Foka
Platonos
Antistaseos
Arkadiou
Dimakopoulou
Tobazi
⑦
Kountourioti
Afentouli
Kallergi
Arkadiou
Venizelou
ⓘ
Bus ■ Station
Igoumenou Gavril
Gerakari
Tim Vasou
Municipal Gardens
⑧
Dimitrakaki
Daskalaki
Hatzidaki
Prevelaki
Moatsou
N
0   300 metres
0   300 yards
Information ⓘ
Post Office ✉
OTE ☎

of Crete – the Humanities and Philosophy Departments of the University of Crete, for example, are based here. It's Crete's third largest town – to give you some idea of scale, Chania is about half the size of Iraklion, and Rethymnon is about half the size of Chania. So whilst Iraklion and Chania do feel like cities, Rethymnon does not.

Another of Crete's wonderful Venetian ports which also boasts

a huge castle, it lacks the space and tranquillity of Chania, but makes up for it in vigour and verve. Noisier than Chania by day, it's quieter by night. Leave the National Road and drive directly into the centre of town.

INSIDER TIP 》

Probably the best place to park is immediately beyond the Public Gardens, which you'll pass on your right, or along the public

Rethymnon Harbour

beach to the east of the town centre if you can find a place. If you visit on a Thursday, the good news will be the large open-air market at the eastern end of the promenade; the bad new is the heavy traffic and parking problems that result.

Rethymnon is a busy port, with a lot of commercial shipping plying to and fro at either end of the large harbour. In between these two busy docks, there's the long and sandy town beach, lined with palm trees, and the delight-fully bijou Venetian Harbour. If you can get the family to the Venetian Harbour, most of what you'll want to see is a short walk from here. And if you don't want to walk, there's a **tourist train** which sets off from the eastern end of the main harbour, and takes in a lot of the main sights without any walking at all (every half hour from 10am to 11pm. Adults €6, children 6 to 14 €3,

children 0 to 6 free). Family members who don't want to sight-see can, of course, simply stay on the beach.

The first place to visit, and the heart of the town, is the tiny **Venetian Harbour** itself. The quayside is lined with restaurants, tavernas and cafés, and of course boats. With pastel-painted, balconied buildings reflected in the calm water, and the attractive **16th-century lighthouse**, it looks like a picture postcard. Which is why, of course, it appears on so many.

The old town curves around the harbour, its narrow streets, houses and shops thronged with people. The fun of wandering these lanes lies not in anything in particular – the **Archaeological Museum ★**, for example, may be worth a visit, although there's no outstanding star exhibit. It's open from 8.30am to 3pm, closed on Mondays, and costs €3 adults, €2 concessions, with children up to 12 free). But the enjoyment of Rethymnon is, rather, in the detail – the balconies, the Venetian and Turkish ornamentation, the fountains and minarets and churches. Look out for the **Guora Gate** – the only remaining bit of the city walls to survive – and the **Rimondi Fountain**. The one attraction that really does merit a visit is the **Fortezza**, the Venetian fortress. It's open 9am–7pm March to November, last entry 6.15pm, with admission charges: adults €3.10, concessions €2.60, children up to 12 free. Built in the 16th century as the result of pirate raids (including one by Barbarossa) at huge cost in time and materials, it proved totally ineffective against the Turks, who took the town in 1645 by simply bypassing it. It's still an impressive building, with massive walls, ruined mosque and church, armoury and water cisterns. The views from the walls are wonderful.

If you don't have a family breather on the town beach, the best place to head for is the **Public Gardens.** Originally a Turkish cemetery, the gardens are now an oasis of shade on a hot day. Towards the end of July the highly regarded **Rethymnon Wine Festival** held in the Gardens is a colourful experience, with food and dancing, and of course wine. Watch out for over-indulgence, though – once in, you can drink as much as you like, at no extra cost.

Arkadi Monastery, Amari Valley and Agia Galini

If there's one tour which covers nearly all the things that make western Crete a delightful holiday destination – stirring history, religious buildings, towering mountains, quiet valleys and pleasant seaside towns – this is it. It begins with one of Crete's most visited sites.

Arkadi Monastery

The Arkadi Monastery, about 25 km southeast of Rethymnon, is the ultimate symbol of Cretan

Arkadi Monastery

The Arkadi Monastery

Long associated with Cretan resistance to Turkish occupation, Arkadi Monastery was involved in a rebellion in 1866 which aimed to join Crete to Greece. The insurgents soon controlled most of the island's rural areas, but the main garrison towns remained under Turkish sway. The Ottoman authorities, afraid that rebellion might spread, put it down with ruthless efficiency. More than 700 women and children fleeing the fighting around Rethymnon took refuge in the monastery, which had a small garrison of just under 300 armed men under the command of **Lieutenant Dimakopoulous**. Also there were 12 of the 16 members of Crete's Revolutionary Committee, led by **Abbot Gabriel Marinakis**.

Refusal to obey repeated Turkish demands that revolutionary activity should cease and the committee expelled led to a force of 15 000 regular Turkish troops with 30 cannons being despatched from Rethymnon. The Greeks refused to surrender and, on 8th November, 1866, the Turkish army attacked.

There could be no doubt about the outcome, yet the Greeks fought ferociously. The battle raged all day, and attempts by the Turks to bring down the main gateway were foiled. By nightfall the area around the monastery was littered with the dead and dying.

During the night the Turks brought two heavy cannons up from Rethymnon. By morning, it was clear the tide had turned against the defenders. The main gateway collapsed and the besieging Turks poured into the monastery compound. **Hariklia Daskalaki**, wife of one of the Cretan chiefs, was indefatigable in snatching weapons from dead men and passing them to the living. The battle entered its second day, but there were ever fewer Cretans left to fight, and ammunition was running out. Surviving men, women and children under the leadership of **Konstantine Giaboudakis** withdrew into the room where the gunpowder was stored. With Turkish attackers hammering on the doors, they ignited the gunpowder, causing a huge explosion that blew the roof off the building and killed attackers and defenders.

This event became one of the great inspirational stories associated with the birth of the Greek nation, but that's not all. Aided by the newly invented telegraph, news of the massacre spread around the world, earning sympathy for the Greek cause. It was a huge public-relations disaster for the ailing Ottoman Empire.

resistance to the Turks, and occupies the place that, say, the Alamo does in US history. Famous for a siege, battle and explosion that took place during the Cretan rising against the Turks in 1866 (see box above for the full story), the monastery is also worth a visit because of its beauty, and for its lovely setting. And this is not just a tourist attraction – when you get there you're likely to find foreigners outnumbered by Greeks paying their respects. Buses run up to the monastery from Rethymnon as does a tourist train – it costs €15 (with reductions for children) and the round trip takes four hours. If you're driving, head east along the National Road from the regional capital and take the turning off to the right signposted Arkadi (it's a sharp right as soon as you get off the main road, up a short hill and then left). The road up to the monastery climbs through lush countryside, with lots of flowers, olive groves and eucalyptus trees, and passes through two villages – Pigi and Loutra. There's a large free car park next to the monastery, which is open from 8am to 7pm all year, and admission is €3.

Entering through the Western Gateway, take a look at the plan on the wall – it'll help you get yourself orientated. Then just wander about among the beautiful pale brown buildings, dotted with urns of flowers and climbing plants. Built around a square, the monastery consists of the gorgeous Venetian monastery church in the centre, surrounded by arched cloisters, monk's cells, store rooms and food treatment rooms. There's a shop selling icons and other religious paraphernalia, a fascinating small museum, and, in the far left-hand corner of the monastery, the famous gunpowder room, with no roof, and with a melodramatic depiction of the event painted on the far wall.

In the courtyard next to the church is a stark reminder of the massacre – a gaunt fire-blasted olive tree in whose trunk you can still see the remains of a Turkish artillery shell embedded. And take a look at the bullet-scarred refectory door.

Returning towards the car park you can stop in the cafeteria for refreshment, or have a look at the 'Heroes' Memorial' (once a windmill), outside which are busts of some of the famous characters associated with the massacre. Inside, up a flight of steps, is a gruesome cabinet of over 60 skulls of people killed in the battle – many of them showing damage from swords or from the explosion. What small boy could fail to be enthralled?

The Amari Valley

After the violent images conjured up by the story of Arkadi Monastery, it's a pleasure to continue through the mountains towards Thronos, the village at the head of the beautiful Amari Valley. This road, from Arkadi to Thronos, is marked on many maps as a dirt road. It isn't – it's brand new. It passes through ancient olive groves, eucalyptus trees and fertile-looking fields – you could be a million miles from the holiday Crete of the northern coastal strip.

Thronos, built indeed on a hill that looks like a throne, was once ancient **Sybritos**, a 13th-century BC Minoan, and later Greco-Roman, town the remains of whose acropolis can be reached along a path behind the church. The village is developing as something of a hiking centre, as well as a place renowned for its raki.

Beyond the village, turn left towards Fourfouras. The road now travels south along the eastern flank of the Amari Valley. The tiny villages, vineyards and olive groves of the valley contrast strangely with the towering grey-brown bulk of the **Psiloritis Mountains** to the east (they sound more like a faintly disreputable disease, it has to be said, than a highland range!). A five-kilometre detour to **Amari**, the village that gives the valley its name, is worth it just to see the village – a pretty hill settlement whose steeply raked roofs, designed to shed snow, and chimneys for wood fires, seem at odds with one's mental picture of what Greece's southernmost island should be like. Indeed, the Venetian clock tower makes it look more Italian than Greek.

Back on the main road, you soon come to **Fourfouras**, one of the few Amari Valley villages to have a petrol station. It also has a taverna called the 'Windy Place'! You're now in the heart of one of Crete's main hiking areas, and dyed-in-the-wool walking families might want to bide awhile.

A few kilometres onwards, after the village of **Nithavris**, the road splits. If you turn right you get to **Agios Ioannis** and the start of the road up the western side of the Amari Valley. Here any tranquillity brought by the peacefulness of the valley and its

succession of villages – **Hordaki, Ano Meros, Vrises, Kardaki, Gerakari** – is destroyed by its blood-soaked history. The villages of the western Amari Valley were systematically destroyed by the Germans in 1944, both as punishment for the kidnap of General Kreipe (see 'The Battle of Crete' on p. 141), and as an anti-resistance measure. All the men were executed, the houses were set alight, and anything then remaining standing was dynamited. So the villages you pass through were all built from top to bottom after the end of World War II.

If, instead of turning west after Nithavris, you continue straight on, you will arrive at a village – **Apodoulou** – which was the scene of a fascinating, and considerably more uplifting, story. Look (or ask a local) for the ruins of the **House of Kalitsa Psaraki** – they're towards the lower end of the village. During the Greek War of Independence, several young women were abducted from the village and taken off to be sold at the slave market at Alexandria, in Egypt. There young Scottish traveller and Egyptologist, Robert Hay, took pity on the plight of the women, bought them their freedom and paid for their education in England. In due course he fell in love with one of them – Kalitsa – and, in 1828, made her his wife. It was obviously a happy match – he said a year later that he would advise all travellers, 'Never to travel with any other companion than a wife. . . .' Whilst in the village look out, too, for a later Minoan 'passage tomb' – you'll see the surviving lintel at the top of the hill, on the left as you enter the village.

Whichever road you take, if you keep bearing south you'll end up at Agia Galini, a delightful small resort and port on the south coast.

Agia Galini

Once an unpretentious fishing village, Agia Galini has developed a tourist dimension perhaps more quickly than was good for it. Yet, with its white buildings stacked up around a little **harbour**, its sandstone cliffs and flowers and palm trees, it's still as pretty as a picture. Many of its buildings are cafés and tavernas, so it's a good lunch-stop to aim for. And many more are small hotels and apartment blocks, so it's easy to stay if you need an overnight stop. Prices – for both food and accommodation – are very reasonable: there's a lot of competition. Indeed Agia Galini might make for an even longer break, though it can get noisy during the season, and, beyond the beach, the boats and the discos, there's not an awful lot to do.

The **beach** is just around the headland to the east from the harbour, and is accessible either via a footpath or by car from the top of the town. If you walk, notice the **caves**, once used as gun emplacements. Excursions run from the harbour to dolphin-watch, along the coast to **Agios Pavlos**, **Palm Beach** and the monastery at **Preveli**, or out to the **Paximadia Islands**.

The main road back to the north coast is new, fast and of good quality. However, the old road (which I discovered by accident) is, though a bit potholed, much more scenic. It really is worth the extra time. Leave Agia Galini and drive to the northwest, towards the village of **Melambes** – you get terrific

Agia Galini

views of the mountains ahead and back down towards the coast.

Spili

Back on the new road, and about halfway across the island, it's worth stopping at Spili, a pretty village built into the mountain-side. In a shady village square just off the main street, water pours out of the hillside below the terrace of a pleasant taverna, and is also diverted to a long trough via **25 lion-head spouts**. The heavy shade, roar of rushing water, block-paved streets and pleasant shops and tavernas make it a good place to stop, or if you're into walking, even stay: Spili is at the centre of a network of footpaths. Look out, too, for eagles, riding the thermals.

The Minoan sites

You really can't holiday in west-ern Crete (or indeed anywhere else on the island) without visit-ing at least some of the Minoan sites. Such is their worldwide celebrity and, indeed, their his-torical importance, that wher-ever you're based there will be excursions available to get you to see them. For adults, this is almost certainly the best way to do it – you don't have to worry about parking, and you'll benefit from the professional knowledge of accredited guides. The mini-mum, and most popular, combi-nation is to visit the site at Knossos and the Archeological Museum in nearby Iraklion.

For families with children though, such excursions can be counter-productive. A long day being herded from pillar to post, no say in where or when you stop for refreshment or toilet breaks, guides who make no allowances for the level of understanding or attention span of children – by the end you're likely to have offspring who are hot, tired and very grumpy! So I've designed this tour specifically for families with youngsters.

Iraklion

The best place to start is Iraklion itself. Whether you're coming in from the west or the east along the National Road, follow the signs for Iraklion, and then for the port. Just after the **ferry dock** and **bus station** (coming from the east) or just after the **Venetian Harbour** (coming in from the west), turn into the large car park next to the Coastguard and Port Authority building (there's a large square building beyond the car park you can't miss – it has huge pictures of footballers on it, and a sign saying 'Welcome to Heraklion'). Though the drive into Iraklion might have its hairy moments, once you're driving alongside the sea it's a doddle – there are lots of roundabouts, so if you overshoot it's easy to double back.

Once parked up, this is an excellent place for a family base. There's a delightful taverna, a first-class modern **playground**, a

IRAKLION

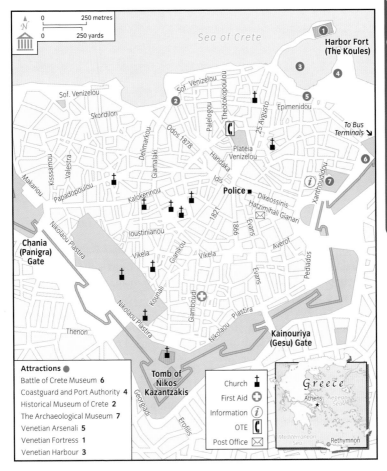

Attractions ●

Battle of Crete Museum **6**
Coastguard and Port Authority **4**
Historical Museum of Crete **2**
The Archaeological Museum **7**
Venetian Arsenali **5**
Venetian Fortress **1**
Venetian Harbour **3**

Church †
First Aid ✚
Information ⓘ
OTE 🎵
Post Office ✉

small **park** with interesting bits
and pieces (a boat, a dilapidated
steam locomotive), nice views of
the ferries coming and going
into the dock to the east, the
boat-jammed Venetian harbour
to the west and the massive
Venetian fortress directly opposite. It's also within easy walking
distance of the main part of the
city centre, and it's easy to find
on your return. Older teenagers
could therefore be allowed off

the leash to explore the capital in
their own way.

A 500m walk south will bring
you to the **Archaeological
Museum** (see p. 164), which has
the most comprehensive collection in the world of Minoan
artefacts, from Knossos and elsewhere in Crete. Whilst it's the
Archaeological Museum that is
the essential ingredient in this
tour of Minoan Crete, it would
be a pity not to take in some of

Iraklion Port

Iraklion's other attractions – the capital usually gets short shrift in guidebooks, I think unfairly, so at least consider visits to the **Battle of Crete Museum** (essential for an understanding of the battle) and the **Historical Museum of Crete** (which covers Crete's non-Minoan history). See p. 165 for both.

Worth a look too are the **Venetian fortress**, overpoweringly massive and beautifully restored, and the **Venetian Arsenali** – like the ones in Chania, they were used to house the building of new ships and the maintenance and repair of old ones.

Apart from specific sights, Iraklion can be a pleasant, if hot and crowded, place to just wander around.

The Archaeological Museum ★★★ AGE 5 AND ABOVE

1 Xanthoudidou, ☎ *28 10 22 46 30.*

The Archaeological Museum of Crete is a must-visit for anybody wishing to appreciate how spectacular Crete's Minoan civilisation was. Some of the exhibits are simply stunning, though you will clearly need to tailor your visit to the ages of your children. The museum has been in the throes of extensive and exhaustive renovation, so no two sources seem to agree when it will be finished, and what limited exhibitions are on show until then (☎ *28 10 22 46 30* or ☎ *28 10 22 64 70* to ask). At the time of writing (July 2007), I was told that it is open from 8am to 7.30pm, admission €4 (€2 for children). But they didn't seem very sure!

Among the most famous exhibits that you're likely to come across are the bare-breasted **snake-goddess** that has spawned a million souvenir-shop copies, the black **bull's head rhyton** (drinking vessel), the carved **draught board**, the **leopard axe**

El Greco (1541–1614)

Renaissance artist Doménikos Theotokópoulos was a real one-off. He didn't belong to any 'schools' of painting, and he didn't found any either. Born in Iraklion in 1541, he moved to Venice, probably in his early 20s, to study painting in the studio of **Titian**. By 1677 he had resurfaced in Spain – at first in Madrid, and finally in Toledo, where he lived for the rest of his life.

Known throughout the world as **El Greco** ('The Greek', though he always signed himself in full), he is famous for his vivid use of colour and as he got older, the elongated shape of his human figures. Though this was probably a stylistic trick, it has been speculated that it was the result of increasing astigmatism. Whatever the reason, El Greco's paintings, though very much a part of the **Spanish Renaissance**, look astonishingly modern.

You'll see El Greco's best work in Spain, or in major collections around the world – he never returned to Crete once he'd left for Italy. But there is an **El Greco Park** to commemorate him in Iraklion, and you can see his alleged birthplace in Fodele, on the road between the main inland Perama to Heraklion road (route 90) and the coast road (route E75). The only El Greco painting on Crete alas is 'The Landscape of the Gods – Trodden Mount Sinai', at Iraklion's **Historical Museum** (see below).

and the **ivory bull-leaper**. A wonderful sense of what life was like in Minoan Crete can be gained from all the **vase-paintings**, **carvings** and **everyday objects** from the period. It just doesn't seem possible that this rich wealth of detail was created thousands of years ago

Open 8am–7.30pm Tues–Sun, 12.30–7.30pm Mon (Mar–mid Oct. From mid Oct to Mar, closes at 5pm). *Adm* adult €4, child €2. Combined ticket for Museum and Palace of Knossos €10. *Amenities* Shop.

Battle of Crete Museum ★★
AGE 5 AND ABOVE

Doukos Bofor/Merambelou Road, ☎ 28 10 34 65 54. Next to the Archaeological Museum.

The Battle of Crete was one of the most important of World War II, notable for the first successful invasion by paratroopers, who landed at Maleme (see box 'Battle of Crete', p. 141). The museum contains a wealth of photographs and artefacts relating to the island's invasion and occupation 1941–1945.

Open 9am–3pm Mon–Fri. *Adm* free.

Historical Museum of Crete
★★ AGE 5 AND ABOVE

7 Lysimakos Kalokerinou, ☎ 28 10 28 32 19, www.historical-museum.gr

Not much visited by tourists, who have eyes only for the Minoans, this museum has a lot of good stuff about the rest of Crete's history. Look out for a painting (the only one in Crete) by the island's famous son El Greco, and the reconstruction of the study of its most famous writer, Nikos Kazantzakis (his tomb is to be found in the city's southernmost bastion, but it's too much of a step to visit on foot unless you have a major Kazantzakis fan in the family).

Open *9am–5pm Mon–Fri,9am–2pm Sat (April–Oct); 9am–3pm Mon–Sat (Nov–Mar), with an evening session 6pm–9pm on Wednesdays.* **Adm** *Adult €5, concessions €3, under–12s free.*

Knossos and around

Part Two of the Minoan tour, and an essential complement to the visit to the Archaeological Museum (like love and marriage, you can't have one without the other) is the **Palace of Knossos** about 5 kilometres south of the capital. It's along a busy, sometimes chaotic but generally well sign-posted road. Park up, pay up and enter the palace (see p. 167).

There are other Minoan sites scattered across central Crete, from individual houses or tombs to full-scale palaces. They're likely to be far less crowded than Knossos, and far cheaper. The two biggest sites, both of palaces, are at **Malia,** east of Iraklion (excavated by the French), and **Phaestos,** to the southwest (excavated by the Italians). Both excavations were carried out in ways far more likely to win the approval of modern-day purists than Sir Arthor Eva's work at Knossos but alas for the non-specialist, and for children, they don't come near Knossos in nurturing the uninformed imagination. So for families with children, bite the bullet, put up with the crowds, and go to Knossos.

If you've followed the main route of the tour so far – you've visited the Archaeological Museum in Iraklion, braved the heat and the crowds at Knossos – and could do with a quiet, under-stated finalé, head south from Knossos towards the village of **Myrtia**. As the hurly-burly around the great palace is left behind, the road climbs up into hilly cultiva-tion-carpeted countryside, through a series of intersections – one of them is where the auda-cious kidnapping of **German General Kreipe** was carried out by partisans and British special forces in 1944 – and then high along the ridge between two valleys. Ranks of olive trees and grapevines line hillside terraces that stretch away like the sea in all directions. It looks like a thick green quilt thrown over the sur-rounding hills.

When you get to Myrtia, park up in the main street and have a wander around. It's a large hilltop village of narrow lanes, pastel-washed houses, little shops and café-tavernas. If you get there in the afternoon, the village will be empty – almost everybody will be taking their siesta. Enjoy the peace and tranquillity.

Finally, follow the signs to the museum dedicated to Crete's greatest writer, **Nikos Kazantzakis** (see p. 167) – it's in a main square paved with pale flagstones and dotted with terracotta pots of shrubs and dramatic pieces of modern sculpture.

To return to the National Road by a different route, follow the signs for 'green road' – it meanders down the hillsides towards the coast, and comes out eventually near Iraklion's airport.

The Palace of Knossos ★★★
AGE 5 AND ABOVE

Knossos Road, 📞 28 10 23 19 40. Knossos the suburb, and then the site, are well signposted on all approaches. As you do so, note the bust of Sir Arthur Evans standing near the entrance.

Until the beginning of the 20th century, Knossos was thought to be mythical. Convinced to the contrary, in 1900 British archaeologist Sir Arthur Evans bought the land where he thought the ancient palace might have been situated and started excavating. Bingo. As the dig continued over the following years, one of the most amazing archaeological sites ever to be discovered was slowly revealed.

There has since been huge controversy among archaeologists about Evans's methods and conclusions. It is alleged that he found what he expected to find, cheerfully jumping to conclusions with very little evidence to support them. He was castigated for his reconstructions, which, it was said, owed more to imagination that to careful scientific analysis. All this may be true. But with children in tow, one can only be thankful for the reconstructions – they bring this 3500-year-old civilisation to life in a way that unrestored ruins never could. So follow the timber walkways, admire the massive columns, marvel at the great staircases, the sophisticated plumbing, the storerooms, the *pithoi* (huge storage jars for wine and olive oil), Europe's oldest throne, the Royal apartments and the incredibly vivid frescoes (suspiciously vivid? I don't know). These last, in particular, make the intervening three-and-a-half millennia dissolve – athletic young men famously jumping over charging bulls, and beautiful girls with long corkscrew-curled black hair and pristine white gowns.

If you're in Knossos at any time from June to September, accept that the site will be packed, and that your visit may largely consist of serial queuing. Accept, too, that you'll be dodging hundreds of organised tours – it's the price you pay for seeing one of the world's greatest archaeological discoveries. Only you can decide if it's worth it, and that will depend on how interested you are, and on the age of your children.

Open Mon–Fri 8am–8pm (April–mid-Oct) and 8am–5pm (mid-Oct–March). Weekends: 8.30am–3pm. Adm Adults €6, concessions €4, under-18s free, Sundays free for all Nov–Mar. Free parking just before entrance. Guides available – make sure they're accredited.

Kazantzakis Museum ★★

FIND   **AGE 5 AND ABOVE**

Myrtia 70100, ☎ *28 10 74 16 89,*
www.kazantzakis-museum.gr/
index.

The museum dedicated to
Crete's greatest writer, Nikos
Kazantzakis, is housed in a substantial villa that once belonged
to the great man's grandfather.
You might well be the only visitors – a notice on the door says
'The Museum is open every day
9.00–19.00. Please knock at the
door'.

It's a lovely house, and the
huge collection of memorabilia
creates a wonderful mental picture of the writer. There are
busts of him at different ages,
masses of photographs, old editions of his books in translation
from around the world, newspaper cuttings, some of his personal effects (pipes, a kettle, a
teapot), and, most interesting of
all, posters, stage-designer mod-
els and costumes from theatrical
productions of his plays, and a
set of stills from different productions of 'Zorba the Greek'
(including the famous film version starring Anthony Quinn
and Alan Bates).

Open 9am–7pm all week Mar– Oct.
10am–3pm Nov–Feb. *Adm* €3 adult,
€1 child. *Amenities* English spoken.

For Active Families

There is no doubt at all that
western Crete is one of the very
best places, not only in Greece,
but in the whole of Europe, for
holidays that involve physical
activity. Here are just a few:

Trekking

*www.greek-travel.info/adventure.
html* (Samaria and Irini Gorge).

Kayaking

*www.greek-travel.info/adventure.
html* (Kournas Lake).

Canyoning

*www.greek-travel.info/adventure.
html* (in all main gorges).

General (mountain biking, trekking, climbing, parascending)

www.icna.gr

Walking

www.hfholidays.co.uk
www.walksworldwide.com
www.exploreworldwide.com
www.responsibletravel.com
www.worldwalks.com

Diving

*www.greek-travel.info/adventure.
html*
www.scubakreta.gr (Iraklion
area).
www.diversclub-crete.gr between
Iraklion and Rethymnon.

Horseriding

www.unicorntrails.com
www.zoraidas-horseriding.com
(stables in Georgioupolis).
*www.greek-travel.info/adventure.
html*

Jeep safaris

www.blueaegean.com offers jeep
safaris, caving and paragliding,
mountain biking, trekking and
yoga.
*www.greek-travel.info/adventure.
html* (in White Mountains).

Skiing

*www.greek-travel.info/adventure.
html* (in White Mountains).

Cycling

www.cycling.gr (useful site, but not complete).

www.hellasbike.net (Opposite the Bank of Cyprus in Chania). Offer a wide variety of cycling tours of different difficulties. Prices range between €35–55, and parent-and-child tandems and baby seats can be provided.

www.adventurebikes.org (Georgioupolis).

Dolphin-watching

www.interkriti.net/minicruise

Sailing

UCPA – on the beach at Almirida (there is a website, but it doesn't cover Crete).

Cooking

www.cookingincrete.com (combines cooking with sightseeing).

Greek language with Greek dancing

www.cactuslanguage.com (Based in Chania – two weeks. Check on UK courses too).

Shopping with Children

Chania has all the usual tourist shops that you'll find on any Greek island. But there are things to look out for. A number of designer jewellery shops line El Greco Street, whilst in nearby Zambeliou Street, in Roka Carpets, you can see Mikaelis Manousakis working at his 400-year old wooden loom. In Kondilaki Street you might buy traditional worry beads (*komboloi*), used to de-stress their owner (and distress everybody else!). For a decent set of *komboloi* expect to pay around €45 (i.e., they're not cheap, and they can go as high as €12 000!). Skridlof Street is famous for its leather goods, and beyond it you might want to wander the huge cross-shaped market hall just to absorb the atmosphere – this is where most Chaniots buy their fish and meat. Beyond the north exit of the market you'll see a lot of wine, herbs and olive oil for sale, and, along Sifaka Street, the knifemakers, who sell anything from ceremonial knives to swords to carving knives.

FAMILY-FRIENDLY ACCOMMODATION

EXPENSIVE

Grecotel Kalliston ★

Glaros, 73100 Nea Kydonia, Chania, 28 21 03 44 00, www.grecotel. com. On the beach side of the coast road west of Chania.

Not too large (it calls itself a boutique hotel), the Kalliston not only oozes quality in every aspect of its provision, but has everything a family with children is likely to need – separate kid's clubs offering morning and afternoon activities for three to 12 and 13–17 year olds, outdoor as well as indoor play areas, a children's pool, a lovely private beach. They will arrange (and supervise!) children's dinners on request, and (again on request) arrange babysitting. On top of all this, there's a range of daytime sport and night-time entertainment put on, and the hotel's location couldn't be better – it's just four-and-a-half kilometres west of Chania (there's a direct bus service from outside the hotel), western Crete's most beautiful town. And along the same strip of road, there are children's play areas, some lovely restaurants, a go-kart track, and the biggest, and newest, play facility in Crete (see 'Golden Fun Park' on p. 142, above). The Kalliston offers the sort of range of services and facilities that you usually get in the large resort hotels, yet remains on a human scale.

Rooms 127. **Rates** €125–325 double (suites €138–836; VIP suite €1239–2147). Rates are per room per night, and include B&B (half board available); children up to 2 stay free in parents' room, 2 to 12 get 60% discount, 13 upwards 50% discount. **Credit** AMEX, MC, V, DC. **Amenities** Babysitting. Bars (3). Children's clubs (one for three to 12 year olds, one for 13–17 year olds). Cots. Disabled access. Gym. Laundry service. Pools (1 indoor, 2 outdoor, 1 for children). Restaurants (3). Shop. Spa. **In room** A/C. Fridge. Internet access. Safe. TV/DVD/Satellite.

Alexandra Beach Hotel, Chania

Agia Marina, 73014 Chania, ☎ 28 21 03 65 99, www.alexandrabeach. com. On the beach side of the coast road west of Chania.

Along the same stretch of coast as the Kalliston, and therefore with the same wealth of children's attractions nearby (there's a play park directly across the road), the Alexandra Beach is child-friendly, with a mini-club, children's pool, playground, daytime activities,

highchairs in the restaurants and so on. Its two greatest strengths are that all rooms have a kitchenette consisting of fridge, microwave, toaster, coffee-maker and kitchen utensils, so that you can eat in when the youngsters get sick of restaurants, and that it can offer tremendously flexible accommodation – from double rooms (with the option of a cot), through suites (two to five people) to family rooms (four to seven people). The latter are particularly useful in that they offer two bedrooms and a separate lounge.

Rooms 138. **Rates** €180–220 per night for suites suitable for families. Accommodation only. **Credit** AmEx, MC, V DC. **Amenities** Bars (2). Children's club. Cots. Pools (1 indoor, 1 outdoor, 1 for children). Restaurants (3). Spa. **In room** A/C. Safe. TV/Satellite.

MODERATE

Kalyves Beach Hotel ★ FIND

Kalyves Apoloronou, 73003 Chania, ☎ 28 25 03 12 85, www.kalyves beach.com. On the left, immediately after crossing the bridge over the river.

The Kalyves Beach is a fine hotel for families with children if what you're looking for is peace and quiet. In the centre of an attractively low-key village on the Drapano Peninsula, and therefore within walking distance of a range of cafés, restaurants and shops, it is beautifully located at the point where a river (the Xydas) runs into the sea. The hotel has its own access to a stunning sandy beach (across a little footbridge), and the

Kalives Beach Hotel

The Louis Creta Princess Hotel, in Maleme has over 400 rooms, just under half in the main building and the rest in 'garden rooms' dotted about the grounds. All rooms are double, and all can be adapted for children with up to two additional (bunk) beds. Cots are available, but are limited, and so need to be booked in advance. Last renovated in 2005/2006, the Louis Creta Princess offers a variety of activities for adults and children. It's particularly strong on sports and games, but also has a terrific playground – check out the wonderful pirate ship – a variety of children's activities and all the bars, restaurants and swimming pools that you're likely to need. There's also an excellent beach with a range of water sports. Although Maleme is very much adapted to cater for holiday-makers, it does have a life of its own, so that, as well as having a sun and sand beach holiday, you can feel that you're learning something about life in Crete. And the sunsets are wonderful!

Rooms 420. *Rates* €44–93.50 per person per day; children 0–one free, older children (two upwards) sharing parents' room 50%. Rates include half board. *Credit* AmEx, MC, V, DC. *Amenities* Bars. Children's club (four to 12). Pools (2 adult, 1children). Parking. Restaurants (2). *In room* A/C. Safe. Fridge.

wrap-around terrace follows the line of the river (with three lovely old boats moored) and the beach. Interconnecting rooms are available for families, and there's a small range of children's toys out on the patio beside the windmill. Not an all-singing, all-dancing hotel, and therefore maybe a little quiet if you have lively teenagers, but a wonderful place for a holiday with younger children.

Rooms 100. *Rates* €120–140 per night, double/suite, depending on size and season. *Credit* AmEx, MC, V. *Amenities* Babysitting. Bars (2). Gym. Parking. Pools (2 outdoor, 1 indoor). Restaurants (2). Spa. *In room* A/C. Fridge. Safe. TV.

Louis Creta Princess Hotel, Chania ★

PO Box 9, 73014 Platanias, Chania, ☎ 28 21 06 27 03, www.louishotels. com. In the village of Maleme, 17km west of Chania.

Best Western Porto Veneziano, Chania

Old Venetian Harbour, 73132 Chania, ☎ 28 21 02 71 00, www.porto veneziano.gr. At the eastern end of the Venetian harbour.

Sky Beach Hotel

The Porto Veneziano's great attraction is its location – on the quayside overlooking Chania's inner Venetian Harbour, right next to several Arsenali. This means that the views from any of its front-facing balconies are just stunning. It also means that you are within walking distance of all the best bits of Chania. In fact, all the cafés, restaurants, shops, and excursions available in Crete's second largest, and I would argue most beautiful, town are right there on your doorstep. The disadvantage of the hotel is that there is little provision for children – no entertainment, kid's club, playground or anything else. There's a pretty garden, and that's about it. Furthermore, if you have more than one child, you're into booking two rooms. So not really viable for an extended stay, especially if you have several children, but a wonderful stop-over to explore Chania if you're touring.

*Rooms 57. **Rates** €113–150 per room per night, triple room (two adults, one child aged 3 to 15). Rates include B&B; children up to two stay free in parents' bedroom. Credit AmEx, MC, V. DC. **Amenities** Bar. Laundry service. Parking. Restaurant (breakfast only). **In room** A/C. TV/Satellite.*

INEXPENSIVE

Sky Beach Hotel, Agia Galini

*Agia Galini, 74056, ☎ 28 32 09 14 15. **www.skybeach.gr**. Just above Agia Galini's beach.*

Any visitor to the pretty southern Cretan seaside resort of Agia Galini has a wide range of hotels to choose from. They're stacked up around the little harbour like a house of cards, and most are clean, tidy and reasonably priced. What the Sky Beach really has going for it is that it's just outside the town proper, and therefore a lot quieter. It tumbles down the hillside overlooking the town's pretty little beach. So although it doesn't have much in the way of facilities, you've got a beach, a beach shop and a taverna right on the doorstep, and the facilities of the town a five-minute footpath walk around the headland. Inside the hotel, there's a café/bar, a lift (important in a hotel which drops all the way from the main road at the top to the beach at the bottom), and all rooms have a large balcony. The rooms are fairly basic, but they're spacious, airy and clean. They all have a kitchenette – ideal when you get bored with eating out.

Rooms 11. **Rates** *two-bedroom apartments €100 per night.* **Amenities** *Bar.* **In room:** *A/C. TV.*

Areti Hotel, Agia Galini

Agia Galini, Rethymnon, 📞 *28 32 09 15 14, www.interkriti.net/hotel/ aggalini/areti. On the right, just as you come into the town from the east.*

If you're happier in a hotel rather than an apartment-hotel environment, then the Areti is a good example of what's available in the village. There are no facilities specifically for children, but a café/bar, swimming pool and satellite TV room will go a long way towards keeping everybody happy. And room rates are so low that booking separate rooms for

adults and youngsters won't break the bank.

Rooms 47. **Rates** *€40–50 per double room per night. Rates include buffet breakfast.* **Credit** *AmEx, MC, V, DC.* **Amenities** *Bar. Parking. Pool (outdoor).* **In room** *A/C. TV.*

Hotel Pal Beach, Paleochora

73001 Paleochora, 📞 *28 23 04 15 12, www.palbeach.gr. The hotel is at the very end of Paleochora's western beach (the one on your right as you enter the town), just before you get to the castle.*

One of 15 small B and C class hotels in Paleochora advertised by the local Hotel Owners Association (*www.paleochora-holidays.gr*), the Pal Beach offers clean and pleasant rooms on two floors facing the beach. Suites have double or twin bedroom with sitting room containing double sofa-bed. In-hotel facilities are limited to a snack-bar, but everything that Paleochora has to offer is within easy walking distance – cafés, restaurants, shops, banks, etc.

Rooms 16. **Rates** *€80–100 double with extra bed, €135–152 suite for four people. Rates include buffet breakfast.* **Amenities** *Cots. Extra beds. Non-smoking rooms.* **In room** *A/C (2.30pm to midnight). Fridge.*

Vamos S.A. Guest Houses ★★★ FIND

Vamos Apokoronou, 73008, 📞 *28 25 02 32 51, www.vamossa.gr.*

If you're looking for a completely different western Cretan holiday from the usual hotel/villa/apartment-based ones, an alternative that's really worth considering is the traditional houses which you can book through the Vamos S.A. cooperative, set up in the main village of the Drapano Peninsula in 1995. What they've done is to renovate old houses and other buildings to let them out to visitors. So you can choose from an inn, a wine storage building, a doctor's house, an old olive oil mill and a variety of renovated 18th, 19th and early 20th-century houses, together with new houses built using traditional methods and materials. Don't worry that this is going to involve some sort of back-to-the-land spartan austerity – the 'guest-houses' as they call them come with all mod cons, and many also have shared or completely private swimming pools. They also come in a variety of sizes, so you should be able to find one that exactly fits your family. And although the name of the game is quiet rest, there's plenty to see and do in the surrounding area, and you can get involved in all sorts of activities, from walking to cooking to helping with the harvest.

Rates *€75–80 per night for a one-bedroom house suitable for a family of four. Bigger houses can be up to €120 per night. For families who just want to stop over for a day or two, there is accommodation in the cooperative's art-café the Liakoto, and meals are available in the taverna 'Bloumosifis'.*

Guest-houses *These have traditional furniture, fully equipped kitchenette, refrigerator, TV, A/C, fireplace, furnished balconies, verandas or garden with views across the village or the White Mountains. Some also have* central heating, so off-season holidays are a definite possibility.

Daskalogiannis Hotel ★ FIND

Loutro Sfakia, Chania, 📞 *28 25 09 15 14, http://loutro.com/daska.htm. You'll need to get the ferry from Hora Sfakion or Paleochora – there's no road to Loutro (which is, of course, one of its delights!).*

A pretty little hotel in the pretty little southern town of Loutro, the Daskalogiannis offers cool, clean bedrooms, all with balconies looking out across the bay. The café has outside tables and chairs next to a small boat dock, and also Internet facilities. The rates below are the ones quoted by the hotel – you may find cheaper through holiday companies. The hotel is closed from November to March.

Rooms *11.* ***Rates*** *€45–65 (doubles), €55–80 (triples). Prices are per room per day, and include breakfast.* ***Credit*** *AmEx, MC, V, DC.* ***Amenities*** *Bar.* ***In Room*** *A/C. Fridge. Television.*

FAMILY-FRIENDLY DINING

EXPENSIVE

Avli Taverna ★★★

22 Xanthoudidou Street, Rethymnon, Crete, Greece. 📞 *28 31 02 62 13. In the centre of the old town, near the Rimondi Fountain.*

In the heart of Rethymnon's old town, the Avli Taverna has been called one of the most beautiful restaurants in Crete. In an old Venetian building that was a soap factory until Katerina

Xekalou turned it into the restaurant, it has the lushest décor, the most intimate lighting and the most beautiful garden you're ever likely to come across. The food is top class – a mixture of Cretan and more general dishes, and it has an extensive wine list. Neither the food nor the wine is cheap, but it's a lovely place to treat yourself. Is it family-friendly? Not particularly, but surely the adults get to have a good time once in a while!

Open *10.30am–12.30am.* **Main Course** *€18.50–25.* **Credit** *AmEx, V.* **Amenities** *Highchairs. Reservations required in August and September, and at weekends.*

MODERATE

Taverna Kosmas ★

Kosmas and Ines Linoxilakis, 74056 Agia Galini, ☎ *28 32 09 12 22, www. kosmas.agiagalini.com. Just behind the harbour.*

Run by a Greek, Kosmas, who does the cooking, and his German wife, who looks after front of house, the Taverna Kosmas has a long history in various guises spanning a century. The menu is largely Greek, though with some more adventurous options such as Thai. The speciality of the house is food cooked in olive-wood-burning ovens. In addition to the provision of a children's menu and highchairs, there's a ton of stuff in the restaurant for the children to look at – photographs, paintings, a ram's horn, antique furniture – all giving a real feel for Cretan history. There are also small toys and colouring books to keep them occupied. Above all, though, what you get at Taverna Kosmas is a very real warm Cretan welcome.

Open *noon–3pm, 5.30pm–midnight, all week.* **Main course** *€5–17.* **Credit** *MC V.* **Amenities** *Children's menu. Entertainment (toys and colouring books). Highchairs.*

Koumos, Stone Garden ★★ FIND

Kalives Apokoronou, Chania, ☎ *28 25 03 22 57. As you enter Kalives, turn right at the IN.KA supermarket, drive under the National Road, then turn left and left again.*

The attraction of the Koumos (it means 'beehive', but also refers to the beehive-shaped huts used by shepherds) is the astounding 'stone garden' created by the taverna's owner, George Havaledakis. You can guarantee that wandering around it will keep the children occupied throughout your visit. If not, there are always animals to look at (chickens, puppies, cats, goats, sheep) – the Koumos is a small farm as well as a taverna. And if the taverna has another unique selling point, it has to be the relaxed and friendly attitude of its owner to his guests – when we were there, it wasn't yet open, and he was busy getting ready for the day, so he let us make our own coffee!

Open *10am till late.* **Main Course** *€9–20.* **Amenities** *Entertainment ('stone garden', farm animals). Highchairs.*

Ostria, Paleochoria ★ FIND

Paleochoria, ☎ *28 23 04 19 86. On the road that runs along the western (sandy) beach.*

The Ostria is a large restaurant which is ideal for families with children. Just across the road from Paleochora's sandy beach and a rather nice tree-shaded playground, it has a caged bird that children flock around (no pun intended), colonial-looking fans that keep the air moving, and, at the back of the restaurant, a little folk museum containing a variety of household implements – a loom, a fiddle, textiles and much more. The man lying asleep on a settee isn't one of the exhibits, though – he's the owner! The food consists of good traditional Greek dishes, well cooked and plentiful, and the service is prompt.

Open 12 noon–1am, all year.
Main course €7–19**. Amenities** Entertainment (Greek evenings Wed, Cretan evenings Fri. Small museum). Highchairs.

Afivoles ★★★

Argiroupolis, 📞 28 31 08 10 11/8 24 52. The first of a clutch of tavernas grouped along a series of waterfalls, just before the road climbs up to the village proper.

One of several tavernas in this lovely setting along a series of waterfalls under the trees, the Afivoles offers a range of traditional Greek dishes, and is happy to split meals and adjust portions to suit smaller appetites. Its strengths for families are the small play area at the end of one of the terraces (a slide and a swing), and the water courses that thread their way between tables and tumble down little waterfalls. I watched a small boy

work his way down from terrace to terrace, following the water and working out where it went.

Open 10am–4pm at weekends till end of June, July–Sept open all week 10am–late. It's all very complicated so phone and check. **Main course** €6–18. **Amenities** Highchairs. Play area.

East of Eden ★★★ FIND

Pirgos Psilonerou, 📞 28 21 06 20 83. On the beach just west of Maleme.

A wonderful traditional Greek taverna, specialising in Cretan dishes, East of Eden has extensive seating in the main building, on a terrace and out on the beach itself. The service is friendly, the food excellent. During the day children can move back and forth onto the beach as the family eats, and at night a slide in the centre of the main building becomes a focus for them to meet and talk. The management and staff go out of their way to make visitors feel welcome – when we were there, a power cut threw the kitchens into disarray, yet the restaurant continued to take orders for the food they could still cook, whilst car headlamps provided the light until a generator could be brought in!

Open 8am–late May–October. **Main course** €7–15. **Amenities** Play area.

Irida ★★ FIND

Kalamaki Kidonias, Chania, 📞 28 21 03 27 22. Right on the beach at Kalamaki, west of Chania.

Offering a good range of Cretan meat and fish dishes, and its own wine, the Irida is usually thronged with Greeks from Chania and the local area – always a good sign. The food's excellent, there's a children's menu, and above all there's direct access onto a lovely sandy beach, with safe shallow water, a lifeguard tower, and rock-pools beyond the beach to explore. The restaurant provides free sun-beds, and will deliver ice-cold drinks, coffee and snacks onto the beach, or you can wander in to order full meals. A lovely spot for a couple of hours or a full day.

Open *9am–late (midnight, 1am) May to October.* **Main course** *€6–12.* **Amenities** *Children's menu.*

INEXPENSIVE

Sirocco

Along Almyrida's main street are numerous cafés and restaurants overlooking the beach, and all have a good reputation. The Sirocco, for example, is Irish run, has a covered terrace on the beach (some of the tables are actually on the sand), and has a wide enough choice of both Greek and English meals and snacks to satisfy even the most picky children. Highchairs are available, and the youngsters can play on the sand whilst parents have a drink or something to eat. There's a karaoke every Friday, and frequent pub quizzes.

Open *8.30am–late all year.* **Main course** *€4.50–8.* **Amenities** *Entertainment (quiz nights, karaoke). Highchairs.*

Mythos Bar ★

Maleme, ☎ 28 21 06 20 46. On the beach at Maleme.

One of a group of bars and restaurants on the beach at Maleme (a good place for children – nice beach, and several bar/restaurants with well-equipped play areas), the Mythos Bar has a children's menu, a children's pool at the rear and a variety of bar games (Connect 4, etc). Adults are catered for with a terrific range of cocktails and tasty snacks, and the owner, Nikos, is married to an Englishwoman (Linda) who is a Sunvil rep, so if she's around, pick her brains – she knows a ton of stuff about good things to do and places to go in western Crete. Their son Danny is often around, too, and keen to play with customers' children!

Open *9.30am till last customer leaves at night.* **Credit** *MC, V.* **Main course** *€4–9.* **Amenities** *Children's menu. Entertainment (children's pool, bar games).*

The Good Heart ★★ FIND

Afrata, Crete, Greece. ☎ 0824 22077. Straight ahead of you as you come into the village.

A typical village taverna/ouzeri, the Good Heart is an experience. Run by a husband and wife team, the setting is delightful – at the top of a flower-bedecked flight of steps, you sit at bright blue tables and chairs in the deep shade of a vine-wreathed roof under which hang brightly-coloured gourds. On the terrace is a charcoal grill and a wood-burning oven. The menu seems almost English greasy-spoon, but you need to ask what's available, and what's good – when we were there, it

The Good Heart

was kid and potatoes done in the oven, and it was absolutely superb. The restaurant has its own chickens, rabbits and goats, and its own vines. So the meat, eggs, cheese and wine are all home-grown or homemade – not only ecologically sound, but fresh and delicious.

Open 9am till late, all year. **Main course** €6–12. **Amenities** Reservations. If you want certain rabbit or chicken dishes, you'll have to wait up to an hour, or you can phone ahead and order.

6 Evia

EVIA

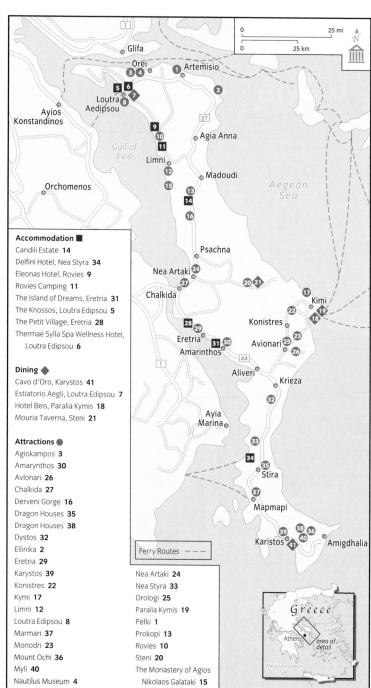

Evia is a very different island to the other three covered here in almost every respect. It is very Greek, where the others are cosmopolitan – you'll come across few non-Greeks in Evia even at the height of the season. It doesn't require a ferry or a flight to get to it – it's joined to the mainland by two bridges. You *can* get there by boat – six ferry crossings bind it to the mainland along its considerable length – and it's the only Greek island you can visit by train.

It's also right at the heart of Greece. Evia is so close to the capital that Chalkida and the southern half of the island have almost become suburbs of Athens. Because of this proximity, it has become a favourite place for Athenians to buy holiday homes, go for weekend breaks or spend longer holidays. Greeks throng to the seaside towns of the island, and the spas of the north. But although Evia has developed a good tourist infrastructure of hotels and beach facilities, it is such a large island (second in size only to Crete) that, even at the height of summer, it never feels crowded. Its mainstay remains farming; as you drive around on its excellent roads, you're more likely to be held up by tractors than tour buses.

Mountainous and well-watered in the north, hilly and windy in the south, Evia is fertile throughout, and very beautiful. Yet it is given only the most cursory of treatment in most guidebooks – some omit it altogether. This is one of its great attractions: it really is that favourite cliché of travel writers, a hidden gem.

There is little in the way of tourist attractions: no water parks or resort hotels, no historical set-pieces like the Old Fortress in Corfu or Knossos in Crete. There's evidence of rule by the Venetians and the Turks – the odd castle, the towers that dot the landscape – but not much that's open to the public. So if lots to do and an active sightseeing programme are a must, Evia's not really for you. For more high-powered sightseeing, you can visit the Sporades to the east (see Chapter 7), the Pelion peninsula to the north (p. 203) or the ancient sites at Marathon to the west (p. 201). Even Athens isn't out of the question.

If you want a quiet holiday, however, in unspoilt countryside offering an insight into authentic modern Greek life, to chill out and learn something of the language and culture, Evia is just the place. It is as close to the 'real Greece' as you'll find on a holiday. When I asked my (Greek) brother-in-law whether he thought Evia was suitable for this book, he nodded and said, 'It's an island for families.'

ESSENTIALS

Getting There

By plane The nearest international airport to Evia is in Athens – British Airways and Olympic Airlines both fly there. From Athens there are buses to all the coastal towns that have ferry links with southern Evia, and trains to Chalkida, the Evian capital. Realistically, though, with a family this is going to cause a lot

Chalkida

of palaver, not to mention the cost of cabs from airport to bus or railway station. So your best bet is to hire a car – the drive from Athens Airport to the ports with Evian ferry links, or to the bridge that links Evia to the mainland, is simplicity itself: the new Attiki Odos motorway (€2.70) sweeps you through the Athens suburbs with no fuss, and it's very clearly signposted. Ask for the excellent free map of the system when you stop to pay your toll.

By car If you want to take your own car to Greece, the best route is across Europe to one of the Italian ports (Venice, Ancona, Bari), a ferry across the Adriatic, then a pleasant drive across Greece from Igoumenitsa or Patras. Once in the vicinity of Evia, you can cross on one of the ferries – Glifa-Agiokampos or Arkitsa-Loutra Edipsou if you're coming from the north, Rafina-Marmari, Agia Marina-Nea Styra or Oropos-Eretria if you're coming from the south. Crossings

vary from 30 minutes to an hour. Alternatively you can follow the National Road to Chalkida, whether you're approaching from the north or south, and cross on the bridge.

VISITOR INFORMATION

Evia is not well served by Tourist Information facilities. If you're having any problems, get in touch with the tourist police:

● Chalkida Tourist Police Service: 153 Arethousis Street, Chalkida, ✆ 22 21 07 77 77.

● Edipsos Tourist Police (Summer only): 3 Okeanidon Street, Edipsos, ✆ 22 26 02 46 55.

As for other sources of information, try:

www.aroundevia.com

www.euboea.de/englisch

Getting Around

Although very long and thin, Evia is a large island – it's almost as big as Crete. So unless you intend to stay in one spot, it is important to sort out your transport.

On foot All Evia's towns are small enough to be explored on foot, even Chalkida.

By bus The bus service on Evia is perfectly adequate, and operates largely from Chalkida. However, the idea of loading a family with all its paraphernalia onto a local bus is somewhat daunting, and not to be recommended unless all other avenues have failed. However, when you've settled into your accommodation, the buses are a convenient way of getting back and forth into town.

By car By far the best way of exploring Evia is by car – either your own or a rented one. The main roads on Evia are good, and the side roads perfectly adequate. Being very mountainous, however, the roads can be extremely bendy – don't bank on an average speed of above 50 kilometres per hour. Parking is usually not a problem, even at the height of summer. Interestingly enough, unlike any other part of Greece I've been to, the main road-kill you'll see on Evia is snakes – I suspect that Greek drivers go out of their way to run them over. You often come across tortoises lumbering slowly across the road as well, but they don't seem to get killed – Greek drivers, I suspect, avoid them, either through kindness, or because they're worried about damage to their cars.

By boat The ferry links that bind the island to the mainland are fast and cheap. You don't need to book – just turn up, buy your ticket from the booth, park where you're told to, then, if you have time, go for a coffee. Some of the ferries are roll-on – roll-off, whereas on others you may have to reverse up the ramp. If you do, obey the instructions of the deck hands – they know their job. Ferry journeys can provide a pleasant break – they're a good opportunity for the children to stretch their legs, buy refreshments and use the toilets. Such is the length of Evia, and the bendiness of its roads, that if you found yourself needing to travel the length of the island, it might be quicker to cross to the mainland, use the National Road, and cross back.

Planning Your Outings

The main thing to remember is the slow speed of travel – if you're used to averaging 80 kilometres per hour and you end up managing 50, the day can seem a lot longer than you expected, and the children can be a lot crabbier by the time they get to the destination. Also try to get the family to have a siesta – afternoons on Evia are dead, with lots of stuff closing down, to re-open in the evening. There are few experiences more pleasant than to have an afternoon snooze followed by a shower, then sally out refreshed as the sun begins to set, to join all the Greeks who are doing the same.

FAST FACTS (SEE ALSO CHAPTER 2)

Airport See 'Arriving by plane'.

Banks and ATMs Bigger towns all have banks and ATMs, and hotels will usually change traveller's cheques. However, in smaller towns you may be caught out, so if you intend to do a lot of hinterland exploring, it's better to stock up with a reasonable amount of cash when you can.

British Vice Consulate There is no British Vice Consulate in Evia – not enough Brits visit to make it worthwhile. The nearest is in Athens: 1 Ploutarchou Street, 106 75 Athens, *21 07 27 26 00*, open 8.30am–1pm Mon–Fri.

Buses *22 21 02 26 40.*

Business hours See Chapter 2. Most of the tourists who visit Evia are Greek, therefore you'll find Greek opening hours (a morning session that starts early and ends around 1–2pm, then an evening session from about 7pm onwards) are the norm.

Credit cards The general reluctance to use credit cards, noticeable in many parts of Greece, applies even more in Evia.

Internet access Bigger hotels usually offer Internet access, either in-room or in a dedicated 'Internet corner' on the premises.

Most holiday towns have Internet cafés, which can vary from a café with a couple of machines to a large, youth-thronged games room with minimal refreshments.

Police Chalkida: *22 21 02 21 00;* Eretria: *22 29 06 11 11;* Kymi: *22 22 02 25 55;* Karystos: *22 24 02 22 52.*

EXPLORING EVIA

Chalkida

Sometimes called by its ancient name of **Chalkis**, the capital city of Evia spreads over hills on both sides of the straits that separate the island from the mainland. Almost exactly halfway along Evia's 160 km length, it is the hub of its transport system.

Often dismissed as too industrial to merit the interest of visitors, it is in fact a lovely city which sets the tone for the island – workaday, yes, but with the atmosphere of a place where ordinary Greeks go about their lives unsullied by mass tourism.

About 50km north of **Athens** just east of the National Road to Thessaloniki, Chalkida is in every way the gateway to the island – if you're visiting Evia by road, you have to pass through the capital. It's joined to the mainland by two bridges – one, a new **suspension bridge**, just south of the city, the other, an older **swing bridge** right at the heart of the city. Arriving at the suspension bridge, it's worth parking just to get your first

CHALKIDA

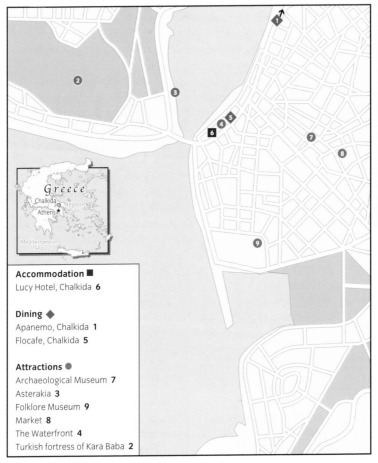

Accommodation ■
Lucy Hotel, Chalkida **6**

Dining ◆
Apanemo, Chalkida **1**
Flocafe, Chalkida **5**

Attractions ●
Archaeological Museum **7**
Asterakia **3**
Folklore Museum **9**
Market **8**
The Waterfront **4**
Turkish fortress of Kara Baba **2**

view of the island. There's an imposing statue to one of the island's most important sons – **Georgios Papanikolaou**, the inventor of the 'pap' cervical smear test. It's absolutely in keeping with the island's unpretentiousness that the man it most honours is little known outside Evia, never mind Greece, but that his fame arises from a mundane innovation that has saved thousands of lives. There's

a nice **view** of the city and the straits and though it is marred by a huge cement works, even this seems in keeping with the island's no-nonsense practicality.

Once across the bridge, and now on the island, take an immediate left and follow the signs for 'Centre', heading downhill towards the waterfront.

Chalkida's **waterfront** is lined with palm trees, hotels, restaurants and cafés – it's the social

Top 10 Family Experiences

1. Enjoying the rides at **Asterakia** against the lovely backdrop of Chalkida's waterfront (see p. 187).

2. Driving through the hill-town-dotted countryside south of **Kymi** (see p. 189).

3. Picnicking on one of the river-beaches north of **Prokopi** (see p. 191).

4. Looking at the seashells and other sea life exhibits in the **Nautilus Museum** at Agiokampos, then having a drink in the café (see p. 193).

5. Bathing in a sea warmed by hot springs in **Loutra Edipsou** (see p. 193).

6. **Standing on deck** as your ferry plies between Evia and the mainland, watching the land you've just left slip behind, and the land you're heading for approaching (see p. 182).

7. Experiencing the peace of the **monastery of Agios Nikolaos** Galataki, listening to the sigh of the wind and the cackling of the chickens (see p. 196).

8. Jumping from boulder to boulder as you cross the stream uphill from **Steni** (see p. 197).

9. Clambering around on the huge monoliths of one of southern Evia's **Dragon Houses** (see p. 198).

10. Playing in one of the **quayside playgrounds** in Nea Styra or Marmari, watching the ferries come and go (see p. 199).

centre of the city, stretching north from the swing bridge. People crowd pavement tables, dangle fishing lines in the water and sit on park benches, taking in the view of the mainland just across the water. Balloon sellers and musicians add a festive air. The water runs so powerfully under the swing bridge that it's hard to believe that this is a marine strait and not a river estuary. Called the **Euripos** channel, it's famous for the bewildering and apparently random changes in the direction of the flow. Wander up and down, or stop at one of the cafés – try the **Flocafé** (see 'Family-friendly Dining', p. 208) – the coffee and snacks are good, and the service excellent.

Though there are few 'must see' attractions in Chalkida, there are several worth checking out as you potter around the city. On the hill behind the waterfront is the **fish, meat and vegetable market** (authentic but smelly), and a bit further up the **Archaeological Museum** AGES 5 AND ABOVE (Venizelou 13, ☎ 22 21 02 51 31). It's open 8.30am–3pm, Tuesday–Sunday; admission is €3. It contains a wealth of finds, not only from the capital, but from all over the island. Further south, the

Parking in Chalkida

Parking in Evia's capital can be difficult. It's a busy city, so you'll need to grab a parking space where you can. Alternatively, when you get to the waterfront, cross the swing bridge (bringing you back onto the mainland) and turn right – there's a free car park on the quayside. In fact, depending how long you've been in the car, this might be a really good place to let the children let off steam, because it's right next to a rather good fun fair (see below).

Folklore Museum ★
AGES 3 AND ABOVE (Frizi, ☏ 22 21 02 18 17) is well worth a look, with its collections of everyday artefacts from guns to guitars, costumes to coins, household implements to hookahs. It's open Wednesday 10am–1pm and 6pm–8pm, Thursday–Sunday 10am–1pm; admission is free.

Finally, on the mainland across the Euripos on the hill above the town are the remains of the **Turkish fortress of Kara Baba**
AGES 5 AND ABOVE (no admission restrictions, free). They're impressive from the outside, and even on the inside, despite everything being overgrown, the broad shallow steps and continuous crenellated walls still have undoubted atmosphere. And the **views** from the walls (accessible via stone ramps) across the capital are excellent (though keep a tight hold on younger children). And on the quayside below the castle, take a look at Asterakia, a lovely little

fun fair on your way back to the swing bridge.

On leaving Chalkida, wherever you're going in Evia, the road travels south for a kilometre or two along the coast (signposted 'N and S Evia'). It then splits – to go to central or south Evia, continue straight; to head for northern Evia, turn left.

Asterakia ★★ FIND ALL AGES
Choc-full of rides and games, Asterakia fun fair has bumper cars, boats, trampolines, carousels, coin-in-the-slot games and rides, table football, gliders, a small train, all overlooking the Euripos and the pretty waterfront opposite. There's also a small café at which to take refreshment.

Central Evia

The area to the east of Chalkida – along the coast to **Lepoura** then north to **Kymi** – has a distinct character of its own, and comes in two parts. Once clear of the capital's eastern sprawl, the

Ending it in Evia

Legend has it that philosopher **Aristotle** ended his life in the Euripos channel when, in despair at not being able to explain the changes in the direction of the water flow, he threw himself in.

Don't get Lost

In Greek script southern Evia is 'N. Evia'. This can cause major confusion – allow for it, or only read the Latin script signs. To travel south and east, the sea should be on your right. To travel north, the sea should (eventually) be on your left. If the sea's on the wrong side, you're going the wrong way!

south-facing coast along the shores of the South Euboean sea is pleasant beach country. Beyond Lepoura, when the road has turned north, the landscape becomes almost mountainous, dotted with hill towns, and very pretty. This whole area is a fine destination for **family holidays**, and central enough to allow a number of touring options.

Eretria and Amarynthos

The first town distinct from the capital is **Eretria**, with a lot going for it. Built on a horseshoe-shaped bay which has been extended to create a harbour for the frequent ferries to and from the mainland (at **Oropos**), it has all the shops and facilities that you're likely to need – banks, supermarkets, an Internet café and a variety of small shops – whilst retaining a small-town feel. The layout of the town is a predictable strict grid-plan and there's an island on the eastern side of the harbour attached to the mainland by a causeway, which gives it considerable individuality. The island not only has some lovely beaches (and a nice hotel-cum-holiday camp – see 'Family-friendly Accommodation', p. 204), but the road along the causeway has

uninterrupted cafés and tavernas that are pleasant by day and lively by night. There can be few greater pleasures than to sit at one of these tavernas, eating, drinking and watching the mainland ferries come and go. Incoming ferries disgorge mainlanders bound for the same strip of tavernas.

Eretria has other family-friendly aspects. It's close to Chalkida – a 20-minute drive, tops – so you've got the best shopping on the island. Before you actually get there, there's a really nice **go-kart track** with cafeteria attached on the left, (though at €6 for 6 minutes, it's not cheap). **Ancient Eretria** was a town of considerable importance, and you'll see remains dotted around the town. In particular, there are the ruins of the baths and some terrific **mosaics** in the centre of town, and the huge theatre to the north of the main road. The **Eretria Museum** (☎ 22 21 06 22 06) is a delight – the Greeks are good at this sort of thing – with a cool garden full of interesting statues and grave stones or 'steles', and nicely displayed artefacts in the museum's two rooms. In fact it's so tastefully done that the awe-inspiring antiquity of some of the things you're looking at might escape you: some of the exhibits are over 3000 years old.

The next town heading east, **Amarynthos**, is by comparison a little anodyne. It's pleasant enough, with a long seafront and an open town square. Just before you get to the village there's a small boat dock and a **children's playground**. In the village itself there's a string of tavernas and restaurants along the front, with views out to sea. There's also a kiosk with a group of coin-in-the-slot rides for children. Before and after Amarynthos are several large hotels, the nearest, apart from the north coast, that Evia comes to a holiday area. After Amarynthos, the road snakes along above the sea, past some serious fish-farms. Down a side road to the coast is **Karavos**, with its little harbour and several typical tavernas.

Beyond Lepoura

At **Lepoura** the route divides – off to the right is the main road to the southern tip of Evia, whilst straight on is the regional capital of Kymi.

Continuing north, the hilltops sport **Venetian towers** or **hill towns**, set in increasingly fertile countryside. Attractive **Avlonari**, off to the right and surrounded by meadows, has red roofs stacked up on a hill, its summit dominated by an imposing tower and magnificent church.

Beyond Avlonari, the road splits again. To the left is the inland route to Kymi, to the right the coastal route to Kymi's port (Paralia Kymis), the only ferryport on Evia's east coast.

Kymi is a picturesque town, crowded onto a hillside. In the platia stands an imposing church, and beside it are an excellent fenced modern **playground** ★ (open 10am–12.30pm and 6pm–11pm; free) and a bust of **Georgios Papanikolaou** – he of the 'pap' test fame, who was born in Kymi. Above the *platia* houses climb up to a Venetian tower; below it the roofs of the town drop down the hillside towards the sea. It's all very Greek, and is far enough off the tourist trail for local children to take an interest in obvious foreigners. Kymi gives an excellent idea of what life is like in a small Greek rural town. You can buy freshly baked bread and freshly ground coffee. Men sit in the *kafenio* talking machine-gun Greek and playing *tafli,* (backgammon), or reading the paper. And to add depth to the picture, just below the town a **folklore museum** (open daily 10am–1pm and 6–8.30pm, free) displays a huge array of objects and photographs from the town's past that have drifted down through time to the present.

A steep winding road snakes down the mountain four kilometres to **Paralia Kymis**, Kymi's port. The ferries nudging in on a crest-flecked sea is a sight to see. Paralia Kymis has a couple of hotels, some tavernas, and ferries to Skyros, the nearest of the Sporades.

A 20-minute drive back down the coast along a scenic road past a long surf beach, an inland stretch through farmland and

The Scenic Route to Kymi

Taking the inland route, the road winds through a series of attractive villages, with lovely views across valleys and hills. **Monodri** has a long main street running up to a river bridge with a weir and clouds of dragonflies. Above it is the upper part of the town topped by a church. Pretty **Orologi**, all whitewashed walls and tree boles, is also dominated by a church on the hillside above it. **Konistres** is a no-nonsense market town with a good selection of shops, cafés and tavernas, and again nice views. All in all, this is an excellent area in which to potter around, adapting to the slow pace of rural Greek life. But you might need your phrase book – not many of the local people speak English.

olive groves, and you're back at Avlonari.

Northern Evia

Chalkida's northern sprawl extends as far as **Nea Artaki**, though you could stop at one of two large **toy shops** along the route if the youngsters are getting mutinous. Beyond Nea Artaki (created during the 'exchange of populations', see p. 191) the road climbs into attractive hills, with extensive views opening up back the way you came. The **Panorama Restaurant**, with fountain and children's playground, makes a pleasant stop after the stress of getting out of the capital. Still the road swings upwards, now among pine forests and alpine meadows; in 1843 Bavarian Ludvic Ros drew comparisons between northern Evia and the Tyrol. It's exhilarating driving – a good surface, lots of sweeping but not too acute bends, fine mountain views opening up on both sides with

glimpses of sunlight reflected off a distant sea.

When you've topped the pass, the road starts to plunge downwards through the **Derveni Gorge**. Deciduous trees now mix with evergreens, clearings are dotted with red, white, blue and yellow beehives, or with logging camps, and the road descends next to a raging stream between towering cliffs – 'Attention – falling rocks!' Then you're out of the gorge, bowling along towards the large village of Prokopi between fertile-looking fields and stalls selling honey, tomatoes and other farm produce.

Prokopi is a pleasant small town with lots of cheap eateries. Its 1960s-built **Church of St John the Russian** is architecturally uninteresting, but has a fascinating story behind it. This St John was a Ukrainian (not a Russian) who was captured by the Ottoman army in the 18th century. He died in Turkey and, it was claimed, his mummified remains started to work miracles. So in 1922, when Muslim and

Orthodox populations in Turkey and Greece were exchanged (see below), Greek Orthodox priests brought the remains with them to Prokopi. The town itself was named after Prokopi in Turkey, where most of its residents originated.

The town is also noted for the **Candili Estate** of the Noel-Bakers, which sits on a bluff overlooking the town. A famous British political family, they bought the estate in 1832 and still run it today (see 'Family-friendly Accommodation', p. 204).

Beyond Prokopi, the road meanders alongside a pretty river, deep in the shade of the trees that line it. There are pebble river-beaches and

wooded islets: lots of places to stop for a picnic and a swim. At **Madoudi** you can either bear right over the bridge into the town (which is worth a stop), or continue on the main road to Agia Anna. You're now in open farmland, dotted with reels of irrigation pipes and plumes of water. After **Kirinthos** the road climbs up once more into the mountains. **Agia Anna** is a pleasant hill-town, with a beach some distance east, which has camping bungalows and a swimming pool (📞 *21 03 60 22 02, www.club agiaanna.gr*) The landscape is alpine once more, with grazing herds of goats, filling the air with clanging bells, the odd little church sitting in forest clearings, the smell of pine coming

Greek Expansion & the 1922 Exchange of Populations

When Greece became independent in 1832, it consisted only of the central and southern mainland, and three groups of islands – the Argo-Saronic islands, the Sporades and the Cyclades. The driving force behind Greek foreign policy from then on was the 'Great Idea' – securing the rest of the Turkish-occupied but ethnically Greek area of the mainland and islands. Things seemed to be going well, with parts of the northern mainland becoming Greek in 1881, much of the rest and several of the islands during the Balkan Wars of 1912–13, and Crete in 1913. Then, after World War I, the Greek government claimed the largely Greek city of Smyrna (now called Izmir) on the coast of Asia Minor and ruled by Turkey. It backed up the claim by sending forces to occupy it. In the summer of 1922 they were heavily defeated by Turkish forces. Many Greeks were evacuated from Smyrna; those who remained were massacred. In the Treaty of Lausanne the following year an exchange of populations between Greece and Turkey was agreed – 390 000 Muslims from Greece were resettled in Turkey, and more than 1.3 million Christians were moved the other way. Though initially housed in shanty towns, they were eventually successfully integrated – the towns that developed from their settlements often start with 'Nea'.

Evia & the Noel-Baker Family

The connection between the Candili Estate in central north Evia and the Noel-Baker family started in 1832, when Edward Noel, a relative of **Lord Byron**, bought the estate. Friendly foreigners had been invited by the new Greek government to buy up property being vacated by departing Turks, since so few local Greeks could afford them. The estate has been owned and run by the Noel-Baker family ever since (the 'Baker' was added in 1919 when Philip Baker married Irene Noel, who had inherited the estate). A very distinguished family – as Liberal and Labour Members of Parliament – probably the most famous was Philip, a prominent Quaker peace campaigner who won the Nobel Peace Prize in 1959 and became a lord in 1977. His son, the honourable Francis Noel-Baker, now owns the estate, which *his* son Philip runs. Famous visitors to the Candili Estate have included author Virginia Woolf and opera singer Maria Callas.

through the windows strong enough to strip paint, and views far across the sea to **Skyros** glimpsed between the trunks of the trees.

The North Coast

As the road comes down from the mountains, you arrive at **Vassilika**, its long beach visible as you approach. Immediately you get the first indications that you've arrived at the north coast, one of Evia's main tourist areas. There's a 'welcome' sign in several languages, and hoardings for hotels and 'studios' (i.e. studio apartments). But we're still not talking ribbon development here – it's all very low key, and each town has its separate character, with the countryside in between fertile and pretty. Everywhere there are ploughed fields, meadows and lanes, dotted with blue-and-white bee hives

and olive groves, with views across an azure sea towards the mainland, and large, very Greek houses – mainly second homes for prosperous Athenians. The beaches are nothing to write home about – dusty and a little down-at-heel. **Ellinika** is probably the best of the bunch – small and clean, with a little islet offshore with the inevitable church. **Pefki**, popular with Greek holidaymakers all summer, has a long and broad beach beside the road, with parasols and sun-beds. The bathing is safe, but again it's very dusty, and there's not much in the way of facilities. Plenty of cafés though, and the odd playground.

Continuing along the coast, it's worth stopping off at **Orei** to see the marble statue of a bull down near the harbour – it dates from the time of **Alexander the Great**. From **Agiokampos** there are ferries to Glyfa on the mainland, and there's also a rather interesting sealife museum.

Nautilus Museum ★★ FIND
ALL AGES

☏ 22 26 0316 62 – *halfway down the road leading to the town from the main coast road, on the right.*

Pleasantly set in its own gardens (a good opportunity for children to run around), the Nautilus Museum's collections are made up of shells, minerals and rocks. It's not really a serious scientific endeavour – displays include shell-mosaics, and the main merchandise on sale in the shop is jewellery made of silver-mounted shells and minerals – but I suspect that youngsters will love it. There's an English-language pamphlet, an audio-visual presentation, a café and toilets.

Open 10am–2pm, daily. **Adm** €4 *adults,* €2 *children.* **Amenities** *Café. English spoken. Parking. Shop.*

Loutra Edipsou

There is no doubt where most Greek holidaymakers are heading when they come to this part of the world. It's **Loutra Edipsou** ★★, long famous for its healing spa waters. When you get to it, you've turned the corner of Evia's northwest coast, and are heading back south towards Chalkida.

With a reputation for being posh and 'top-end', it can seem on first acquaintance a bit downmarket, especially if you arrive during the afternoon. Everything's dead, the shops shut, the cafés and restaurants empty. But as the sun sets the town blossoms, fishing boats return to the harbour, traffic builds up, teenagers beep each other on their mopeds and motorcycles, or play cards at café tables, Greek tourists come out for the night, and the **large playground** on the beach is suddenly thronged with children and their parents. The frequent ferries from **Arkitsa** on the mainland add to the merriment, and the whole town comes to life. So, do what Greek parents do in Loutra Edipsou – park yourselves in one of the cafés

Pefki

Statuesque

West of Pefki is the site of a major naval battle between the Persians and the Greeks in 480BC. It's also the area where one of the most famous statues of Ancient Greece was hauled out of the sea – the one of a bearded **Poseidon**, left arm stretched forward, right arm clearly about to launch his trident. The original is now in the National Museum in Athens, but there's a copy at the docks in Chalkida.

around the playground and watch the sunset while your children play and make friends.

Because it has been popular with Greek holidaymakers for such a long time, Loutra Edipsou has a good stock of hotels and restaurants. The resulting competition means that, off-season at least, it's not too expensive – you can often negotiate a good deal.

The great magnet is the hot springs, whose alleged health-giving properties have drawn visitors to the area since ancient times. Facilities for modern health-tourists centre on the **Thermae Sylla Wellness Hotel**, perched on a promontory at the eastern edge of the town. The restaurant and wellness centre are open to the public (for details, see 'Family-friendly Accommodation', p. 204). The area around the hotel is delightful. There's a palm-fringed promenade, a terrace overlooking the sea, steamy water flooding across the salt-stained rocks below the hotel, and shady playground, whilst, just up the road is a small beach and taverna, with hot spring water flowing down chutes and pouring over

sulphur-stained rocks into the sea. This is one of the pleasantest places on Evia, perhaps in the whole of Greece.

Though the Thermae Sylla is the best known of the spa hotels, it isn't the only one – many of the hotels offer at least some of the services, and the spa water itself can be sampled in several places where it floods out onto the beach – look out for the steam. The rest of the town, behind the broad ferry dock, is built on a grid plan, and has all the shops and services you're likely to need. All in all, Loutra Edipsou makes a fine base for a family holiday.

South from Loutra Edipsou: Rovies and Limni

From Loutra Edipsou, drive past the Thermae Sylla Hotel and join the road just after the viaduct you'll see overhead. Enjoy the drive along the coast – it's invigorating. The next village of any size is Rovies, just off the main road.

A large and pleasant village, **Rovies** is another possible base for a family holiday. Important since classical times, it was destroyed by an earthquake in 426 BC (a disaster mentioned by Thucydides), rebuilt to become the regional centre in Byzantine times (hence the **13th century tower**), and remained significant during the Ottoman occupation. Known mainly for its olives, Rovies has been slowly attracting an increasing number of holiday-makers, who stay in small-scale apartments or the excellent **campsite** (see 'Family-friendly Accommodation', p. 204). It's also making inroads into the relatively recent development of **Agritourism**: holidaymakers can, for example, take part in the olive harvest (see 'Family-friendly Accommodation', p. 204).

To get into the centre of Rovies turn left when you get to the village, and follow the signs for 'Medieval Tower'. This will bring you eventually to a little square with a church with the tower beyond it, a war memorial and a few swings. There are paths down to the beach.

Nine kilometres or so south of Rovies is **Limni** ★, a pretty fishing village with a consider-able history. Important enough to have its own ships in the past, it was also rich enough to attract a number of envious attackers. In 1821 it was the first town on Evia to proclaim the Revolution, and contributed ships to the cause during the War of Independence. After independ-ence, Limni enjoyed a 'Golden Age', with its merchant fleet enriching the town. Towards the end of the 19th century the coming of steam brought sharp decline. Limni also played a con-siderable part in resistance to the Nazis during World War II.

Limni today is a pleasant and relaxing place to stop. A sea of red tile roofs set on a curved bay below the main coast road, it has a small dock lined with fishing boats, and a lovely prom-enade of trees and benches, interrupted by a series of taver-nas and cafés. Just behind (and

Loutra Edipsou

Folk Museum, Limni

The road out is well surfaced, twisting along tortuously between the sea and the cliffs. Watch out for fallen rocks. At the end of this tarmac section is a delightful glade – heavily wooded and echoing with the sound of rushing water – sheltering a restaurant, a small church and a shingle beach. Even if you go no further, it's worth the drive. Beyond the restaurant the road becomes a rock-strewn unsurfaced track – drive accordingly! However, the road is wide, and the views stunning. Continue past a brand-new church, and you come out onto a wide, sharply-curving shingle beach backed by woodland. A nice place for a picnic. Five kilometres after starting on the unsurfaced road, you arrive at the monastery itself.

clearly signposted) is the excellent little **Folk Museum** ★★ **AGES 3 AND ABOVE**, open daily 9am–1pm, Sundays 10.30am–1pm. Admission is €2. In a handsome balconied house, it consists of a series of rooms containing household implements, furniture, textiles, a loom, a traditional dining room, costumes, and even some mosaics and statuary. A bit of a mish-mash, perhaps, but certainly of interest to the inquisitive child! It's an authentic flavour of Evia's past.

Agios Nikolaos Galataki

AGES 5 AND ABOVE ★

Signposted off road 3 km south of Limni.

Before continuing down the coast road, it's worth visiting the monastery of **Agios Nikolaos Galataki**. Said to be the oldest monastery in Northern Evia, it is now home to a group of nuns.

As is often the case with working monasteries and convents in Greece, the site is very prosperous and well looked after. Perched above the sea at the foot of Mount Kankili, it has imposing whitewashed walls, pristine red roof-tiles, white-boled olive trees, tidy chicken enclosures and well-tended gardens, all clustered around a 13th-century tower built as a defence against pirates. Bags suspended on the trunks of trees collect sap, apparently used in the production of retsina.

It really is worthwhile for families with children to look around at least one monastery whilst in Greece – they play such an important part in the Greek psyche. And there's almost always a fresco which depicts what happens to the ungodly on the 'Day of Judgement', with sufficient bloodthirstiness to keep even the most demanding small boy happy. On that score, Agios Nikolaos Galataki doesn't disappoint.

Open 8am–midday and 5–8pm daily. **Adm** free.

Steni

Before returning to Chalkida, it's worth visiting Steni, one of Northern Evia's best-known mountain villages. At Nea Artaki, a left turn brings you onto a road that climbs up into the foothills of Mount Dirfys. After 24 km of almost constant climbing, beautiful views and shepherds supervising their flocks, you'll arrive in Steni itself. It can be difficult to know that you *have* arrived, since the village straggles up the mountain, and the town square is long and thin. There are tavernas on both sides of the road, a bridge across a tumbling stream, and, on the left, a lane up to the village's two hotels (see 'Family-friendly Accommodation', p. 204). The village square becomes busy in the evening as locals gather on café terraces to drink coffee, eat ice-cream and gossip. The favourite venue with the locals is the Café Elati. You'll often see a table of mums sitting chatting whilst their children sit at a separate table, messing about or playing on Game Boys. Other youngsters ride their bikes on the street. You may also see the local priest taking the air with his wife,

with local people greeting him and kissing his ring.

Higher up the mountain, the upper part of the village has a group of restaurants and tavernas with, beyond them, stalls set up at the roadside where women sell honey. On the right the river hurls itself over large boulders, among a woodland of gnarled trees. This is a well-known beauty spot, and you'll find lots of Greek couples strolling under the trees, school parties being disgorged from coaches, or boy and girl scouts drinking in their leaders' words of wisdom.

Beyond Steni the road continues to wind up the mountainside, every bend with its clutch of colourful beehives. If you continue on this road, it eventually descends to the east coast. But it's a long, slow drive and better to return the way you came to get back to Chalkida (p. 184).

Southern Evia

To explore southern Evia drive east from Chalkida (see p. 184), through Eretria, Amarynthos and Aliveri (see p. 188) to Lepoura, then turn right. You are now on the road that travels along the spine of the island to the southernmost tip at Karystos (see p. 199).

Driving south

Within minutes you drive through the pleasant village of Krieza, past two Venetian towers, one with a cap of greenery set at a

Lake Dystos

At your feet as you exit Krieza, a hill dotted with olive trees and vineyards falls away to a marsh cupped by the surrounding mountains. This is – or was – **Lake Dystos**. In the 1950s water was drained from the lake to act as coolant for the power station in Aliveri, substantially reducing the size of the lake and increasing the amount of land available for farming. In the 1980s reclamation continued, with debris from fires being used as landfill. But then, just when the lake seemed to have all but disappeared, heavy rains gave it a reprieve, and it became the marshy wetland that you see today. From the centre of the marsh rises a conical hill. This is **Ancient Dystos**, dating from the fifth century BC. Later medieval remains are still visible.

raffish angle, then down a long hill. It's worth stopping at one of the lay-bys on the hill to take in the **view ★★** of the valley that holds Lake Dystos (see above).

The road continues downhill across the rich farmland of the valley floor. Along the ridges of the surrounding mountains, hundreds of **wind-turbines** stand and wave – you'll see a lot more as you drive down through southern Evia, offering a clue to one of the region's most noted characteristics: it is very, very windy!

At the far side of the valley you pass along a ridge dotted with these giants, and get a good idea of how narrow this part of Evia is – you can see both coasts, their bays and islands laid out on a deep-blue sea. Halfway along the ridge is a crossroads, and a right turn brings you down a long steep hill into the little port and resort of Nea Styra.

Lining a nice sandy beach, **Nea Styra** has lots of cafés and tavernas, several small hotels,

a little, slightly down-at-heel children's playground (primarily for locals, but open to all) and the ferry and fishing boat quay. Though it gets short shrift in several popular guidebooks, I liked it. It makes a good base for exploring southern Evia and the mainland opposite – the ferries from Nea Styra go to **Agia Marina** on the mainland, just outside **Marathon**, an hour out of Athens. The best hotel in Nea Styra for families is the **Delfini** – it overlooks the town's pleasant little beach (see 'Family-friendly Accommodation', p. 204).

Back on the main road, there are more wind-turbines, facing out to sea like Easter Island statues. Just before Styra (the old part of the town, 5km or so from Nea Styra), a road off to the left is signposted '**Dragon Houses**' (*drakospita*). Brand-new tarmac soon gives way to boulder-strewn red shale and bare scraped rock. As you inch your way upwards (take care of your exhaust and sump) the **views** ★★ across sea, headlands and islands are increasingly spectacular.

When you finally get to the *drakospita* you'll find them worth the climb. Constructed out of huge slabs of stone, some time around the sixth century BC, they are spectacular in their bulk – they get the name because it was thought that only mythological creatures like dragons could have had the strength to move the massive stones. Indeed, it's hard to imagine how early man, with only very primitive technology at their command, could have managed the huge monoliths. Nobody is really sure who built them or why. With more of them beyond Styra, at Kapsala, and also on Mount Ochi above Karystos (see p. 200), a hint as to their provenance might be given by the fact that they are all close to quarries. The theory is that they were temples built by immigrant or slave labour from Asia Minor who worked in the quarries.

Beyond **Styra** (pleasant square, church, trees and tavernas) another of Southern Evia's little ports lies off to the right. **Marmari** is similar in size and atmosphere to Nea Styra, with the difference that it has two really excellent **children's playgrounds** along the front, and that its ferries sail to **Rafina** rather than Agia Marina. This makes it the closest place on Evia to **Athens**.

INSIDER TIP ❯❯

Beyond Marmari, on the road to Karystos, there are seemingly permanent road works as the final leg of the route to the southern end of the island is brought up to scratch. It's high, with a succession of wonderful views, but regularly subject to gale-force winds.

Karystos and Mount Ochi

A handsome white town and seaport (Evia's southernmost), **Karystos** sits at the foot of Mount Ochi (see below), Evia's third highest peak. Built on a grid plan, modern Karystos was largely designed in the 19th century for **King Otho**, who contemplated establishing it as the capital of Greece. You're greeted as you enter the town by a large blue-domed church and a substantial children's playground. To the right, the streets lead down to a pleasant **promenade**, at one end of which (the western end) is the **commercial harbour**, whilst at the other is a little **park** with a statue of a mariner, a wartime mine and a huge anchor. Between the two, rows of picturesque fishing boats are moored on the quay. Beyond it is the **Bourtzi** or Venetian fort, which though slightly soiled by graffiti, is still a picture against the deep blue of the sea. Opposite, in the Cultural Centre, is the town's **archaeological museum** (📞 *22 24 02 56 61*), open every day except Sunday from 8.30am to 3pm (adm €2).

Karystos

Karystos has excellent **beaches** ★★ – a small one to the east and a seemingly never-ending one that stretches westward from the town out towards a distant headland. With the road right next to this beach, it is just asking for you to park in the shade of a tree and go for a swim. Further along the road the beach breaks up into a series of coves of golden sand looking out towards a tiny islet with a church on it. Perfect for a quick dip or a long day on the beach, and never crowded, though you'll have to take everything you need with you – there are no cafés or tavernas. Eventually you'll come to an enormous tangle of roads, each labelled with a number – Odos 1, Odos 8, Odos 164, etc. This is a development, where the roads are built, and the parcels of land enclosed and put on sale. There's a similar one on the distant eastern headland – it looks like a plate of spaghetti, or one of those sinuous

chalk figures on England's South Downs.

Mount Ochi ★ AGES 10 AND ABOVE

Towering behind Karystos, 1400m **Mount Ochi**, bare and forbidding, is only for the serious walker. But you can drive up to the village of **Myli**, clinging to the foothills, for wonderful views across the town. From the church it's a 20-minute scramble up a steep path to **Castel Rosso**, the blasted shell of a medieval fortress which should be more imposing than it is – although it dominates Myli village, it is dwarfed by the great mass of mountain behind it. Once you're up there, there's not much to see inside – just rubble and the church of **Profitis Ilias** built over the cistern. But the views are even more special than they are from Myli. Further up the mountain is another **Dragon House** – more impressive than the ones near Styra, but not as accessible unless you're very fit indeed.

If you want to make an attempt on the summit, and you're happy to stay overnight on the mountain (and preferably have a 4×4), drive east out of Karystos to Metochi, and then bear left up the mountain to a **shelter**, built in 1962, which can accommodate up to 15 people. For rates and bookings, phone Mr N. Gika (📞 *22 24 02 64 17/69 36 36 54 35*).

THREE TOURS OF THE MAINLAND

Evia is a delightfully unspoilt place to have a holiday, where you can immerse the family in Greek life and the language, and get away from the hurly-burly of tourist Greece. But it can't be disguised that, beyond visiting little towns, admiring magnificent scenery, spending time on the beach, or enjoying one of the island's embryonic active holidays, there isn't an awful lot to do. Such attractions as you'll find on Evia are pretty small-scale.

Luckily, however, the mainland is full of attractions that are **world class**, and right on your doorstep. Below you'll find brief details of three short tours from Evia. The first two are most easily accessible from the south of the island, the third from the north.

A Trip to Athens

To enjoy a day out in the capital, drive to **Marmari** and park near the ferry dock. The trip across to **Rafina** takes an enjoyable hour. From Rafina catch a comfortable, air-conditioned bus from the bus station next to the quay, into the capital – a further 45 minutes. The delights of Athens are much more accessible than they were, thanks to infrastructure improvements made for the 2004 Olympic Games. For timetables and prices, contact the Rafina Port Authority (📞 *22 94 02 33 00*). For bus timetables and fares into Athens, contact KTEL (BUS) Terminal Office in Athens (📞 *21 08 31 71 53*).

Marathon & Around

Easily done in a day by car is the ancient site of the **Battle of Marathon**, where a heavily outnumbered force of Greek soldiers defeated the Persian army in 490 BC (see 'The Battle of Marathon', below). Get the car ferry from **Nea Styra** to **Agia Marina** on the mainland – it takes around three-quarters of an hour. For timetables and prices contact the Nea Styra Port Authority (📞 *22 24 04 15 33*) or the Agia Marina Port Authority (📞 *22 94 06 38 88*).

Once in Agia Marina, drive the 4 or so kilometres up to the main road. All the signposts at the intersection point to the right. Ignore them – *turn left*. This road will bring you to a large dual carriageway past the small town of **Marathonas**. You are now on the **Plain of Marathon**, where the battle took place. Head for **Nea Makri** and Athens. Just past Marathonas you

The Battle of Marathon

In 490 BC, the Greeks, against all the odds, defeated a huge invading Persian army on the Plain of Marathon. The battle was fought on flat land bounded by three hills to the west, marshes to the north and south, and the sea to the east. The Persians, led by Datis and Artaphernes, landed near Marathon beach and set up camp. With the help only of the city of Plataea, the Athenian army of around 10 000, led by Miltiades, faced a much bigger Persian force – estimates vary between 18 000 and 200 000.

After several days' standoff, the Greeks attacked. Miltiades had withdrawn soldiers from the centre to strengthen the wings, and when the Persians seemed to be prevailing in the middle, the wings closed in, causing panic in the Persian ranks. The Persians broke and tried to get back to their ships, pursued by the Greeks. By the end of the battle, 6400 Persian invaders lay dead on the battlefield, and many more drowned in the marshes. The Greeks lost 192 Athenians and 11 Plataeans. For the first time, the mighty Persian army had been defeated on land by the Greeks.

A warrior in full armour – Thersippos or Eucles, or even the runner Pheidippides, depending on which account you read – was despatched to Athens to bring news of the great victory. He ran the full 26 miles, said the famous words, 'Hail, we are victorious,' and expired on the spot.

After the battle, the Greek and Plataean dead were cremated and buried with full military honours, under two separate tumuli on the battlefield. The Persian dead were interred in a mass grave. A monument – called the 'Trophy' – was erected over a pile of weapons and armour taken from the defeated Persians.

will come to another T-junction – turn left again. From now on, along this long stretch of dual carriageway, you will see brown ancient monument signs to sites associated with the battle on both sides of the road. One, on the left, points to **'The Trophy'**, a victory column in a clearing next to a church a few hundred metres down a lane between tall reeds. This is a reconstruction – you can see the actual remains of the column in the **Battle of Marathon Museum.** All museums and sites are clearly signposted from the dual carriageway.

The museum is just two rooms, but well worth it. Another sign (on the left again) takes you to the **tumulus** under which the Greek dead were buried – near it there's an excellent relief map explaining the layout of the battle. Sites/museums are open Tuesday to Sunday 8.30am–3pm. Admission is €3 (children €2), and your ticket covers all the Marathon sites.

After your visit to the battle-field you could complete your day out in one of two ways – by doubling back to the town of Marathonas, or by going on to Nea Makri.

Marathonas itself is well worth having a look around – you can see where the **2004 Olympic Marathon race** began, or go around the **Museum of the Olympic Games**. A couple of kilometres above the town is a reservoir (signposted '**Marathon Lake**') overlooked by a restaurant which is usually thronged with Greeks from Athens and around. If you've stayed in the Marathon area, return to Agia Marina to get the ferry back to Nea Styra.

Alternatively, further along the dual carriageway towards Athens, head for the fishing port of Nea Makri. Follow the signs down to the front from the main road, to a promenade lined with bars and tavernas, **a sandy beach** and a **children's playground**. A tourist train whisks around the town from the promenade.

INSIDER TIP ≫

The restaurants in the town square, beside the through-road to Athens, are excellent, and there's another fine children's playground here as well.

If you've visited Nea Makri, then you have a choice of ferry routes back to Evia – you can either backtrack to Agia Marina and return to Nea Styra, or go on to Rafina and catch the boat to Marmari.

The Pelion Peninsula

If you're staying in northern Evia, it is just about feasible to visit the beautiful Pelion penin-sula in a day, though it would be even better if the trip could be extended.

Take the car ferry from **Agiokampos** to **Glifa** on the mainland. A half-hour crossing and a couple of kilometres' driv-ing, and you'll be on the National Road that runs from Athens to Thessaloniki. From here, 40km driving on a fast road brings you to the city of **Volos.** From here explore one or more of three very different areas – the city of Volos itself, the stunning mountain villages of **Mount Pelion**, right next to the city, or the long **Pelion peninsula** with its beaches and villages.

Shopping With Children

Almost everything that's for sale on Evia is aimed at local people: chic shoppers may be disap-pointed. However, if you can find stuff that you want – toys, olives, preserves and embroidery are local specialities – be assured there's no tourist mark-up: you won't be ripped off. Two local produce (food and drink) shops worth making a detour for are **Artoparadosis Bakers** ★ (☏ *22 29 06 01 02, www.artoparadosis. com*), a traditional bakery in Eretria, and **Cava Minahilis** (☏ *22 26 03 17 34, www.minahilis. com*), a small wholesaler who operates retail outlets in northern Evia; look out for them in Agios

Geogios and Edipsos. Bread and cakes from the first, and a huge range of wines and beers in the second, are particularly good if you're packing a picnic/planning a BBQ/having a day in the car. Both are easy to find.

FAMILY-FRIENDLY ACCOMMODATION

EXPENSIVE

Thermae Sylla Spa Wellness Hotel ★★★

Edipsos, Evia, ☎ 22 26 06 01 00, www.thermaesylla.gr. At the eastern end of the promenade.

The Thermae Sylla is a really top-end luxury hotel whose unique selling point is the hot chemical springs over which it was built in 1897. It offers, at a cost, a huge range of beauty and wellness treatments, massages, hydrotherapy and physiotherapy. The most expensive I could find

on the list includes full body massage with four hands (€136), pumpkin seed treatment (€106), lomi-lomi massage (€113) and a basic facial treatment (€130). Not cheap then, even if you know what they all mean – it's enough to persuade you that you're beautiful enough! Everything in the hotel is plush and luxurious, the setting over the sea is lovely and you get the sort of service you'd expect at these prices. There's a children's playroom and a pleasant public playground right next to the hotel, and it's an easy walk along to where all the restaurants and cafés are.

Rooms 108. Rates €73–119 twin, €322–641 junior/ Executive/ Presidential suite. All per person per night. Rates include breakfast and use of pools; children up to 2 stay free (no meals), first child 2 to 12 sharing parents' room – free, except during high and super high season, then 60% reduction. Children 2 to 12 in own room – 20% discount.

Thermae Sylla Spa Wellness Hotel

TIP ›› **Evia for Active Families** ‹‹

Though nowhere near as well developed in its active holiday provision as Crete, Evia is just beginning to realise its possibilities. Keep an eye out for local signs, especially for **walks** in the mountainous areas and water sports and **sea-fishing** trips in seaside towns. It's a good idea, too, to ask at your hotel. For **water sports**, including scuba diving off northern Evia, try **Diving Travel** (📞 *22 26 03 32 12, www.divingtravelgreece.com*). **Thalassa Sports** (📞 *69 74 41 00 39, www.thalassasports.com*) rents jet skis, banana boats and motorboats in Amarynthos. For something a little different, enrol the family on a Thai Massage course at **Thai Yoga Massage** (📞 *22 21 05 51 09, www.thaimassage.gr*) in Chalkida. It's not terribly 'Greek', I know.

Child sharing with adult – 30% discount. **Credit** *AmEx, MC, V, DC.* **Amenities** *Babysitting. Bars (4). Cots (free). Extra beds. Gym. Laundry service. Non-smoking rooms. Parking. Pools (2, medicinal). Restaurants (2). Spa.* **In room** *A/C. Internet access. Safe. TV/Satellite.*

Candili Estate ★ ★ ★

Candili Prokopi, Evia 34004, 📞 *69 44 20 21 12, www.candili.gr. After the town of Prokopi, heading north, turn left after 500m (signposted Dafnousa). Next left, and the black gates of the estate are on your left.*

If you want a totally unique family-friendly experience of Evia, you could do no better than to consider the house, out-buildings and grounds of the Candili Estate. How to describe it? With its communal dining, book-lined library and craft workshop, it has the air of a minor English public school. The outdoors – the tree house and plunge pools, the alfresco dining and wide vistas of hills and forests – are somehow very 'Swallows and Amazons', but in the centre of a Greek island. It provides delightful accommodation, and manages to combine a

'we all muck in together' approach with lots of quiet corners where you can just sit and read. The Candili Estate is not a hotel – you can't book your family in just for a night or two. What Philip Noel-Baker, who now runs it, prefers is to rent out the whole lot – 12 en suite bedrooms, public rooms, gardens, swimming pools, everything – to visiting groups, on a half or full board basis. He already does so to music groups, yoga courses, that

Candili Estate

sort of thing (see the website). So if you wanted to have a holiday with family and friends, or organise a 60th birthday or golden wedding celebration, in a beautiful 19th-century farm set in the wonderful countryside of central northern Evia, get in contact and negotiate a price.

Rooms 12. **Rates** On application. **Amenities** Babysitting. Pools (3). Garden. Table tennis. Tree house. Games field. Use of a Land Rover.

MODERATE

The Island of Dreams, Eretria ★ ★ ★ FIND

Eretria, Evia 34008, ☏ 22 29 06 12 24, www.dreamisland.com.gr. As you enter Eretria, drive through the town, keeping the sea and harbour on your right. When you get to a roundabout, turn right, then at the end of the road, turn right again.

Yes, a whimsical name I know. But it really does what it says on the tin. Located on a small island off the eastern arm of Eretria harbour, joined to the mainland by a bridge, it really is dreamy! More holiday camp than a hotel, its facilities are spread under the trees all over the island – restaurant, lounge with board games and continental billiards table, outdoor theatre, delightful blue flag beach with its own bar, small boat harbour – it even has its own very pretty church. Add to this that it's at the end of Eretria's main restaurant road (so there's a huge choice of places if you want to eat out), that the rest of the town is also within easy walking distance, and that, if you use the

ferry from Eretria to Oropo, you're only 45 kilometres from Athens, and you begin to see the possibilities of the Island of Dreams as a place to stay.

Rooms 94 rooms and bungalows/ chalets. **Rates** €123–160 per double/suite, 1st July–30th Sept. **Credit** AmEx, MC, V, DC. **Amenities** Bar. Laundry service. Parking. Restaurant. **In room** A/C. TV.

The Knossos ★

19 Vizantinon Aftokratoron, 34300 Edipsos, ☏ 22 26 02 24 60 or 2 25 60, www.knossos-spa.com.

Tucked away just behind the promenade in Loutra Edipsou, the Knossos is a good choice if you want the kind of treatments offered in the Thermae Sylla at a fraction of the cost. You will not, of course, get the same level of luxury, but it's still perfectly comfortable, and there's a very pleasant garden bar on the roof. The beauty and wellness treatments are provided, from March to October, by the CitySpa franchise, which operates in other hotels in various parts of Greece and Cyprus (and indeed, in London). As with all the other hotels in Edipsos, there are often bargains to be had, especially outside the high season (when I was there – in May 2007 – the tariff charged was much lower than any of those quoted).

Rooms 37. **Rates** €85–120 double/ triple, room only: breakfast €10; there are often offers (e.g. €65–75, including breakfast). **Credit** AmEx, MC, V, DC. **Amenities** Bar. Extra bed. Gym. Non-smoking rooms; Pool. Restaurant. Spa (Mar–Oct). **In room** A/C. Internet access. Safe. TV.

The Petit Village ★★ FIND

Eretria, 34008 Evia, ☎ *22 29 06 00 70, www.petitvillage.gr. On the road from Chalkida to Eretria 17km from the former, 2km from the latter, on the right.*

Between the main Chalkida–Eretria road and the sea, the Petit Village is something between a hotel and an apartment complex. Indeed, it is thinking of becoming purely an apartment complex for the 2008 season, so do ring to ascertain the state of play. Made up of 26 rooms in two-storey and 29 in one-storey blocks set in beautiful gardens, with the reception/restaurant/bar block down near the swimming pool, the hotel is immaculately maintained and very peaceful. It has its own sandy beach, boules and tennis courts, basketball pitch and children's playground. Ideal for families with younger children, it's a five-minute drive into the pleasant port/resort of Eretria.

Rooms 55. Rates €50–60 double. Families can have two rooms sharing a balcony. Rates include breakfast. Credit AmEx, MC, V, DC. Amenities Bar. Non-smoking room. Parking. Pool (outdoor). Restaurant. In room A/C. TV.

Delfini Hotel, Nea Styra

Nea Styra, Evia, ☎ *22 24 04 12 10. When you get to the harbour at Nea Styra, drive along with the sea on your right. The hotel is at the end, overlooking the beach.*

Nea Styra would make a good base for a family holiday – it's a pleasant seaside town with a nice beach, lots of cafés, restaurants and shops, and ferries to Agia Marina on the mainland, which is a 15-minute drive from Marathon and just over an hour from Athens. And being halfway down narrow southern Evia, Nea Styra is in a good position for exploring this part of the island. The town has several small hotels, but the pick of the bunch has to be the Delfini, because it's actually on the town's pleasant little public beach – the children can be in the water two minutes after getting up! It offers clean, attractive basic accommodation at reasonable cost, with a choice of double rooms and studios (with kitchenette and dining area).

Rooms 50. Open May–Sept. Rates €50–75 double rooms. Rates are per room, per night. Amenities Cots. Extra beds. Laundry. Parking. Restaurant. In room A/C. Fridge. Internet access. TV/DVD/Satellite.

Lucy

10 Voudouri Avenue, 34100 Chalkis, ☎ *22 21 02 38 31, www.lucy-hotel. gr. On the waterfront in Chalkida, just north of the Old Bridge.*

One of the Best Western chain (though each hotel is separately owned and operated), the Lucy provides good basic accommodation right on the lively waterfront in the heart of the city. Two-bedroom suites are available specifically for families. The views across the Euripos from the restaurant and the balconies of the outward facing rooms are superb. Ask for a room on one of the upper storeys – they're high enough above the busy waterside to be nice and quiet.

The Lucy's a particularly good option for families with teenagers – the road along the quayside is thronged with young people and with families.

Rooms 90. **Rates** €67–143 per double/suite. Rates include breakfast; for every two paying adults, one child is free if sleeping in parents' room. **Credit** AmEx, AC, V, MC. **Amenities** Bar. Extra beds. Laundry services. Parking. Restaurant. **In room** A/C. TV.

Eleonas Hotel ★★★ GREEN

Rovies, Evia 34005, 📞 22 27 07 16 19/ 30, www.eleonashotel.com.

The Eleonas Hotel is peace-and-quiet personified. A beautiful building set in acres of olive trees (it's still a working olive farm), its owners Stefanos and Marina Vallis have developed it along 'agritourism' lines, offering very high grade accommodation, simple décor, homemade food and the chance to unwind. For parents with one child double rooms are available with an extra bed, while bigger families can book maisonettes on two floors with two bedrooms, two bathrooms and their own balcony and garden. There's a small 'activity centre' for youngsters (TV plus video games, board games and books), and a small outdoor playground, table tennis table and enclosed football area. There's even a loom, if you fancy a crack at weaving! But don't expect kid's clubs, paddling pools or any of the other stuff that big holiday hotels offer – this hotel is really only suitable for children aged six or above. In the list of in-room facilities the hotel brochure includes,

'books instead of a television'. That says it all.

Rooms: 10 twins – 5 with connecting doors. **Rates** €100–110 per night for double with extra bed, €155–170 for a four-bed maisonette. Open all year; high season is 20/7–20/8. Prices include breakfast. **Credit** V. **Amenities** Restaurant. **In room** AC. Internet access.

Rovies Camping

Abouria, Rovies, Evia, 📞 22 27 07 11 20, www.campingevia.com. Just outside the village, between the road and the sea.

Rovies Camping is a lovely site – pitches are heavily shaded, facilities are immaculate, there's a lovely shingle beach along the length of the site, and there's a small playground on the grass under the trees. Even if you don't have a caravan, it is possible to rent one on site.

Rates Adults €5–6, children €3.50–4.50, car €2.50–3.50, caravan €5.50–8, tent €5–8, depending on size; electric hook-up €4. Charges are per night. Open April–Oct. **Amenities** Café/bar. Restaurant. Mini-market (from 1st July to 30th August). Shingle beach. playground. Basketball court. First aid post. Information centre in reception. Excursions. Horse-riding. Water-sports and other activities can be arranged. Boats can be launched from the beach.

FAMILY-FRIENDLY DINING

Because there's so little foreign tourism in Evia, the tavernas and restaurants you're likely to come across are almost exclusively traditionally Greek. Most villages will have several, often with a charcoal grill outside, and the standard of food is generally very good – look out for the ones that most of the locals seem to use. But don't expect highchairs, children's menus or play equipment – most don't have them. What you will get is a warm welcome, a keen interest in where you come from, and a lot of attention for the youngsters.

Hotel Beis

Paralia Kymis, 34003 Kymis, Evia, ☎ 22 22 02 26 04. A modern hotel, the Beis overlooks the harbour – if you're coming from Kymi, it's on the left as you get to the quayside.

Popular as an overnight stop for those arriving or departing on early or late ferries to or from Skyros, the Hotel Beis is indeed a possible overnight stay, though it does rather lack character. But even if you're just on your way through, its restaurant is well worth looking out for – it is widely known for its fresh fish. So if it's dinner time, pop in and ask what's on. A mixed plate of different sorts of fish and shellfish will set you back between €20 and €25, but it's worth it. Watch out for the bones, and don't be surprised if the proprietor is watching the telly as you eat.

Open 'Day and night'! *Main course* €15–40 (breakfast from €6). *Credit* AmEx, MC, V.

Apanemo ★

Chalkida, Evia, ☎ 22 21 02 26 14.

An excellent, and therefore very popular, restaurant at the far end of the shoreline near the lighthouse, Apanemo has tables on the beach, so the youngsters will be perfectly happy digging in the sand or paddling in the water. The staff are friendly and helpful, and there are fish, spaghetti and chicken meals suitable for children. There are no highchairs, but plenty of room for buggies if you've got one with you. It is very popular, though, so it'd be as well to book.

Open 12 noon–1am. *Main course* €8–18. *Credit* AE, V.

Estiatorio Aegli

Loutro Edipsou, Evia, ☎ 22 26 02 23 50. On the seafront towards the eastern end.

If you want a more relaxed, lively atmosphere, try the Aegli, just down the road. Popular with Greek tour parties (whose arrival can slow the service down considerably!), the menu offers a wide range of Greek dishes, from meat to fish to cheese to pasta. The food's excellent, the music's Greek, and when the waiters sing along with the customers and women get up to dance, you feel at last that you're getting a glimpse of the real Greece.

Open 6am–1am. *Main course* €5–12. *Amenities* Children's menu.

Mouria Taverna

Steni, Evia, ☎ *22 28 05 12 34.*

A good basic taverna under a mulberry tree (that's what a 'mouria' is) in the town square. No nonsense: no highchairs, no children's menus, no credit cards. But good food and, as ever in Greece, nice attitudes to little ones.

Open *8am–1 or 2am.* **Main course** *€5–14.*

Flocafe ★★

Voudourni, Chalkida, Evia, ☎ *22 21 07 87 01, www.flocafe.gr. On the waterfront overlooking the Euripos channel.*

The Flocafe in Chalkida is obviously Chalkida's top place for socialising. One of a chain of

Flocafe

coffee shops to be found all over Greece and Cyprus, it does a good range of club sandwiches, baguettes and mini-pizzas, as well as the cakes, ice-creams, puddings and drinks you'd expect. If you have a buggy with you, grab a table that borders the pavement. The service is terrific – despite being busy, you'll find iced water plonked in front of you within seconds of sitting down, and your order taken and filled within minutes. In summer the bulk of the customers sit outside, watching the world go by, being serenaded by itinerant musicians or being chivvied to buy balloons. A lovely place to sit with the family, and the food's delicious.

Open *8am–2am all year.* **Main course** *€5–8.* **Amenities** *Highchairs.*

Cavo d'Oro ★

Karystos, Evia, ☎ *22 24 02 23 26.*

A well-reckoned and pleasantly old-fashioned restaurant down a narrow alley west of the main square, the Cavo d'Oro is heavily used by locals. Serving traditional Greek food, the staff will be very happy to help with explanations and advice, and they're magic with children. Not much in the way of bells and whistles, but family-friendly up to its eyeballs.

Open *9am–midnight, but closed 3.30pm–7pm.* **Main course** *€3–8.*

7 Other Islands

OTHER ISLANDS

Mountain ▲▲

Other Islands ●
Ionian Islands **1**
Argo-Saronic Islands **2**
Sporades **3**
Northeastern Aegean Islands **4**
Dodecanese **5**
Cyclades **6**

I would be doing an injustice to the huge number and variety of Greek islands if I claimed that the four I've covered so far are the only ones worthy of consideration for family holidays. When planning the book, I went for my own preferences – islands with a substantial tourist infrastructure, a fascinating history, lots of interesting days out; islands which are big enough to offer a variety of attractions, accommodation and places to eat, and are reasonably easy to get to from the UK. All these things certainly apply to three of my choices – Corfu, Rhodes and Crete. The fourth – Evia – I included because it meets most of the criteria, yet offers a contrasting holiday experience. I believe that a family with children, not knowing anything about Greece, wouldn't go far wrong if they chose to holiday on one of these four.

That having been said, half the fun of going to the Greek Islands is exploring their infinite variety. There will be lots of families who already have their own favourites, and who will be incensed (or perhaps relieved) that I haven't chosen them for detailed treatment. When I talked to colleagues and friends about which islands I'd chosen, I was immediately met with a barrage of 'You have to include x, or y, or z'. There are some islands which are ideal if you've got young children but not teenagers. Others might appeal to older families looking for a lively nightlife. Yet others are perfect if you just want to chill out, far away from the hurly-burly of modern life.

If you've had wonderful family experiences on islands that I haven't chosen, please e-mail us at: *frommers@wiley.co.uk* and perhaps you can persuade us that your favourite should be included in upcoming editions.

In the meantime, here is a run-down of the other major island groups, and what they have to offer.

The Ionian Islands

Of all the Greek island groups, the Ionian Islands are probably, across the board, the most family-friendly. Dotted along the length of the Greek mainland's west coast, from **Corfu** (see Chapter 3) at the top to Kythera at the bottom, the Ionian Islands are unique in a number of ways. Greener than most, and wetter, blessed with a wealth of flora and fauna, they are (apart from Lefkada) the only ones never to have been a part of the Ottoman Empire. They therefore lack the types of Turkish architecture – especially mosques, aqueducts and Turkish houses – notable on so many other islands. What they do have in abundance is buildings originating in their periods of Venetian and British rule – particularly mansions, public buildings and statues. Because they are not very far off the Greek coast, they are linked more closely to the mainland than to each other.

The Ionian Islands are among the most heavily used by the UK travel industry. Apart from Corfu, both Kefalonia and Zakinthos appear in a lot of holiday brochures, and, because of their popularity as destinations for charter flights, are easy to get to from most parts of the UK. Both are therefore desirable for certain types of family holidays: **Kefalonia** enjoys the glamour associated with the novel and film 'Captain Corelli's Mandolin', but through no fault of its own somewhat lacks character (almost all its buildings were destroyed by an earthquake in 1953), and **Zakinthos**, all mountains, fertile valleys and lovely beaches, is not only very beautiful, but has earned a reputation for dusk-to-dawn partying. Both are good for diving, snorkeling and water sports generally, together with a variety of other outdoor activities.

Cathedral of Agios Dionysios, Zakinthos

Of the rest, **Paxi** (and little brother **Antipaxi**) are tiny, delightfully unspoiled and perfect for families that just want to chill out. **Ithaca** is relaxed and, because of its indented coast and natural harbours, ideal for sailors, while **Lefkada** offers not only miles of beaches and excellent windsurfing on its west coast, but easy access to the Greek mainland, to which it is attached by a bridge. The disadvantage of **Kythera** as a holiday destination is also its advantage. Traditionally included in the Ionian group but now administered from Athens, it is one of the most difficult Greek Islands to get to, and is therefore one of the least affected by tourism. Enthusiasts try not to talk up its charms too much, since they want it to stay that way!

The Argo-Saronic Islands

Tucked into the angle between northern Greece and the Peloponnese, the Argo-Saronic Islands are the group closest to the capital. This is probably why they're among the artiest and trendiest in the whole of Greece. They're also among the most historic. Their greatest strength as a holiday destination is that they offer a taste of island life while giving easy access not only to Athens itself, but to some of the most important sites of Ancient Greece. They do get horrendously crowded in summer, and can be very expensive.

Pick of the bunch is undoubtedly **Hydra,** famous for its motor transport ban ('To invent the wheel is talent, to ignore it is genius' – novelist Frederick Raphael), yet its reliance on donkey transport shouldn't make you think of it as a lazy backwater – it combines a lively nightlife with cosmopolitan chic and been called the St Tropez of the Greek Islands. Famous past visitors include Leonard Cohen, the Rolling Stones, Pink Floyd and Joan

Collins. Though the focal point of any holiday on Hydra is sure to be the beautiful main town, dotted with sea-captains' mansions and curved around a pretty harbour, there are also pleasant walks to the island's extremities and a couple of nice beaches.

Of the rest of the archipelago, each has its own character. **Salamis**, almost a suburb of the national capital, is rather pedestrian but might appeal to searchers after non-touristy Greece. **Aegina**, despite its huge popularity with tourists, has retained a lot of its atmosphere, and its farming and fishing traditions. Famed for its pistachio orchards, nut nuts will be nuts about Aegina! **Poros** is quaint and, separated from the mainland by straits a mere 400m wide, easily accessible from the mainland. The throngs of cadets from the island's Naval Academy might be a definite selling point for families with teenage girls.

Spetses is calm and beautiful, and will appeal to fans of John Fowles' 'The Magus'. The furthest of the Argo-Saronic Islands from Athens, it attracts mainly water-borne holiday-makers and independent travellers.

The Sporades

Scattered (like spores, which is where they get their name) off the north and east coast of Evia (see Chapter 6), the Sporades are late developers in the international tourism stakes. Without having played any dominant part in the story of Greece, they seem to have been passed from hand to hand between the great players in Mediterranean history, more often spoils of war than movers and shakers. Undoubtedly beautiful, with lovely beaches, forests, crystal waters and pleasant sea breezes, they were originally very much off the beaten track, but started to become transformed by

Skiathos Town

tourism in the latter part of the 20th century after an airport was built on Skiathos. They now offer a balance of tranquillity and lively nightlife, holiday facilities and traditional Greek life, and so are a definite possibility for family holidays – especially for families with young children.

The brashest of the Sporades, **Skiathos** is the easiest to get to, courtesy of that international airport, has the best beaches and the widest range of leisure activities. The most heavily affected by tourism, it can be noisy and boozy in summer, with little room for escape. **Skopelos** is quieter, prettier, greener and more sedate, but getting there requires flying to Skiathos, or the mainland, then transferring by sea. Still, its combination of tourist infrastructure and placid pace of life make it very appealing to families. **Alonissos**, a late developer by even Sporades standards, was until the 1990s a declining and dispiriting place. Since then the push to preserve the rare monk seal (one of Europe's most endangered mammals) has led to an eco-resurgence of the island's fortunes, with the establishment in 1992 of Greece's first 'National Marine Park' covering Alonissos and its uninhabited satellites. **Skyros** is in many ways the odd one out of the Sporades, with closer connections to Evia than with the rest of the group, and with physical and architectural similarities to the Cyclades. Famous for its tiny indigenous ponies, its remoteness has

ensured the survival of traditional costume and culture.

The Northeastern Aegean Islands

Clustered in the angle between Asia Minor and northern Greece, the islands of the northeastern Aegean are not the first to spring to mind when looking to book a family holiday. Apart from Samos and Lesvos they're not particularly easy to get to. A lot of them are not really holiday destinations, and have other priorities and workaday, rather unattractive, towns. Add to this that, being so close to the Turkish mainland, access to parts of many of the islands is limited by military installations, and also their tendency to be consumed by forest fires, and you'll begin to see why no members of the group are covered in this book.

Having said that, there are beautiful villages and pockets of lovely countryside in most of them, and quite a few UK holiday companies include some of them in their catalogues – certainly the big two of the Aegean Islands, Samos and Lesvos, because of their airports. **Samos**, the most visited and package-orientated of the islands, has countryside which balances the dramatic with the lush and a well-developed infrastructure, while **Lesvos**, the third-largest Greek island after Crete and Evia, has unspoiled countryside, numerous villages officially designated as traditional settlements, and friendly people renowned for their love of horses, strong drink, singing and dancing. It's also the best endowed with opportunities for physical recreation. It's true that getting around can be very time-consuming because of two enormous unbridged inlets that penetrate deep into its heart, but this ensures that you get to see a lot of the island as you travel about.

Of the other islands, **Thassos**, right up in the north opposite the mainland town of Kavala, has recreational opportunities that almost rival those of Lesvos, and has wonderfully varied forests and, courtesy of a calm yet moist climate, a misty, magical feel – perfect for dreamers but also, alas, for mosquitoes. **Ikaria** is one of Greece's most mountainous islands – long and thin, with sandy beaches on the north coast and rocky ones in the south. Considered a model of how inhabitants can relate to their environment sustainably, Ikaria is a good choice if you want a quiet holiday untroubled by the pressure to party, tour or see sites. **Chios**, despite a tragic history of massacre, fire and earthquake, is attractive in both the variety of its topography and in the unaffected, uncynical enthusiasm of its people to share their love of the island. **Limnos** is notable mainly for its agriculture (especially, oddly, for its scarecrows and beehives) and (being close to the passage through Turkey into the Black Sea) its military installations. **Samothraki**, with its 1500-m peak and cliffs that drop straight into the sea, is probably the most dramatic island in the group, but

is unlikely to attract any but the most adventurous family – it is one of the most remote of the Greek islands, with access that is very much at the mercy of the weather. However, for families who like to make their own travel and accommodation arrangements, it's an unspoilt and dramatic destination that very few others will have visited.

The Dodecanese

Being the furthest group from mainland Greece, and the closest to Turkey, the Dodecanese have experienced a roller-coaster history. They didn't become a part of Greece until 1948, and before that were occupied by the Crusaders, the Ottomans and most recently the Italians. Though the words 'May you live in interesting times' are usually seen as a curse, the interesting times experienced by the Dodecanese, while horrible for the people who lived there at the time, have left a wide and seductive legacy of culture, architecture and history that makes them fascinating to visit.

The greatest of the Dodecanese is **Rhodes** (see Chapter 4), which has the best contacts with the UK, the most varied tourist infrastructure, and the widest range of attractions and things to do. But several others are possibilities for family holidays. Chief of these is **Kos**, which is in some ways a sort of 'mini-me' to Rhodes – similar in relics of the Knights of St John and of the Fascist Italian occupation in the first half of the 20th century, similar even in atmosphere.

Far less well-known than either Rhodes or Kos, **Karpathos** has a lot going for it as a family destination. Midway between Rhodes and Crete, its geography – narrow mountainous north, flatter, fertile and beach-edged south – offers the possibility of a balanced holiday, with interesting exploration (though it has to be said that the roads are not brilliant), varied places to eat, and villages (especially in the north) that have retained their character and culture. There's a fair range of outdoor activities as well.

Many of the remaining Dodecanese are ideal if all you want to do is to eat, sleep, swim and get to know the locals. Butterfly-shaped **Astypalaia** feels and looks Cycladic, with white-painted cuboid houses spilling down rocky hillsides, but its notoriously unreliable links with the outside world, and paucity of accommodation, make it one only for families really determined to get away from the crowds. Rocky **Kassos**, the southernmost of the Dodecanese, is equally inaccessible, and with a population scattered among five tiny villages, offers a handful of rooms to let and nothing much to do – ideal for chilling out and seeing what Greece must have been like before the tourist revolution, but not if you want entertainment and sightseeing. **Lipsi** is widely thought to be Homer's Ogygia, where the temptress Calypso kept Odysseus in thrall

for seven years. You can see the attraction – it's a green and pleasant land with, again, nothing much to do.

Other members of the Dodecanese group are magnets for excursion boats and the sailing fraternity, and are ideal if you're looking for islands which are buzzing and up-market. **Symi**, one of the prettiest of all the Greek islands, has a striking main town with a wealth of restored mansions climbing up from the sea. Although packed and very hot in August, it is pleasant in spring – you've still got the prettiness, but without the crowds of day-visitors. All this is true too of nearby **Chalki** and (further north) **Patmos** – pretty, nice out of season, but packed during the summer. Patmos has the additional cross to bear that its crowds of day-trippers are swollen by religious tourists visiting its famous monastery. Somewhere in between, little **Nissyros** is defined by its volcano, which, though now dormant, created the island's landscape of moon-like rocks, lush fruit orchards, pumice-quarries and coastal volcanic rocks and sand. Again more noted for day-visitors than longer-term holiday-makers, Nissyros offers a number of unspoilt villages, good walking and, its unique selling point, the sulphurous and vent-dotted volcano.

Sponge-producing **Kalymnos**, in decline since disease wreaked havoc on eastern Mediterranean sponges in the 1980s, might attract because it has stayed relatively unspoilt. Understated **Tilos**

Castle of the Knights

provides peace and good walking, while **Leros** has yet to overcome its reputation throughout Greece for prisons and mental institutions.

One to look out for, though, if you want a really away-from-it-all holiday that may be the next thing is **Kastellorizo**, Greece's most easterly island. It's attractive in an understated sort of way, and so far off the beaten track that its position on maps of Greece is usually indicated by an arrow on the right-hand edge. Once a prosperous island with its own schooner fleet, it was until recently in apparently terminal decline, kept afloat only by politically motivated support from the Government – it's a long way from the rest of Greece, and only a mile or so off the Turkish coast. Although there are still a lot of derelict houses, many are being renovated by islanders who have moved abroad, and by the odd foreigner, and celebrities like Eric Clapton and Jeremy Irons have apparently been spotted there. Definitely one to watch!

The Cyclades

Named it is said because they encircle the holy island of Delos, the Cyclades are the islands most associated with the image of the Greek islands – tiny white-domed churches, dazzling cuboid houses with blue doors and window-shutters, poised on barren rocks above an azure sea. And there can be no argument – the Cyclades are very, very beautiful. Yet in many ways they are the least suitable for family holidays. Relatively far from the land masses of Greece and Turkey, most are very small, with a limited range of things to see and do.

There are two ways of overcoming these limitations – either island-hop, so that you can enjoy the different sorts of thing each island can offer, or if you have a limited number of very clear requirements, choose your island carefully to meet them.

Island-hopping with a family wouldn't be everybody's cup of tea – the logistics, the amount of time spent travelling and the uncertainties caused by the very windy Cycladic weather make it an option for only the most adventurous. However, with good preparation and after consulting *www.greekislandhopping.com*, you should be able to make use of the excellent ferry and hydrofoil connections between the islands to visit several during your holiday.

As for choosing a single island, Paros and Naxos are undoubtedly the ones which offer the widest range of activities. For more specialist tastes, diving and snorkelling are good on Mykonos, Amorgos and Santorini, with Mykonos, Paros, Santorini and Serifos offering good water sports generally. Horse riding can be arranged on Paros, kayaking on Andros and Paros, cycling on Syros, Paros, Naxos and Milos, and golf on Kea. Most islands are good for hiking. And if archaeology's the family thing, visit the wonderful ancient site on Delos, the island at the heart of the Cyclades. You can't, however, stay on the island itself: there's nothing there but the vast archaeological excavations. Most of its thousands of visitors stay on Mykonos.

8 History

You really can't get full value from a holiday in Greece without knowing something about its history. Without it, Greece is simply one of the poorer members of the European Union, made up of a rocky mainland surrounded by a scattering of islands on the southeast margin of the continent. It's beautiful, it offers lovely weather and fine beaches, a terrific tourist infrastructure, an expanding menu of holiday activities. But then so do most other sunshine destinations.

Take Greek history into account, though, and it's a different matter. Greece is unique, one of the most important countries on the planet. It's the rock upon which Western Civilisation was built. Its spirit is soaked into every aspect of Western philosophy, science, mathematics, art, history, architecture and literature, not only directly, but through its enormous influence on those who came after its decline, from the Romans onwards. The Renaissance and the Enlightenment would have been unthinkable without the rediscovery of Greek civilisation after its eclipse during the Dark Ages.

As you holiday in Greece, therefore, you'll come across names and places which are familiar – world famous – together with evidence of the cultural diversity caused by its tumultuous past. You can only appreciate it if you have a broad historical framework into which to fit what you see. Below I've tried to sketch out such a framework – if at least one member of the family knows the historical background, the enjoyment for all will be enhanced. So try to get one of the children to take this on. If all else fails, you'll have to do it yourself!

First, a few health warnings:

● The history of Greece is so long that a lot of the stories and people in it tend to get jumbled up in our minds. The siege of Troy happened almost 1000 years before the Golden Age of Athenian civilisation, which was itself 1000 years before Venice and the Ottoman Empire vied to control Greece.

● The historical experience of different parts of Greece varies enormously – parts of the Greek mainland were ruled by the Ottoman Empire for around four centuries, while Corfu never was; Greek independence was gained in the 1830s, but Crete didn't become part of Greece until 1913. So, although I've tried to provide a continuous, if brief, history of Greece below, bear in mind that the experiences of individual islands can be very different from that of Greece as a whole. You'll find sketches of the individual history of each island in the relevant chapter introductions.

● Far from being a succession of accepted facts, Greek history abounds with the unknown and the disputed. So what appears below is a gross over-simplification – the alternative was an account full of 'it is believed that ...' and 'some experts claim that ...'. I don't think we need that amount of detail in a guidebook: life, frankly, is too short.

THE GREECE TIMELINE

In many ways it's easier to deal with Greece's expansive history in significant blocks of time, rather than as a continuous chronicle of events – it makes it all the more manageable.

Cycladic/Mycenaean/ Minoan Civilisations (2000–1200 BC)

The semi-mythic, pre-historical civilisations revealed through archaeology and through the writing, centuries later, of stories passed down orally. The Cycladic civilisation flourished in the Cyclades, the Mycenaean on the mainland, and the Minoan in Crete.

Look out for

● Cycladic statues – beautifully simple and incredibly modern-looking.

● The saga of the Trojan Wars between the Mycenaeans and the Trojans, involving great names like Paris, Menelaus, Agamemnon, Odysseus, Hector and Achilles. And, of course, Helen, whose face launched the thousand ships of the Greek invasion.

● The story of King Minos of Crete, his palace at Knossos, the Labyrinth and the Minotaur.

The Dark Ages (1200–750 BC)

A chaotic period of migration, depopulation and a reversion to subsistence farming.

The Greece That Changed the World (750–338 BC)

During this period city states with a variety of forms of government rose to the fore, and Greek civilisation spread to Italy, Sicily, Asia Minor and the shores of the Black Sea. (Plato described the Greeks in the Eastern Mediterranean as 'like frogs around a pond'. Don't you love it?)

Look out for

● The written account of the Siege of Troy (in the *Iliad*) and of Odysseus' long journey home to Ithaca (in the *Odyssey*), written by blind poet Homer, summarising, in around 725 BC, 500 years of oral tradition. Available in translation at all good bookshops. These two books were the foundation of Greek (and later) civilisations.

● The Persian Wars (490–478 BC), which produced some of the greatest stories of Greek history – the Athenian defeat of a massive Persian force at Marathon (490 BC), for example, or the holding of the pass at Thermopylae by a tiny group of Spartans ten years later.

● The work of the great men of Athens' golden age: Socrates, Plato and Aristotle (philosophy), Herodotus and Thucydides (history), Euripides, Aeschylus, and Aristophanes (drama), Themistocles and Pericles (politics), and many more.

● The building of the Parthenon in Athens, and the holding of the first Olympic Games in the Peloponnese.

● The Peloponnesian Wars (431–404 BC) between Athens and Sparta, which marked the beginning of the end for Greece's greatest period of civilisation.

The Greece That Conquered the World (338–146 BC)

During the squabbling and open warfare between city states that characterised the final years of the Golden Age, the northern kingdom of Macedonia, which many Greeks denied was Greek at all, rose to prominence under its formidable King Philip II. He united the city states by force and announced a great invasion of the Persian Empire. His assassination in 336 BC didn't stop the plan – his 20-year-old son Alexander proceeded to conquer most of the known world – not only Persia, but a swathe of territory that included Egypt and parts of India.

Look out for

● The defeat by Philip II of combined Athenian/Theban

forces at Chaironeia, showcasing the effectiveness of the Macedonian 'phalanx'.

● Alexander the Great's Asian Campaign (335–330 BC), during which Asia Minor, Syria, Egypt, Babylon, Susa, Persepolis and Pasargadae fell to him.

● The Colossus of Rhodes, built around 290–280 BC, one of the seven wonders of the Ancient World.

Roman Greece (146 BC–330 AD)

Greece, like Britain, became a part of the mighty Roman Empire. Though at that time (again like Britain) something of an outpost, Greece was (unlike Britain) very influential, with many Romans touring the country to admire its classical remains. In due course the Roman Empire took on much of what Greek civilization had to offer, including its mythology, gods, science, art and architecture.

Look out for

● Julius Caesar's defeat of Pompey at Pharsalus in Thessaly (49 BC), in Central Greece.

● Mark Antony and Ocatavian's defeat of Caesar's assassins at Philippi, near present day Kavala in northern Greece.

● Octavian's defeat of Mark Antony and Cleopatra at the naval Battle of Actium, which he celebrated by establishing the town of Nikopolis (Victory City) on the west coast of the northern part of Greece (31 BC).

● The sacking of Rhodes by Cassius during the Roman Civil Wars.

Byzantine Greece (330–1460 AD)

When the Roman Empire split in two (the west ruled from Rome, the east from Byzantium – later called Constantinople) and the western half was overrun by barbarians, the eastern half became the Christian Byzantine Empire. Though it survived for 1000 years, it was racked by plague, attacked by barbarians from the north, and squeezed by the advancing Muslim Ottoman Empire to the east. Despite early success against the Ottoman Empire during the early Crusades, the Byzantine Empire disintegrated, being occupied first by Franks, Lombards and Venetians from the west, and finally by the Ottomans themselves.

Look out for

● Many of the greatest churches, monasteries, convents and icons to be found in Greece, which date from the Byzantine period.

● The ruins of the great Byzantine city of Mistras in the Peloponnese.

● The great Crusader castles on Rhodes and other Dodecanese islands, and Venetian and Frankish castles on Corfu, Crete and many other places.

Ottoman Greece (1460–1821 AD)

Although usually referred to as the period of Turkish rule, or even 'slavery', the period during which Greece was part of the Ottoman Empire is not quite as clear-cut as that. The Ottoman rulers were not always Turks, and they were far more interested in taxation than cultural domination. Therefore, as long as the Greeks paid the 'tribute' to the Ottoman Empire, they were allowed to keep both their religion and their way of life. Ruled by the Patriarch of Constantinople, Greece became almost a state-within-a-state. There is no doubting the underlying resentment caused by not only being subject to an outside authority, but to a non-Christian authority at that. It is also certain that the Ottoman authorities did little to improve the lot of their Greek subjects – there is remarkably little surviving evidence of the Ottoman occupation, considering that it lasted for over 350 years.

Look out for

● The fall of Constantinople to the Ottoman Empire in 1453, which not only marked the approaching dismemberment of the Byzantine Empire, but, oddly enough, helped to kick start the Renaissance as the contents of the great classical libraries of the Byzantine capital were scattered across Christian western Europe.

● The ousting of the Knights of St John from Rhodes by Suleiman the Magnificent.

● Mosques (often converted into churches) and 'Turkish Quarters' in many towns.

● Turkish-built aqueducts (for example, in Chalkida on Evia).

● Other buildings, such as the Turkish Baths (Mustafa Hamam) in Rhodes Town.

● The sacking of the Arkadi Monastery in Crete by Turkish troops in 1866. (Crete didn't become independent, then part of Greece, until the 20th century).

The War of Independence & the Formation of Modern Greece (1821–1939 AD)

The impetus towards independence came initially from Greeks settled abroad. When it spread to those living in Greece, the banner of freedom was raised in 1821, and fighting started all over the country. By the end of the decade, and with the help of Western powers and individuals like Lord Byron, the core of the country had thrown off the Ottoman yoke. The areas covered by the new Greek state consisted only of the Peloponnese and the area around Athens on the mainland, and the Argo-Saronic, Sporades and Cyclades islands, but over succeeding years other areas were added, until the borders as we know them today were formalised. An attempt to include Greek settlements in Asia Minor in 1922 led to ignominious defeat (known in Greece as 'The Catastrophe') at the hands of the Turks, when Greeks in Smyrna were massacred, after which an exchange of populations was agreed whereby around 400 000 Muslims left Greece for Turkey, and over 1 500 000 Greek Christians moved into Greece from Turkey.

Look out for

● The Battle of Navarino Bay (1827), in the south-western Peloponnese, during which the Ottoman navy was destroyed by a combined British/French/Russian fleet. This marked the beginning of the end of Ottoman control of Greece.

● Stories of massacre and counter-massacre in many parts of the Greek mainland and islands.

● The Philhellenic movement across Europe which mobilised support for the War of Independence.

● Most famous by far of the Philhellenes – Lord Byron, the British poet. His influence was more inspirational than practical, but the fact that he gave his life to the cause (if by fever rather than battle) at Missolongi made him popular throughout Greece – Byron is still widely used as a Christian name, and most towns have streets named after the great man.

World War II & the Civil War (1939–1950)

Having repelled an Italian invasion from Albania in 1940, Greece fell to a German invasion the following year. Occupied by German/Italian/Bulgarian forces, the Greeks suffered horrendously both from starvation provoked by the seizure of food by the invaders, and from brutal reprisals, carried out when resistance fighters inflicted damage on occupying forces, often including the destruction of whole villages and murder of civilian populations (one of the worst examples took place in Crete's Amari Valley). Thousands of Jews were also deported to the death camps (look out from the memorial in Rhodes Town's Place of Martyrs). Then the tide of war turned, and when the Germans withdrew from Greece in 1944, the uneasy alliance between the resistance groups of the left and right broke down, and Civil War ensued. This continued, with atrocities committed by both sides, until 1949. The scars left by this decade – by the occupation and then the civil war, which between them reduced the Greek population by more than a tenth – are still in evidence today.

Look out for

● The Italian invasion of northern Greece in 1940, following an ultimatum from Mussolini's Fascist government and the Greek reply of '*Ochi*' (no). Greek forces were so successful that they not only repelled the Italian invasion, but also took parts of Italian-occupied Albania.

● The Nazi invasion of Greece in 1941, followed by the German/Italian/Bulgarian occupation.

● The Battle of Crete later in 1941 – the first successful invasion in history from the air.

● Highly effective resistance to the Axis occupation organised by ELAS (National Popular Liberation Army) and EAM (National Liberation Front), supported by the British SOE (Special Operations Executive).

● The Civil War between left- and right-wing Greek partisans. With the right supported by the British and Americans, and Stalin sticking to an agreement not to support the left, the result wasn't really in doubt. By 1949 it was all over, with Greece now dominated by the right and its supporters.

Modern Greece (1950–Present)

Greece has, since 1950, had its ups and downs. Major issues have included American intervention in the country's politics and the role of US bases, the dictatorship of a military Junta, continued friction with Turkey, especially over Cyprus, disagreements with a former Yugoslav republic over the use of the name 'Macedonia', modernisation of the Greek economy, membership of the EU and European Monetary Union, a thawing of relations with Turkey after mutual earthquake support, and a successful Olympic Games. Today, Greece is a modern state with an efficient infrastructure.

Look out for

● Rule of the inept Junta from 1967 to 1974, with left-wing organisations banned, opponents imprisoned and tortured, and many famous Greeks settling for exile.

● Invasion of Cyprus (1974) – bad news for Cyprus (it led to the partition of the island which continues to this day), but good news for Greece (it led to the downfall of the Junta).

● The Macedonian Problem (1991–1993), involving the former Yugoslav republic's use of the name 'Macedonia' (associated with Greece since the time of Alexander the Great), its use of the 'Star of Vergina' on its flag (Vergina, in Northern Greece, was Philip II's capital), and vague references to its claims to Aegean territories occupied by Greece. After much argument and a Greek trade embargo, the ex-Yugoslav republic remained 'The Former Yugoslav Republic of Macedonia' (FYROM), but dropped the rest.

● Membership of the EU, which led to millions of euros in European aid flooding into Greece. All over the country, road building and other infrastructure improvements are progressing with EU financial support.

● Twin earthquakes in 1999, which devastated parts of Greece and Turkey, and which led to cooperation on an unprecedented scale. Relief and rescue teams were sent by both into each other's territory, and the thaw in relations was so marked that Greece dropped opposition to Turkish EU candidacy.

● The Athens Olympics (2004) were a triumph for Greek public relations. Despite widespread predictions that the building work wouldn't be ready in time, everything went like clockwork – a fact satirised in the opening ceremony by a little figure in dungarees rushing about the Olympic stadium with a giant spanner, making last minute adjustments! Although doubts have been cast as to the long-term value of the Games, they undoubtedly led to a huge infrastructure boost involving a new metro and motorway system in Athens, new stadiums, and great improvements in the national road system, not to mention a shot-in-the-arm for national pride and self-confidence.

The Insider

There's no escaping it – Greek isn't an easy language to learn. For a start, there's the alphabet. You either have to learn it, or deal with its imperfect transliteration into more familiar Roman script. Then there are the difficulties caused by pronunciation, and by the rapid-fire delivery of Greeks speaking their own language. Add regional dialects and accents (look out for this in Crete), and you might decide that it's not worth making the effort. That would be a big mistake.

OK, let's face it – most of us aren't going to become fluent in Greek before setting off on holiday. But it's really worth making an effort to learn at least the basics: Greeks are proud of their country and their language, and they'll be delighted with any effort that you make to learn about either. And believe it or not, there are some pluses with the language:

● Pronunciation, especially if you've learned the Greek alphabet, is regular and unchanging. Letters and letter combinations are always pronounced the same.

● Pronunciation is made even easier by the fact that the stressed syllable in each word is marked by an accent – though only, alas, in lower case. So where all the letters are capitals – on many road signs, for instance – you're on your own when it comes to deciding which syllable to emphasise.

● Because Modern Greek is descended from Ancient Greek, and because Ancient Greek is the root of lots of other European languages (including English), it's easy to make reasonable guesses at the meaning of Greek words because of their similarity to English. For example, the Greek for menu is Katalogo – just like the English word catalogue.

To get ahead:

● Learn a few general greetings – they always go down well (see p. 233).

● Learn some general-purpose phrases which you can adapt to a variety of situations. Then, with a small pocket English/Greek dictionary and phrasebook, you're armed for most holiday situations.

● Speak English. Don't be overwhelmed by the Greek language – with a few general phrases and greetings the vast majority of Greeks involved in the tourist trade speak English and will be happy to converse in it.

● Go one further (especially if you intend to holiday in Greece often) and spend some time with a conversational Greek course. My favourite is the BBC's 'Greek Language and People', which combines useful phrases and information about life in Greece, all done through a variety of scenarios, games and so on.

Whichever of the above routes you take, you could learn the Greek alphabet in a week or so, and this is extraordinarily satisfying – you can then quickly read Greek with a great degree of fluency, even if you don't understand a word!

Learning the Greek alphabet also means that you can read road signs. In some parts of Greece – northern Evia, for example – all the signs are in Greek script, with no transliteration. Elsewhere, the Greek script sign usually precedes the Latin script sign by 30 or 40 yards, so it's a good test of your accuracy – try to read the place names, then check your efforts when you get to the Latin equivalent.

USEFUL TERMS & PHRASES

Alphabet	Transliterated as	Pronounced as in	
A α	álfa	a	father
B β	víta	v	viper
Γ γ	gámma g before α, o, ω, and consonants		get
	y before αι, ε, ει, η, ι, οι, υ		yes
	ng before κ, γ, χ, or ξ		singer
Δ δ	thélta	th	the (not as the th- in 'thin')
E ε	épsilon	e	set
Z ζ	zíta	z	lazy
H η	íta	i	magazine
Θ θ	thíta	th	thin (not as the th- in 'the')
I ι	ióta	i	magazine
	y before a, o		yard, yore
K κ	káppa	k	keep
Λ λ	lámtha	l	leap
M μ	mi	m	marry
N ν	ni	n	never
Ξ ξ	ksi	ks	taxi
O o	ómicron	o	bought
Π π	pi	p	pet
P ρ	ro	r	round
Σ σ	sígma s before vowels or θ, κ, π, τ, φ, χ, ψ		say
	z before β, γ, δ, ζ		
	y before λ, μ, ν, ρ		laz

Alphabet	Transliterated as	Pronounced as in	
Τ τ	taf	t	take
Υ υ	ípsilon	i	magazine
Φ φ	fi	f	fee
Χ χ	chi	h	hero (before e and i sounds; like the ch- in Scottish 'loch' otherwise
Ψ ψ	psi	ps	collapse
Ω ω	ómega	o	bought

Combinations	Transliterated as	Pronounced as in
αι	e	get
αϊ	ai	aisle
αυ before vowels or β, γ, δ, ζ, λ, μ, ν, ρ	av	Ave Maria
αυ before θ, κ, ξ, π, σ, τ, φ, χ, ψ	af	pilaf

What's your Name?

Understanding Greek is complicated by the fact that many Greek words and names have entered our language not directly but by way of Latin or French, and so have become familiar to English speakers in forms that owe something to those languages. When these words are directly transliterated from modern Greek (and that means from Greek in its modern pronunciation, not the ancient one that Romans heard), they almost always appear in a form other than the one you may have read about in school. Perikles for Pericles or Delfi for Delphi are relatively innocent examples; Thivi for Thebes or Omiros for Homer can give you an idea of the traps in store for the innocent traveller. The bottom line is that the names of towns, streets, hotels, items on menus, historical figures, archaeological sites – you name it – are likely to have more than one spelling as you come across them in books, on maps, or before your very eyes.

Sometimes the name of a place has simply changed over the centuries. If you think you've just arrived in Santorini but you see a sign welcoming you to Thira, smile, remember you're in Greece, and take heart. (Santorini is the name the Venetians used, and it became common in Europe for that reason. Thira is the original Greek name.) You're where you want to be.

Talking Heads

Do remember that *óhi,* although it can sound a bit like 'okay', in fact means 'no', and that *ne,* which can sound like a twangy 'nay,' means 'yes.' To complicate matters, some everyday gestures will be different from those you are used to: Greeks nod their heads upward to express an unspoken *óhi* and downward (or downward and to one side) for an unspoken *ne.* When a Greek turns his or her head from side to side at you—and you will see this despite your best efforts—it is a polite way of signalling, 'I can't make out what you're saying.' And remember: Almost any 40-year-old Greek can read Greek, and most people under 30 can also make out some English. If you find that your attempts at speaking fall on deaf ears, show someone the word for what you want and if you stumble over *efharisto* (thank you) you can place your hand over your heart and bow your head slightly.

Combinations	Transliterated as	Pronounced as in
ει	i	magaz*i*ne
ευ before vowels or β, γ, δ, ζ, λ, μ, ν, ρ	ev	*ev*er
ευ before θ, κ, ξ, π, σ, τ, φ, χ, ψ	ef	le*f*t
μπ at beginning of word	b	*b*ane
μπ in middle of word	mb	lu*mb*er
ντ at beginning of word	d	*d*umb
ντ in middle of word	nd	sle*nd*er
Οι	i	magaz*i*ne
Οϊ	oi	*oi*l
Ου	ou	s*ou*p
τζ	dz	roa*ds*
τσ	ts	ge*ts*
υι	i	magaz*i*ne

Useful Words & Phrases

When you're asking for or about something and have to rely on single words or short phrases, it's an excellent idea to use *sas parakaló* (if you please) to introduce or conclude almost anything you say.

Airport	Aerothrómio
Avenue	Leofóros
Bad	Kakós, -kí, -kó*
Bank	Trápeza

The bill, please	Tón logaryazmó(n), parakaló
Breakfast	Proinó
Bus	Leoforío
Can you tell me?	Boríte ná moú píte?
Car	Amáxi/ aftokínito
Cheap	Ft(h)inó
Church	Ekklissía
Closed	Klistós, stí, stó*
Coast	Aktí
Café	Kafenío
Cold	Kríos, -a, -o*
Dinner	Vrathinó
Do you speak English?	Miláte Angliká?
Excuse me	Signómi(n)
Expensive	Akrivós, -í, -ó*
Farewell!	Stó ka-ló! *(to person leaving)*
Glad to meet you	Chéro polí**
Good	Kalós, lí, ló*
Goodbye	Adío *or* chérete**
Good health (cheers)!	Stín (i)yá sas *or* Yá-mas!
Good morning *or* Good day	Kaliméra
Good evening	Kalispéra
Good night	Kaliníchta**
Hello!	Yássas *or* chérete!**
Here	Ethó
Highchair	Psiló karekláki
Hot	Zestós, -stí, -stó*
Hotel	Xenothochío**
How are you?	Tí kánete *or* Pós íst(h)e?
How far?	Pósso makriá?
How long?	Póssi óra *or* Pósso(n) keró?
How much does it cost?	Póso káni?
I am a vegetarian	Íme hortophágos
I am from London	Íme apó to Londino
I am lost *or* I have lost the way	Écho chathí *or* Écho chási tón drómo(n)**
I'm sorry	Singnómi
I'm sorry, but I don't speak Greek (well)	Lipoúme, allá thén miláo elliniká (kalá)
I don't understand	Thén katalavéno

I don't understand, please repeat it	Thén katalavéno, péste to páli, sás prakaló
I want to go to the airport	Thélo ná páo stó aerothrómio
I want a glass of beer	Thélo éna potíri bíra
I would like a room	Tha íthela ena thomátio
It's (not) all right	(Dén) íne en dáxi
Internet	Diadiktio
Left (direction)	Aristerá
Ladies' room	Ghinekón
Lunch	Messimerianó
Map	Chártis**
Market (place)	Agorá
Men's room	Andrón
Mr	Kírios
Mrs	Kiría
Miss	Despinís
My name is . . .	Onomázome . . .
New	Kenoúryos, -ya, -yo*
No	Óchi**
Old	Paleós, -leá, -leó* (pronounce palyós, -lyá, -lyó)
Open	Anichtós, -chtí, -chtó*
Pâtisserie	Zacharoplastío**
Pharmacy	Pharmakío
Please or You're welcome	Parakaló
Please call a taxi (for me)	Parakaló, fonáxte éna taxi (yá ména)
Point out to me, please . . .	Thíkste mou, sas parakaló . . .
Post office	Tachidromío**
Restaurant	Estiatório
Toilet	Tó méros or I toualétta
Right (direction)	Dexiá
Saint	Áyios, ayía, (plural) áyi-i (abbreviated ay.)
Shore	Paralía
Square	Plateía
Street	Odós
Show me on the map	Díxte mou stó(n) chárti**
Station (bus, train)	Stathmos (leoforíou, trénou)
Stop (bus)	Stási(s) (leoforíou)
Telephone	Tiléfono
Temple (of Athena, Zeus)	Naós (Athinás, Diós)

Thank you (very much)	Efcharistó (polí)**
Today	Símera
Tomorrow	Ávrio
Traveller's cheques	Taxidiotikí epitagí
Very nice	Polí oréos, -a, -o*
Very well	Polí kalá or En dáxi
What?	Tí?
What time is it?	Tí ôra íne?
What's your name?	Pós onomázest(h)e?
Where is . . . ?	Poú íne . . . ?
Where am I?	Pou íme?
Why?	Yatí?

* Masculine ending -os, feminine ending -a or -i, neuter ending -o.

** Remember, ch should be pronounced as in Scottish loch or German ich, not as in the word church.

Numbers

0	Midén	21	Íkossi éna
1	Éna	22	Íkossi dío
2	Dío	30	Triánda
3	Tría	40	Saránda
4	Téssera	50	Penínda
5	Pénde	60	Exínda
6	Éxi	70	Evdomínda
7	Eftá	80	Ogdónda
8	Októ	90	Enenínda
9	Enyá	100	Ekató(n)
10	Déka	101	Ekatón éna
11	Éndeka	102	Ekatón dío
12	Dódeka	150	Ekatón penínda
13	Dekatría	151	Ekatón penínda éna
14	Dekatéssera	152	Ekatón penínda dío
15	Dekapénde	200	Dhiakóssya
16	Dekaéxi	300	Triakóssya
17	Dekaeftá	400	Tetrakóssya
18	Dekaoktó	500	Pendakóssya
19	Dekaenyá	600	Exakóssya
20	Íkossi	700	Eftakóssya

800	Oktakóssya	3000	Trís chilyádes*
900	Enyakóssya	4000	Tésseris chilyádes*
1000	Chílya*	5000	Pénde chilyádes*
2000	Dío chilyádes*		

Days of the Week

Monday	Deftéra
Tuesday	Tríti
Wednesday	Tetárti
Thursday	Pémpti
Friday	Paraskeví
Saturday	Sávvato
Sunday	Kiriakí

The Calendar

January	Ianouários
February	Fevrouários
March	Mártios
April	Aprílios
May	Máios
June	Ioúnios
July	Ioúlios
August	Ávgoustos
September	Septémvrios
October	Októvrios
November	Noémvrios
December	Dekémvrios

Menu Terms

arní avgolémono	lamb with lemon sauce
arní soúvlas	spit-roasted lamb
arní yiouvétsi	baked lamb with orzo
astakós (ladolémono)	lobster (with oil-and-lemon sauce)
bakaliáro (skordaliá)	cod (with garlic)
barboúnia (skáras)	red mullet (grilled)
briám	vegetable stew
brizóla chiriní	pork steak or chop
brizóla moscharísia	beef or veal steak
choriátiki saláta	village salad (Greek salad to us)
chórta	dandelion salad
dolmades	stuffed vine leaves
domátes yemistés mé rízi	tomatoes stuffed with rice
eksóhiko	lamb and vegetables wrapped in filo pastry
garídes	shrimp
glóssa (tiganití)	sole (fried)
kalamarákia (tiganitá)	squid (fried)
kalamarákia (yemistá)	squid (stuffed)

kaparosaláta	salad of minced caper leaves and onion
karavídes	crayfish
keftédes	fried meatballs
kokorétsia	grilled entrails
kotópoulo soúvlas	spit-roasted chicken
kotópoulo yemistó	stuffed chicken
kouloúri	pretzel-like roll covered with sesame seeds
loukánika	spiced sausages
loukoumádes	round doughnut centre-like pastries, deep-fried, then drenched with honey and topped with powdered sugar and cinnamon
melitzanosaláta	aubergine salad
moussaká	meat-and- aubergine casserole
oktapódi	octopus
païdákia	lamb chops
paradosiakó	traditional Greek cooking
pastítsio	baked pasta with meat
piláfi rízi	rice pilaf
piperiá yemistá	stuffed green peppers
revídia	chickpeas
revidokeftédes	croquettes of ground chickpeas
saganáki	grilled cheese
skordaliá	hot garlic sauce/dip
soupiés yemistés	stuffed cuttlefish
souvláki	lamb (sometimes veal) on the skewer
spanokópita	spinach pie
stifádo	stew, often of rabbit or veal
taramosaláta	fish roe with mayonnaise
tirópita	cheese pie
tsípouro	aki *what's that?*
tzatzíki	yogurt-cucumber-garlic dip
youvarlákia	boiled meatballs with rice

* Remember, ch should be pronounced as in Scottish *loch* or German *ich,* not as in the word *church.*

TOUR OPERATORS

The list of tour operators seems endless. Some offer traditional 'sun and sand' packages, others go in for activity or special-interest breaks. Some are huge, others small and select. Here are a few pointers.

Thomas Cook

☎ 0870 111 1111,
www.thomascook.com

One of the industry giants cater largely for the mass package-holiday market. Their 'Greece and Cyprus' brochure, which contains succinct summaries of what each hotel or complex offers families. Corfu, Rhodes, Crete and lots of others.

Thomson

☎ 0870 165 2602,
www.thomson.co.uk

Another giant, offers wide range of destinations, prices and types of holiday in Corfu, Rhodes, Crete and more.

Sunvil

☎ 020 8758 4758,
www.sunvil.co.uk/greece

Concentrate on small mid-price hotels and apartments offering an authentic experience of Greece. Corfu and smaller islands.

Ionian Island Holidays

☎ 020 8459 0777,
www.ionianislandholidays.com

Started by Greeks keen to share the beauties of their homeland, now cover Corfu and the other Ionian islands, but also some in the Sporades and Cyclades.

James Villa Holidays

☎ 0870 055 6688,
www.jamesvillas.co.uk

These Mediterranean specialists, offer villas in Corfu, Rhodes, Crete and other islands.

General Holidays

Abercrombie & Kent

☎ 0845 070 0600,
www.abercrombiekent.co.uk

Crete, Zakynthos, Mykonos. From small hotels to large villas. Top end.

Airtours

☎ 0870 241 8933,
www.airtours.co.uk

Corfu, Rhodes, Crete and others.

Inntravel

☎ 01653 617949,
www.inntravel.co.uk

Crete and variety of smaller islands: Chios, Hydra, Lesvos, Kefalonia, Ithaca, Samos. Walking, cycling and horseriding.

Kosmar

☎ 0871 700 0747,
www.kosmar.co.uk

A good choice of budget hotels and apartments in Corfu, Rhodes, Crete and others.

Kuoni

☎ 01306 747746, www.kuoni.co.uk

Greece. Mykonos. Santorini. Variety of types of holiday.

Manos

☎ 0870 753 0530,
www.manos.co.uk

Holidays in Corfu, Rhodes, Crete and other Greek Islands at very reasonable prices.

MyTravel

☎ 0870 238 7777,
www.mytravel.com

Hotel packages to Corfu, Rhodes, Crete and several other islands at mass-market prices.

Olympic Holidays

☎ 0870 429 4242,
www.olympicholidays.com

Hotels and villas in Corfu, Rhodes, Crete and elsewhere.

Owners Direct

☎ 01372 229330,
www.ownersdirect.co.uk

Puts you in touch with property owners. Corfu, Rhodes, Crete, and Evia.

Simply Travel

☎ 0870 166 4979,
www.simplytravel.co.uk

Apartments, villas and farmhouses with character. Top-end, 'out-of-the-mainstream' destinations. Crete Ionian and Sporades islands.

Sovereign Villas

☎ 0871 664 0011,
www.sovereignvillas.co.uk

Quality villas in rural locations, all with pools. Corfu, Crete, Kefalonia, Zakynthos and Lefkas.

Travel Matters

☎ 020 8675 7878,
www.travelmatters.co.uk

Family specialists with self-catering properties in Crete, Lefkas and Zakynthos.

Vintage Travel

☎ 0845 344 0460,
www.vintagetravel.co.uk

Villas from the bijou to the massive, all with private pools. Corfu, Kefalonia, Ithaca, Skopelos.

Specialist Holidays

Hidden Greece

☎ 020 8758 4707,
www.hidden-greece.co.uk

Rep-free, off the beaten track holidays in Rhodes, Crete and a few of out-of-the-way islands.

Sunsail

☎ 0870 770 4839,
www.sunsail.co.uk

Sailing holidays, in Ionian islands and Sporades. Also shore-based 'club' holidays with water sports and child care.

Sailing Holidays

☎ 020 8459 8787,
www.sailingholidays.com

Flotilla specialist, offering cruises in the Ionian islands.

Headwater

☎ 0870 066 2650,
www.headwater.com

Walking holidays in Crete and several other islands.

Exodus

☎ 020 8675 5550,
www.exodus.co.uk

Family cruises around Evia, and walking in Evia, Crete and Lesvos.

Limosa

☎ 01263 578143,
www.limosaholidays.co.uk

Birdwatching in Kos and Lesvos.

The Travelling Naturalist

☎ 01305 267994,
www.naturalist.co.uk

A mixture of nature and history in Crete, Kos and Lesvos.

Index

See also Accommodations and Restaurant indexes, below.

Accommodations

Restaurants